JOURNALS

EARLY FIFTIES EARLY SIXTIES

JOURNALS

EARLY FIFTIES EARLY SIXTIES

Allen Ginsberg

EDITED BY GORDON BALL

Grove Press
New York

Grove Press
841 Broadway
New York, NY 10003

Published in Canada by General Publishing Company, Ltd.

Special thanks to the University of California, Berkeley, Moffit Undergraduate Library.

Library of Congress Cataloging-in-Publication Data

Ginsberg, Allen, 1926–
Journals: early fifties, early sixties.
Includes bibliographical references and index.
ISBN 0-8021-3347-9 (pbk.)
1. Ginsberg, Allen, 1926– —Diaries.
2. Poets, American—20th Century—Biography.
I. Ball, Gordon.
PS3513.I74Z516 1978 818'.5'403 78-50785

Manufactured in the United States of America

Designed by Stevan A. Baron

First Grove Press Edition 1977
First Evergreen Edition 1978
Second Evergreen Edition 1992

APPRECIATION

Thanks be to the author of these journals for writing them and working generously and hospitably with our editing; to Fred Jordan, at Grove Press, for securing them and waiting patiently while they slowly became a single volume; and to Aileen Lee, for typing most of their earlier drafts.

Thanks to Kathy Zobel for editing advice and for adding—through her artful eye—to my own appreciation of these pages; to Kenneth Lohf and Polly Bolling and associates at Butler Library, Columbia University, for providing access to and duplicating photographs; to my roommate, library scientist Richard Hinson, for much enduring helpfulness—from forwarding mail while I was working with Allen, to patiently and generously advising whenever asked, to driving me to the predawn train to get this ms. to New York on time.

To C. T. Ludington for his interest and encouragement, and to Lewis Leary for similar helpfulness; Naropa Institute and its resources for permitting summers' long work; the University of North Carolina at Chapel Hill, its library and English Department; to Richard Elovich, Allen's secretary in New York, for always coming through in work assistance I was too far away from to do myself.

To James Grauerholz, for providing needed background information on William S. Burroughs; to William S. Burroughs, for responding helpfully to the brief questions I put to him directly; to Gary Clemmons (who also assisted with research) and Stuart Phillips, who came through bravely in the closing hours of 1976 and 1977's snowy beginning with invaluable typing assistance.

I also wish to thank Nancy J. Peters at City Lights for making available Allen's photograph of Paul Bowles; Jonas Mekas, for providing me with the script of *Guns of the Trees;* Carl Solomon; and Alan Ansen, for his charming letter. Thanks be to all, and to all other helpful friends and family.

G. B.

CONTENTS*

* This Table of Contents lists the longer entries of major interest.

READER'S GUIDE

Biographical Note: The Decade Preceding These Journals

In the summer of 1943 Allen Ginsberg left Paterson, New Jersey, for Columbia University, where he remained a student on and off till the end of 1948. During this period he first met and developed deep relationships with Jack Kerouac, William S. Burroughs, Neal Cassady, Herbert Huncke, and classmate Lucien Carr.

Suspended in 1945 at age nineteen for writing "Butler has no balls"[1] on his dorm window and for sharing his room overnight with Kerouac (who had entered Columbia in 1939, quit in 1942, and was by this time *persona non grata* on campus), Ginsberg moved across the street to a communal apartment where Burroughs and Kerouac would soon take rooms. Burroughs, thirteen years Ginsberg's senior, served as mentor for Allen and Jack, introducing them to Mayan codices and the works of Spengler, Korzybski, and Céline, among others. At the same time came Ginsberg's first exposure to the Times Square netherworld, through Burroughs and Herbert Huncke.

Soon after his return to campus, Ginsberg became prominent there literarily, winning poetry prizes with rhymed verse and working on the *Columbia Jester Review*. But for the mild exceptions of Mark Van Doren, Raymond Weaver, and Lionel Trilling, Columbia English professors didn't inspire Ginsberg, who learned much more from Burroughs and companions, the lives they shared, and their occasional collaborative writing experiments.

Around the end of 1946 Neal Cassady appeared in New York. Almost immediately Allen fell deeply in love with him. Kerouac was of course also immensely affected by Cassady, and was to use him as

[1] Nicholas Murray Butler: then president of Columbia.

character model in *On the Road* and other novels. Extended all-night rhapsodic exchanges of soul and confusion between Kerouac, Cassady, and Ginsberg ensued for weeks on end.

The following summer Allen took a bus to Denver with high hopes, only to be greeted by Neal with a girl friend. Nevertheless, his relationship with Neal remained close. During his brief stay, Ginsberg began recording daily thoughts and impressions in his first notebook diary. "The Bricklayer's Lunch Hour," [2] a notation made while waiting for Cassady to return from work, is its only entry now surviving in print (the original journal, and other early notebooks not represented in this volume, may be among the Ginsberg Special Collections at Butler Library, Columbia University).

From Denver Allen and Neal hitchhiked to East Texas, where Burroughs had a farm on which a friend grew marijuana. All were indigent; and so, in September, Allen shipped out from Galveston as a yeoman storekeeper to Dakar, intending to make money and meet Neal back in New York at year's end. When he returned, Ginsberg learned Cassady had left for the West Coast and married.

In June 1948 an event (now almost legendary to those who have followed Ginsberg's career) occurred which was to carry an enormous long-term impact on Allen. With most friends gone, Jack somewhat isolated in Long Island completing his first novel, *The Town and the City,* and with one fall semester to complete at Columbia, Allen lay alone on his bed in his East Harlem apartment one afternoon. A book of William Blake, open to "Ah! Sun-flower" (a poem he'd read many times before) lay next to him. He had just jacked off, and as his mind died momentarily he heard an ancient-sounding voice—which he took to be Blake's—recite the poem. Immediately, he looked out his window and saw in the old, intricately corniced buildings and the ancient blue sky above the sign of a Creator, and sensed behind each particle of being the presence of a vast, immortal, intelligent hand. This amplified his own sense of self as he recognized this present existence on earth as "that sweet golden clime" of the poem, Eternity. Varieties of this epiphany recurred that summer and fall, and their import has remained with him.[3]

---

[2] P. 32, *Empty Mirror* (New York: Totem/Corinth, 1961).

[3] For the most thorough discussion of the Blake epiphanies see the A.G. interview in *Writers at Work,* Third Series, George Plimpton, ed. (New York: Viking, 1967), pp. 301–311. In later years Ginsberg has come to view the voice as that of his own mature self.

During the fall Huncke reappeared out of jail and in very poor health, and Ginsberg gave him sanctuary. As good health returned, Huncke and two friends began using the apartment for hot goods storage. Allen eventually blew the whistle, but all four were found by police while moving the goods out in a stolen car. About to graduate from Columbia with an A-average while working as a copyboy at Associated Press, Ginsberg was sent to New York State Psychiatric Institute in lieu of jail.

During his eight months at the Institute he met Carl Solomon (via the famous exchange–C.S.: "Who're *you?*" A.G.: "I'm Myshkin." C.S.: "I'm Kirilov."). Solomon introduced Ginsberg to French surrealist writing and later became the principal dedicatee of *Howl.* Both wrote while together at the Institute; a number of the rhymed poems in Ginsberg's *The Gates of Wrath* (Bolinas, California: Grey Fox Press, 1972) were composed from within N.Y.S.P.I.

In the summer of 1949 Allen relocated at his family home in Paterson with his father Louis and stepmother Edith (his mother Naomi had been in asylum most of the previous twelve years). During this limbo period in Paterson, Ginsberg worked for a while in a ribbon factory downtown, and spent much of his time examining his own (and society's) perceptions of "reality," as well as his own uncertainties about life-work. He wrote the Paterson prose poems in *Empty Mirror,* and gradually began making his way back to New York.

I. New York City 1952

As these journal entries begin, Ginsberg has established himself in a small furnished room on 15th Street between Eighth and Ninth Avenues opposite the Port Authority building. While at home in Paterson in 1949–51 he had been in touch with William Carlos Williams, who already had begun to admire the younger poet from whom he had received poems and letters.[4] The first journal entry, then, records a late-afternoon-evening visit with Williams.

During these first years back in New York Allen held several different jobs (copyboy, market researcher, opinions analyst) and was

---

[4] Williams wrote Robert Lowell on March 11, 1952: "I've become interested in a young poet, Allen Ginsberg, of Paterson–who is coming to personify the place for me"; p. 312, *Selected Letters,* ed. John C. Thirlwall (New York: McDowell, Obolensky, 1957).

also unemployed part of the time. His continuing uncertainty over a professional life-role for himself is reflected in his notes after one of many intense conversations with Lucien Carr: "What do I want to *do* in the world aside from 'be a poet.' " (p. 25.)

Simultaneously, Ginsberg was quite active in an underground literary-musical culture for which the San Remo Bar was one of the meeting places. At the San Remo Allen met Bill Keck, Anton Rosenberg, Aileen Lee, and "very beautiful Jewish girls who read Ezra Pound and were into grandma dresses and sewing and amphetamine and junk and bebop and poesy and kept journals and painted—Iris Brodie, Shirley Goldenberg." [5]

It was at the San Remo that Allen's "Chance meeting with Dylan Thomas" took place a year and a half before Thomas died, a meeting interesting for its brief glimpse of Thomas in his latter days and of Ginsberg in his somewhat jejune mid-twenties. Today, Ginsberg encounters similar "genuine but uncooked egg" treatment himself.

At that same time Charlie Parker played in the Village, highlighting Sundays with $1.00 performances at the barnlike Open Door, and Kerouac was seeing Al Cohen and Zoot Sims. John Casper had a bookstore around the corner from the San Remo on Bleecker Street where he sold the Square Dollar pamphlet series inspired by Pound; painters Sheri Martinelli and Bill Heine came up from Washington, where they had visited Pound at St. Elizabeth's. Many others—Philip Lamantia, Frank O'Hara, Carl Solomon, Mason Hoffenberg, and Stanley Gould among them—appeared from time to time, and in 1951 Ginsberg and Gregory Corso first met.

Ginsberg and Kerouac called the people they met at the San Remo "The Subterraneans" (which Kerouac used as the title for his novel, changing the setting to San Francisco), partly

> . . . because there was a whole anti-police ethos and a sort of mystical search, so it was sort of like Dostoyevsky's underground man—a certain art of psychology with spleen, but the main quality was sensitivity and gentility among all those people, perhaps more reserve than Jack and I had.

Such qualities are reflected in the colloquy with Bill Keck (p. 5), who

---

[5] A.G. in conversation with G.B., Naropa Institute, Boulder, Colorado, August 1976. Subsequent quotations not otherwise attributed are also from this conversation.

impressed Allen with his modernist poetry of a common spiritual search.

Ginsberg's particular spiritual preoccupations at the time still referred all thought to his 1948 Blake vision; yet, partly through his talks with Lucien Carr, he was beginning to recognize his attachment to it as an isolating trap: "... I must abandon again this whole metaphysical urge that leads me further each month back to an uncreated world of bliss of my own making in my own head...." (p. 25.)

Even so, substantial passages in this New York section come from direct attention to the world in front of the author, such as "Memorable Glimpses: Faces on the Street," with its exquisite descriptions of strangers from everyday life, and "We're Flowers to Rocks." The latter, an account of Ginsberg's first peyote exercise in the backyard of his family home, is remarkable for its accurate description of phenomena externally seen and inwardly thought, and is an early example of essentially Buddhist-style appreciation of space the author has developed further in recent years.

From the late 40's through 1952, Allen wrote poetry in both rhyme (see *The Gates of Wrath)* and the kind of Williams-like reality notation in *Empty Mirror.* Within the next year he was to write "The Green Automobile" (p. 9, *Reality Sandwiches),* a semi-realistic romantic declaration of independence of imagination which pointed to some of the directions he was to follow two years later in *Howl.*

In 1953 William S. Burroughs returned from Mexico and South America and joined Ginsberg in an apartment Allen was renting at 206 East 7th St. Working in marketing research, Ginsberg maintained a cozy lower East Side pad where Bill could stay and which other friends—Kerouac, Alan Ansen, Gregory Corso, Aileen Lee, Lucien Carr—visited. Kerouac (with *The Town and the City, Visions of Neal,*[6] and versions of *On the Road)* and Burroughs (with *Junkie, Queer,* and letters to Allen from South America which were edited that fall on East 7th St. to form the first part of *The Yage Letters)* had also already accomplished significant early work. Yet only Kerouac's *The Town and the City* (through Mark Van Doren, who then called Robert Giroux at Harcourt, Brace) and Burroughs' *Junkie*[7] (through Ginsberg's efforts as agent and Carl Solomon's as editor at Ace Books) had been published. Allen's initial

---

[6] Published posthumously as *Visions of Cody* (New York: McGraw-Hill, 1972).

[7] Republished this year (1977) unexpurgated and unadulterated as *Junky* by Penguin, with introduction by A.G.

efforts on behalf of *On the Road* were not successful, and his own *Empty Mirror,* with a preface ("the craft is flawless") by William Carlos Williams, had not found a publisher, while the manuscript of *The Gates of Wrath* was lost by a well-intentioned friend.

II. Mexico and Return to U.S. December 31, 1953–July 1954

Thus while he thought of himself and Bill and Jack (and Gregory) as literary souls already "published in Heaven,"[8] Ginsberg concluded after basically very futile efforts that little could be done in New York. Neal Cassady was on the West Coast and Allen was still enamored of him; he'd had an extended glimpse of Mexico in 1950 on a trip with Lucien and thought to see more of it, then to move up the West Coast to see Neal in San Jose, California. In December 1953 he hitchhiked to Florida, passing Christmas with Burroughs' friends and family, and then by way of Cuba (see "Havana 1953" in *Reality Sandwiches)* arrived in the Yucatán.

Spending much of his time on a coffee *finca* in the state of Chiapas as a guest of Karena Shields, a former actress in Tarzan films who had met him at the Palenque ruins, Ginsberg was still to a large extent preoccupied with capturing or recapturing a vision of eternity, and perhaps came closest to doing so in the following passage from page 52:

> & palmtrees appearing again in the balmy wind presaging a rain—shifting their fronds in the wind with a dry soft rattle sound, so much like animal hairy windmills—insectlike in fact, like monstrous insects long white bodies encased in scales and at the top conglomerated in the head nerve center all these rattly animal feelers move lethargically in the direction of the wind, settling and unsettling as in water.

This passage, along with many others in this second section, was later incorporated in "Siesta in Xbalba." In the case of the above, the prose became:

palms with lethargic feelers
rattling in presage of rain,
shifting their fronds

[8] A.G. in dedication of *Howl.*

in the direction of the balmy wind,
monstrous animals
sprayed up out of the ground
settling and unsettling
as in water. . . .

(p. 25, *Reality Sandwiches*)

Thus what often becomes poetry one or more years later may be initially entered in journals such as these as prose, or as poetry. "Siesta in Xbalba" represents for Ginsberg an extreme example of synthetic composition, of drawing from blocks of epiphanous moments spread throughout a fairly lengthy notebook to arrive at a single unified poem. In the case of most of his other poems, it is a simple matter of transcribing what was entered (as poem or prose notation) in a notebook into poetry to be published in a book. In the journal texts that follow, a note is given, for the benefit of omnivorous readers, whenever the first notation of a poem already published appears.

Though (with few exceptions) what appears in this volume as poetry was not "lifted out" by Ginsberg for his poetry books, the journal poems have a life of their own. Moreover, the prose itself is impressive. In the passage that follows, each image or word informs its neighbors till the total picture is completed, and it is one of great strange soul:

> . . . vasty armadas of white fragmentary clouds in bright blue sky aerial blue transparency—a few pink trees in flower—recurring crow of cocks from this side and that challenging in various cockly hoarse tones as if they existed in a world of pure intuitive sound communicating to anonymous hidden familiar chickensouls from hill to hill. (p. 47.)

And in a nearby shorter sentence Ginsberg develops in a few words a portrait immediately recognizable or familiar: "The Kiosk proprietor a civilized looking citizen in a disgusting sort of way—acne & fatso glasses." The choice of words seems peculiarly inevitable, yet is entirely unpredictable.

After half a year in Mexico, Allen returned to the United States to rejoin Neal, whom he'd not seen for several years. During that period of time Cassady had settled down—somewhat—with marriage and children, and so we find Ginsberg, just turned twenty-eight, revolving in confusion in the midst of his beloved's household: "I feel like a strange idiot, standing there among wife & children all to whom he gives needs of affection and attention, aching for some special side extra sacrifice of attention for me. . . ." (p. 76.)

III. Berkeley 1955–56

Such confusion—and vulnerability—is replaced in part by Allen's meeting poet Peter Orlovsky, who would become his lifelong love companion, beginning around Christmas 1954 in San Francisco. It is also supplanted by the work represented in this Bay area journal, which includes the first notation of "America" (p. 91), but, more importantly, the assimilation of haiku—for Ginsberg "the crucial discovery of haiku and ellipsis in the haiku, which really serves as the base in *Howl.*" At the same time he was reading more Pound *(Pavannes and Divigations, ABC of Reading)* and Arthur Waley's translations of Chinese poetry. During this period he wrote *Howl,* the single poem which perhaps has had greater repercussions and influence than any other in American literature and culture since *The Waste Land.*

IV. New York January 1959—March 1961

The journals now resume in 1959. Thus there's a jump in time from the period which first heard *Howl* to, appropriately enough, that in which *Kaddish* was completed. Allen's mother Naomi had died in 1956, half a year after the legendary Six Gallery reading in San Francisco when Ginsberg (with *Howl),* Michael McClure, Kenneth Rexroth, Philip Whalen, Philip Lamantia, and Gary Snyder read together, urged on by Kerouac and his wine.

Part IV ("O mother") of *Kaddish* was written in Paris 1958; the rest, in Allen's East 2nd Street New York City apartment in 1959. That period (1958–60) in the Lower East Side saw the beginning of what became the amphetamine plague of the early sixties, and also bore witness to much renewed cultural communion. Alex Trocchi, author of *Cain's Book,* lived a few blocks up from East 2nd. Ginsberg was seeing LeRoi Jones (now Imamu Amiri Baraka), who was then publishing *Yugen.* Don Cherry, Cecil Taylor, and Ornette Coleman were playing at LeRoi's and elsewhere on the Lower East Side; Thelonious Monk was at the Five Spot. Many poetry readings were held, including the first public ones in the West Village.

Kerouac, Corso, and Peter Orlovsky's sister Marie and brother Lafcadio stayed over at East 2nd from time to time; Herbert Huncke had a dig upstairs. Living rather penuriously as he always has, Ginsberg was by this time, having already been to Europe,

> sort of what I dreamt myself to be as a kid—somebody who'd come back from Paris speaking French and some kinda continental culture—but there I was stuck on the Lower East Side broke anyway.

Even so, he'd already given major public readings on the West Coast (was in San Francisco from late January to September 1959), in Chicago, and in New York. Robert Frank and Alfred Leslie had shot their film celebration of the Beat Generation, *Pull My Daisy;* Corso's *Gasoline* and Kerouac's *On the Road* had won print at last. Burroughs' *Naked Lunch* had survived University of Chicago seizure of printing plates (see "Subliminal," p. 153) by appearing in part in *Big Table* and in entirety in a Paris edition.

While many of the poems appearing in this section reflect Ginsberg's private ravings of public spokesmanship, others are mementos of moments or days spent with closest friends. Some, such as Ginsberg's and Kerouac's "I Saw The Sunflower Monkeys of the Moon" (p. 171) are collaborations. "Shot in the Back by a Fallen Leaf" is a memorial of a week spent in Cherry Plains, New York, with Francesca and Lucien Carr, Peter Orlovsky, and Jack Kerouac, where the phrase "Mind is shapely, Art is shapely" [9] was devised. But the culmination of such memorializing occurs, at least for this reader, in the poem that immediately follows—"Sunrise":

> The Sad Light of old Decade,
> Angel Bone

it begins, bidding a bittersweet adieu to the 1950's at a New Year's Eve party. What follows is a time capsule picturing everyone there:

---

[9] See Donald M. Allen's *The New American Poetry* (New York: Grove Press, 1960), p. 415; or Donald Allen & Warren Tallman's *The Poetics of the New American Poetry* (New York: Grove Press, 1973), p. 319; or *Howl and Other Poems,* Fantasy L.P. 7013 jacket notes.

> Look how Peter and Lafcadio behave
> in penthouses
> whispering together & comparing hands
> on sofas—
> Jack rolling on the floor in a lumber
> cap...

The poem ends with a summing up of the poet's work which fulfills the poem's beginning:

> this lone scribble in the margin of my days.

The following month, Ginsberg left for his *yage* excursion to South America (letters from which are recorded in his and Burroughs' *The Yage Letters* [San Francisco: City Lights, 1963]), and returned to New York in August with a gallon bottle of liquid infusion of the hallucinogenic vine *ayahuasca,* which he shared with Peter and Jack (see "Kerouac on Ayahuasca.") Simultaneously, Allen was reading *The Tibetan Book of the Dead* while preoccupied with ideas of immolation, annihilation, and nescience, and thus considered a vaster *yogachara* consciousness as the substratum of both life and death. Consequently there follows a lot of musing about who the Knower is, and what sentience is, similar to notions expressed in entries written under laughing gas. Oddly, this may have led to a dream of the presence of Bill Burroughs in Tibet, wherein Burroughs is in some kind of friendly but perhaps ambiguous relationship with lamas, a dream breakthrough into actual future life.[10]

Soon thereafter occurred visits from and to Timothy Leary (pp. 165, 168). Visiting Leary, Allen took psilocybin with him in experimental cocktail environments. In the midst of one session, Allen phoned Kerouac to demand he come up for a big conference of seraphs. (Said Jack: "I can't. My mother won't let me go." Allen: "Bring your mother.")

It was on a visit to Leary's that Ginsberg wrote "Police," one of the many poems addressed to contemporary political problems, many of which are itemized in the letter to Gregory Corso (p. 137). The background for these political poetic ravings is entirely to the point: the banning of *Lady Chatterley's Lover;* the entire mythology of "the Cold

---

[10] In the summers of 1975, 1976, and 1977 William S. Burroughs was a visiting member of the faculty at Naropa Institute, Boulder, Colorado. Naropa was founded by and is under the direction of Tibetan lama Chögyam Trungpa.

War," support of dictatorships in Spain, Asia, and South America; the invasion of Cuba; the overthrow of Mossadeq; the drug police state which persists today—to name a few. Four lines from "Politics on Opium" (p. 151) demonstrate one aspect of the drug police problem:

—two Cops stopt me Peter & his kid brother in the middle of our dream across the street from my house in 1960 off East Second Street & Avenue A
Forced us in a doorway, flashed their badges, rolled up our sleeves, made us show our behinds,
asked for my Being Papers and destination. . . .

Within a few years agents approached Herbert Huncke, among other friends, attempting to entrap the author in a drug bust, as a file was being built in his name by the Federal Bureau of Narcotics.

Thus, in these "ravings," Ginsberg is pointing to many conditions that only a decade later gained even semi-conscious public recognition. Part of the problem, as Allen saw it, was an astonishing internalization of the police state on the part of citizens. When he told a once-radical uncle of his about his desire to visit Cuba, Allen was warned, "You'd better report to the F.B.I. first."

At the same time, there are odd personal and even prophetic political notes: the strange prophecy of Kennedy's death in 1959 ("he has a hole in his back. Thru which Death will enter," p. 111); the dream of Richard Nixon, full of humane prophetic considerations for him and strangely presaging his "post-Watergate" life ("an absurd prisoner alone in his breakfast nook nervously being self-contained reading the papers"); and the dream meeting with Eleanor Roosevelt, followed soon after by an unexpected meeting with her in real life.

V. The Mediterranean 1961–62

By this time Allen saw himself as an international poet, traveling around the world, extending Kerouac's travels across the U.S. throughout the planet. On the earlier visit to Europe, Gregory had written some of his best work of the time ("Bomb," "Death," "Army," "Hair," "Power"); Allen, in addition to Part IV of *Kaddish,* "At Apollinaire's Grave," "Poem Rocket," "Ignu," "To Lindsay," all of which were to appear in *Reality Sandwiches.*

Thus the notion of returning to Paris—and journeying thence to Asia—was accompanied by a certain nostalgia, especially since Kerouac and Corso were there already, and "the idea of seeing Jack along the old bastions of Europe was really beautiful." Moreover, Bill Burroughs was in Tangier and had been expecting Ginsberg. With the idea of visiting Paris en route to Tangier en route to India and points further East, Allen and Peter broke up their East 2nd St. apartment and took the *S.S. America* to Le Havre.

The first entry of length in this section, "I could issue manifestoes . . ." (p. 191), represents the writer's carry-over of thoughts on American and international politics (and his self-conception as spokesman-poet) to Europe. Similar attentions arise from time to time in these journals from Paris through Tangier down the Red Sea into the Indian Ocean along the coast of Africa. "Bay of Pigs" (p. 198) is a response to the U.S.-supported invasion of Cuba. In a later entry, "Rhythmic Paradigm: *National Anger*" (p. 276), Ginsberg achieves a powerful rhythmic incantory breath reminiscent of *Howl.* (He'd long thought to combine all political ravings into one long poem, "The Fall of America.") Among other poems are "One Day," a return once more to the first Blake visions, which complements "Psalm IV" in the preceding New York journals.

After two months in France, Ginsberg and Orlovsky left to join Burroughs in Tangier. Other friends—Kerouac, Paul and Jane Bowles, Tennessee Williams, Brion Gysin, Alan Ansen, Francis Bacon, Leary—were also there or passed through. Within two months a split—largely amicable—developed between Peter and Allen, with Orlovsky taking off for Greece, resolved to rejoin Ginsberg in Tel Aviv in November. Within a couple of weeks, Allen himself prepared for his own trip, his wistfulness of heart reflected in the small poem written in the room they had shared:

The sadness of goodbye again— the melancholy sunset—
Bach pathos on the phonograph— the singer chants his farewell in baritone—
The door is open, and the warm wind blows into the house—
the bread is piled on the cookstove— the drum stands empty, the waterjug has lost its top—. . .

(p. 219)

Soon Allen sailed for Greece on the *S.S. Vulcania,* "to bake my head in the classical sun" where "This is the land of marble and skin/This is the love of man."

The Room Dreams

Entries in Greece, as well as those following in the Red Sea and the east coast of Africa, include many dream records. There is the wonderful Mycenae dream of the poetry contest and surrealists (p. 239); but more significant perhaps is the dream which soon follows Ginsberg's exploration of the caves and tombs of the Mycenae ruins. "The Brain Damage" (p. 243) is perhaps the best single example in these journals of all dreams of one kind, "the room dream." Though he recorded dreams in notebooks just as he did other phenomena, he had no specific intentions with dream records (though some become poems). Thus the recognition that a series of dreams over the years contained recurrent motifs came as a pleasant surprise.

From Columbia times on, Allen had dreamt of a room or house or apartment he once lived in but which in the dream is lost or unrecognizable, utterly changed. Similarly, his father, the poet Louis Ginsberg, had a single recurrent dream for years which sheds some light on Allen's.

Louis' dream: Louis was lost in the suburbs outside of Newark (where he drove to teach at Rutgers extension). His car was lost, or he couldn't find it; night darkened; he didn't recognize where he was. Something had happened but he didn't remember how he'd lost his car or why his keys weren't on him, or why he didn't have his wallet or any money. Finally he found a dime, and a phone booth in a dark corner, his last hope. He went in, tried to phone home, and the dime clicked but the phone didn't work.

Louis had this dream on and off over many years, but it recurred several times during the spring of 1976 before his death in July. He told it to Allen, who recorded it but didn't realize Louis had written a poem about it until he found it while going through his father's papers after his death. The poem ends with a moldy telephone clicking and the poet concluding, "The phone was dead. And was I too?"

Allen recognized the sensation of referenceless disorientation accompanied by an (unremembered) event having taken place, a sense of amnesia and an anxious, confused struggle to return to a place the dreamer was certain he had only just left, as similar to parts of the Bardo

Thodol (planes of existence encountered by the entity after death) described in *The Tibetan Book of the Dead.* The features, then, of Allen's room dreams include:

1. A dwelling place of security, safety, often associated with earlier life.

2. Presence of brother Eugene or archetypal extended family members, soulmates—Burroughs, Kerouac, Lucien Carr.

3. Sometimes Allen is lost in the vast subway arcades looking for home.

4. Sometimes friends, family have gone.

5. The dwelling may be peopled with strangers.

6. Sometimes the key can't be found, or the landlord doesn't recognize him.

7. Sometimes the building is found but the apartment is either not there or completely changed, and the returnee gets lost in corridors looking for his home.

8. Sometimes the dwelling's a vast theater Allen owns or once owned.

9. Sometimes seemingly endless trips on elevators or subways in Paris or Brooklyn or the Bronx are taken in search of it.

10. Sometimes he never arrives there.

11. Sometimes the dwelling place represents safety, security, anonymity, from police state or an unknown or known crime he's dreamt he committed.

While many of his dreams in this volume incorporate some of these characteristics, the principal ones in Sections II, IV, and V are so indicated by title in the Table of Contents. The gist then of the room dreams may be the urge to cling to what one has departed from forever, even without knowing it. ("Some people may not notice they're dead," filmmaker Harry Smith once remarked.) The room/apartment/theater-dwelling place thus suggests the plane of material existence which the separated entity may wander around looking for, bewildered, trying to get back in emotionally, unwilling to give up or let go and enter Dharmakaya. Allen's own conclusion, as he told me last summer, is that:

"The disorientation and wandering in the labyrinthine dream leading to the old habitation is not much different from the sensation of wandering through the world now from Naropa to New York to Berlin—to tantric meetings to father's funerals to passing love affairs to . . . actually, as just now I went downstairs to the living room and switched on the light to this motel-like room with a huge glass window at the end large and commodious and familiar now after a summer, I suddenly had a flash of being a transient ghost in that very room of the dream. 'Cause I realized I'm leaving this place tomorrow.

"So it's not very dissimilar to actual life feelings in the sense that we die every day, or change—that is, continuous change—we die every day and leave our rooms and bodies behind and our minds behind.

"So oddly the subtle sense of space and presence of the body and its houses and apartments in actual waking life now is parallel somewhat to the dreams'. Actually the dream may be about life rather than death—but I'm sure death in that sense is only an extension of life—in that sense. And when one is near death, it would be foolish to cling to worry and anxiety and pain and fear of losing this life when in a sense it's just moving apartments . . . probably been doing it for billions of millions of years, innumerable times, and forgetting every time.

"I don't know where I'd go if I don't have the apartment. It'd be like that anxiety I was talking about before of having to go out and look for a job—start all over again from scratch and build a social existence and economic existence and find a place to live—it's finding a place to live, really. It's just a very commonplace everyday life dream—finding a place to live—superimposed on trying to cling to life and stay in the accustomed normal youthtime life—there's an element of nostalgia for what now appears to be youthtime glories and presences around Columbia with Jack and Bill and Lucien, all of whom I had tender feelings for, reliance on spiritually and emotionally."

Appropriately enough, this repository of dreams, odd minutiae of daily life, ship notes and conversations, travels and returns, ends with a brief room dream of sorts on the *S.S. Amra* en route to Bombay where the dreamer finds himself in a strange Siberian studio where "a big geography is going on" (p. 302).

Prose Style & Influences

In his early days at Columbia Allen was influenced of course by Jack Kerouac, who was already keeping small notebooks every day of key phrases, exchanges, and dramatic moments for later use in his novels. Simultaneously Lucien Carr was writing notebooks, and his youthful notion of "tortured introspection" appealed to Allen at the time.

Ginsberg finally began his own journal-keeping, as mentioned above, at age 20–21 on his 1947 visit to Denver.

Allen, Lucien, and Jack of course admired the prose (as well as poetry) of Arthur Rimbaud, his *A Season in Hell* and *Illuminations* (especially "Matinée d'ivresse"—"Morning of Drunkenness"). Of those younger days, Ginsberg has said:

> I wanted to be like Rimbaud and just write perfect things—slim volumes of perfect things where every word would be glittering and elegant and brilliant and erotic and romantic and mystical . . .

Though the older realistic Ginsberg confesses,

> I find myself saddled now with huge bags of prosaic descriptions, sometimes incomprehensible scenes of incommunicable moments of dreams.

Another early influence was Hart Crane, who used the dash greatly in jumping from thought to thought. A unique example is his "Havana Rose," a drunken note left to himself, Ginsberg surmises, in a late-night near-hypnogogic state, which mixes abstract judgment on himself and others with quick flashings of details of his environment aboard ship leaving Mexico.

Ginsberg's own accuracy in rendering a multi-planed picture is illustrated in numerous passages, such as this, from Greece: ". . . sat for coffee at iron table & watched girls run after cows, trucks unload, & old men lean on canes and blink on main street" (p. 249).

One senses the presence of a certain Cézanne-like attention, and we find the writer directly conscious of it (and of Kerouac as well) at the moment of composition in his long notation of his first peyote experience in the family backyard: "I am like Cézanne, sketching, or Kerouac's idea of prose sketching a personal originality of his . . ." (p. 8). Kerouac had impressed Ginsberg with his practice of accurately recording on the spot whatever was in his mind's eye; Cézanne, in a letter to his son, wrote that he could stand in the same spot and turn his head an inch left or right and the whole landscape would change as he was composing its structure for his canvas.[11]

---

[11] See *Paul Cézanne Letters,* John Rewald, ed. (London: Bruno Cassirer, 1941), pp. 262–3.

Certainly, some of Allen's best writing in these journals arises from similar attention to present external phenomena (see, for further examples, the Salto ball and parade, pp. 59-60, and the description of playing children in Durango, p. 71). Sometimes, such attention catalyzes a very powerful epiphany of self, as in his walk near Mycenae: ". . . reaching the flat rocky dust road my sandals broke & I plodded on thru the solitude bordered by olive groves and hills with the elevation of Hera's ruins on the right hand distance, singing to myself and the sky till the tears came to my eyes while I lifted my voice, desolate in all that history, without any name for what I was– " (p. 257).

A Note on the Text

This book represents edited transcriptions from eighteen separate notebooks ranging incompletely in time from March 1952 (when Ginsberg was twenty-five) to February 1962. In 1967 Fred Jordan at Grove Press asked Allen for all available notebooks for transcription. It is thus to him, and to Aileen Lee, who typed most of the first transcriptions, that thanks is owed for this single-volume publication ten years later.

It should be noted that the writings are not continuous; the years 1955–56 are scantily represented, and journal writings from the late fifties, having not been located (but presumably at Columbia), are not represented. Further gaps in time, cited above, appear when the author left New York for San Francisco (January–August 1959), and from January 5 through July 1960 when he made his *yage* excursion to South America, keeping notebooks that constitute a volume by themselves.

My role began in November 1974 when I appeared at Grove with a duffel bag to take these and later notebooks and their first transcriptions back to Ginsberg for an initial inventory. We decided to begin with the earliest writings and to cover all available material (with the exception of the aforementioned South America notebooks) until 1962, the year of Allen's trip to India (which is already represented in *Indian Journals* [San Francisco: Dave Haselwood/City Lights, 1970]).

As editor I've incorporated entries from these eighteen separate records (some small pocket notebooks used on walks, bus rides, subways, etc., that interleave with larger notebooks used at home, bedside) into a single volume reflecting the diversity of the author's situations, selecting blocks of passages of greatest general or literary interest, suggesting emendation and deletions to the author. Some irregularities of spelling (for instance, Ginsberg's preference of the Spanish *Tanger* for *Tangier)* and punctuation are preserved to present more accurately the poet at work. Emendations (mainly condensation by editor and author) reduce unnecessary repetition.

Footnotes identify significant names, terms, allusions, etc., and are at a minimum, especially in the poems. The many dreams, when not identified as such within the immediate text, are identified by headings. Initial footnote references to other books by the author include customary bibliographical information; subsequent references consist of book title, poem, and page. The card page facing the title page presents a complete listing of all Ginsberg books referred to in this text. First notations of poems already published are so indicated by note as they occur in these journals. Published poems written mostly or entirely on other notebooks or pages during these same years (1952; 1954–6; 1959–62) include: "In Back of the Real," "Wild Orphan," "An Asphodel," "In the Baggage Room at Greyhound," "Sunflower Sutra," "Transcription of Organ Music," "A Supermarket in California" (all in *Howl and Other Poems*—the title poem was typed on separate pages); *Kaddish,* "Laughing Gas," "Mescaline," "Magic Psalm," "The Reply," "The End" (all in *Kaddish and Other Poems);* "Malest Cornific Tuo Catullo," "Dream Record: June 8, 1955," "Fragment 1956," "A Strange New Cottage in Berkeley," "Scribble," "Afternoon Seattle," "Psalm III," "Tears," "Ready to Roll," "Battleship Newsreel," "To an Old Poet in Peru," "Aether" (all in *Reality Sandwiches);* and "Television was a Baby Crawling Toward that Deathchamber," "This form of Life needs Sex" (in *Planet News*).

The editor hopes this selection of minute irregular observations, dream confusions, self-anxieties and revelations, X-rays of consciousness, household talk and kitchen conversations, illuminations, bedside notes, elegies, proclamations and celebrations, meetings and departures of many years ago presents the poet making, as he says,

> this lone
> scribble in the margin of my days.

Gordon Ball
December 19, 1976—February 9, 1977
Carrboro, N.C.

I

NEW YORK CITY

March 12–June 30, 1952

March 12, 1952

Notes After an Evening with William Carlos Williams

Met me at the door; he said, gee I was just going out now. Going to a party, but come in, maybe you can go along? How are you now? I wondered if you had forgotten the alphabet, I said.

O I'm O.K. but the only thing (he said later) is this—my speech is slow.

Did you get to use my letter? I said. He: Have you seen Book 4? (He'd asked my ok to incorporate some letters to him as part of Paterson text.) O yes I used it, after I got your postcard—carte blanche. I used a few of them. I said: Really? He: Were you mocking me? I: No, why no. He: Did you get my card? I: No.

He: While you were sick. I: O yes, but I was sick in the hospital then. (I'd spent 8 months in N.Y. State psychiatric institute 1949 and not received post cards he'd sent.)

Riding to the party ("Party" was afternoon gathering at house of Clayton Hoagland, a Rutherford neighbor poet who worked on N.Y. Herald Tribune editorial page.), sitting on porch, introduced, Williams talking about his first long early poem like Endymion, liking Keats, read an enormous amount. That poem about prince born on foreign land, trying to get back home. Do we ever get home?

He: The more you go out, the more it seems like here—I've tried to get to know my own home territory—The more it seems like people and things I know . . . O yes, that Italian woman, reminds me of that lady I know on Cedar St. Try to wake her up (After someone says "nasty Cedar St. woman") she's conscious.

Talk about Auden at Church reading, invited me (WCW) out for drink. And talk about Spender as off beam, and uninteresting autobiography. My own auto: I tried to write it straight. It's not profound, just a story. How I fell in love with a pair of legs, a pretty pair of legs, that's all. I wrote it out in long hand. I wrote fifty pages, finished it up like this after I got out of hospital (Points meticulously and stubbornly in the air before his eye to show how typewriting fumbling earnest he was to finish). My life is over, I've lived all now, my life is through now, why shouldn't I tell the truth?

Interest in Southwest Indians. Talk about Mayans. Why write? Long disconnected failing conversation. It's all to tell truthfully why people act like they do. (He sweeps arm) Everybody here, we know them, we are afraid to act like ourselves.

Long talk on couch about reason for writing—only by finding ourselves—

Description of Auden's apt. Clutter and dirt, boy cooking food at other end of table. We had nothing to say to each other, except formalities.

Talk about meter, measure, etc. Sitting in garage in car at his home, him tired, now talking straight more: It's a matter of time. Get local speech accents and rhythm, write in that idiom. I don't even know if Paterson is poetry. I have no form, I just try to squeeze the lines up into pictures.

Liked Auden's Nones. All the lines different rhythm, varied, clear thought, mainly all the lines (He holds two hands parallel placed in air) all different, with little variations in each.

My letters: I was embarrassed seeing them. First time I've ever been in print, I said. They are egotistical. He: Well, look at Stevens' first letters, early letters to Marianne Moore.

I was up in the air then. He: Yes, you were. But that's a thing about that, you can look back on it. When you're a young man that's how you are. A young man can't think about anything but himself, that's how it has to be.

Is it all right, the letters? O sure, I said, I'm pleased, delighted. It just looks strange. No great apocalypse to be in print. Is A. P. Allen Paterson? He: No, A. Poet. Maybe I should have put in your name? I'll be sure to tell people. I said: I don't get a cut out of this? He: O well, I'll promise you a copy. Autographed? I said.

Long talk about next generation's work: need to make some standard for the line. There is nothing written to the point, I said. You should, that's necessary so that people like me won't go looking for a pattern when there is none. Maybe I will, he said . . . Flossie, she's tired. That's how she is sometimes.

She said, Thank god the Yankees lost. Also, seeing me out, I'm sorry I couldn't go, but I just can't stand that kind of party.

April 17, 1952

Still at furnished room, once more in halls of Solitude I enter this notebook—

Broke my key last night so went around looking for place to stay, wound up at Bill Keck's.

Big warm loft on 2nd Street—Bolt in door, shouted up, came down to let me in—sat down—"I'm glad to see you in your home," he smiled & grimaced & said, "What am I supposed to say, I'm glad to receive you?" saying it.

Looked at his clavichord under construction, discussed Dolmetsch [1] & Reich, and also "square hipsters." Dolmetsch: a magic name under those conditions—the primitive harkening & evoking fellow magicians.

"What are you a black magician or a white magician?" I said.

"To order," he smiled.

He spoke of God (in reference to peyote) and later I asked him (in the Jewish all night cafeteria around the block where we had vegetable soup that I bought, and macaroons & coffee & cakes)—"You spoke of God before: what's that to you?"

"When the universal order seems organized—when everything I see seems to belong to one organism, when everything about me swings, together."

Difference between T God & Peyote god:

"With T you are observing everything in unison order harmony swinging organized organism—with peyote you are part of it."

He gave me, without my realizing it was sitting there beside us on the improvised table of a solid block of wood or box—three cones or buds of peyote: I was shocked and awed by their appearance—lifelike and large—cones or vortexes consisting of a seemingly alive vegetable.

They are ranged on the paper in front of me as I write: the most perfect is about 3 or 2½ inches long from tip to head; the tip & outer sheath of the cone to the head is made of a brown soft bark, as on a wrinkled potato type root or tuber. The head is chiefly astounding: it looks like dusty malachite in color: green that is perhaps bright, and if

---

[1] Arnold Dolmetsch built clavichords & harpsichords; he was credited by Ezra Pound for resurrecting harpsichord and clavichord music.

wetted goes deeper green—a center of white fuzz, like a fungus growth, and spotted in each section of the head, centered, a tuft of fuzz. The head looks like soft curvy rock; or like green martian flesh, wrinkled or creased: and the whole bud is soft under the surface, so that one dares not squeeze too hard for fear of injuring the plasm or animal. The bottom of the cone, or tip, is harder: the centre of the root seems most vulnerable. It apparently grows much larger; grows underground in the cone, with the head above the desert flatness gaping unreally at the sun.

One of the buds has a double root like a cactus. The last has tip cut off & looks injured & stunted, but center still good.

I was told to eat the pulp, peeling away top & bark & all rot parts from injury to head.

Hard to digest, so eat with milk or juice or especially with fruit salad.

I carried the god (small peyote god) around in my briefcase for 2 days wandering in New York, & saw the burning of the early Christian martyrs in *Quo Vadis* with Gene the next night.

He (Keck) said he read Lao-Tse—in 8 or 9 translations & finally began to get the drift—disliked Bynner translation, liked one in Yutang anthology (Waley). Said he liked poets like Whitman, Blake, Lawrence (didn't know about Rilke), also had been awakened by Kenneth Rexroth as I myself by Rimbaud. Also liked one of Jeffers' longer poems.

I noticed whiteness of dawn street, he noticed blueness of it.

His loft has a window on the stairway overlooking a cemetery—stairway dark & old & deserted, rubbish filled—3 flights in unused bldg. $15 a month rent pipes electric up from next floor, has candles also & kerosene lamp. Tacked on wall—Song by Moondog—

> "I won't go to your dark bed,
> if I do there be many eternities
> of night I'll regret it"—a round.

Mail advertising circular from Magic Gardens, Laredo Texas. Pictures from newspapers & headlines on newspapers.

Feeling of Keck of awe and seriousness—

He rejected Vedanta & other self-dispossession type cures as bad—saw world itself as to be seen either way as in 1st verse (he mentioned) of Lao-Tse. Described & recommended St. John of the Cross' dark night of soul.

Awe & seriousness & slightly sinister maniacal overtones as all subterraneans, but what quality of depths and mysteries unfathomed ever by me—

Can't describe charm of such life & its objects of awe & contemplation—the glass bowl (blue) filled with steel wool (which broke up his cold he said) which holding to the ear I heard a dead silence of the void—robbed air of its infinite music & motion.

He put me up for nite on his couch—one cover (top) of which is a flag, Union Jack, he said. He came to bed later on, crawled in dressed. I slept far over in narrow couch on my side uncomfortable troubled by dreams of god fright and sexual battle between us—he perhaps wanting me (in my dream) to make love to him or we make love together, I resisting & rejecting him.

I came on very square, I am an old fool to these subterraneans.

Keck also read poems:

"Life is the graveyard
Life is the sea
Life is the lime green tree [1]"

"Awe" poems. Used word eternity, referring to the sky.

Dream

With W C Williams at party in my family mansion—Edith my mother—thru the windows into the sun porch arboretum statue room I see bust of goddess? and statue of Hermes & Eros—and statue moves, Hermes is lifting Eros' small boy's marble white behind from his loins in a single gesture upward & outward (to shoulder?). Hermes had been fucking the child Eros. I want to go into sunroom to look closer—apparently statues say something, or some poem is written there, but mother objects—I'm crashing around well-arranged disposition of statue exhibits & flowers & plants & stems.

April 1952

We're flowers to rocks. That was last nite's note. Took Peyote at 8:30 AM—very unpleasant bitter metallic taste, I gagged at second chunk—the yellow insides. Worst part of peyote the metallic imaginary aftertaste &

[1] There was a lime green tree in the graveyard downstairs—A.G., 1975

feeling of stomach sickness and heaviness of body, nearly nausea. I walked my father immediately to the corner, & lay down in bed.

After awhile, when sickness passed—first thing I noticed: eyes closed toward light leaves in eye a golden glow hue—which darkens when you pass hand over lidded eye. It made me feel like a very transparent sort of organism.

I noticed the pillowcloth (inside the white slip) was very beautiful pattern of yellow and green. Classic russian primitive.

When the wind rushes thru the grass you can see the green grass vibrating on the brown ground.

I went to the window, looked at the Cherry Tree in bloom. (Menstruating cherry tree, Louis said).

I'm sitting outside under the tree.

"Heavens, the universe is in order"—It is a wonderful day, in the backyard. The sky is a solid light blue,—I look up at it and it appears the atmosphere of a planet, which it is—pretty white clouds, like static semen, floating very purposefully away in front of me to god knows what Gotter-dammerung of Clouds at the end of the world.

Of course, heavy feeling in stomach and bitter aftertaste.

I am like Cezanne, sketching; or Kerouac's idea of prose sketching a personal originality of his . . .

I can't stand the smell of my hands—ink which smells like metallic peyote tastes—only that nausea haunts me—I keep blinking my eye—my head is heavy and constricted—

This poor journal, which later will seem to be nothing—is *now* so much part of the world, that it seems to be sufficient—to put down only such sparse details—I would like to fit the whole world and its very solid and apparent mysteries here.

The great mystery is that of Being. It is a beautiful day, the houses appear solid and in miniature "open unto" the sky . . . Paterson backyard.

Everything is full of activity—a bee just dropped down on my page (which is light blue or greenish cast ruled lines).

There are flies and butterflies—I saw a white one before but the air is otherwise clear all the way up to the sky is "like a crystal"—it's true air, space—*space is a solid.*

The houses around here seem so primitive, with their poor television antennae tacked on to the patched up chimney—

The neighbor next door, Dr. A—, comes up from his basement inside his house and says in a heavy voice,

"Dear, I feel as if I detect a slight odor of gas down here"

Man so busily occupied sniffing out details of their amazing being that surrounds him on a spring sunny sunday—I hate to even conceive of the weekly world and its rules, complexities, violences—lack of repose—involvement—I am after all looking only thru a plateglass window at the world.

The clank of garbage pails—a hollow sullen roar like that of a dog, calling attention to themselves, too—gaily—

The wind making noises at the top of the tree, laundry flapping in a tree of laundry too—the window-shade cord with the silly ring-holder at the bottom hanging & swinging in the open window.

I am merely looking up at details & noting them down as they come to my attention. But to turn the mind to something fixed and contemplate (I should like to go in and hear music—I started writing, and heard a burst of music from the ill-adjusted radio being turned on . . . then volume down)—

To contemplate that rock, for instance, that my mind? who? *I* imagined last nite suddenly in the dark—(the rock lasting longer than a man)

The world is full of strange noises, I turn on music which is the most strange—I'm walking around house at a mad pitch, doing things and writing—must go back to that rock—am at kitchen table now.

"Stream of consciousness"—the other (in books) is literary. But quite an interesting concept.

I have been going around grinning idiotically at people—almost afraid they'll ask "What's the matter with you this minute?" But they seem to me also—so strange in their momentary consciousness—M— reserved talking to her brother didn't understand my intrusion: "What are you bothering with practical politics again?"—didn't even understand my language.

Louis's head characteristically peers from the back window. I nod and he withdraws.

Rock. Serried & worn by years, so old, a huge stone tear. I can't even see you under your shroud of dirt.

A bird just shat on me! It must have been on purpose.

My father came to the door—I said, "You know what? A bird just flew by and dropped on me. I'm a victim of the birds out here"—he couldn't hear and turned away.

Imagine being in the literal presence of one's father.

The rock is grey and has a film of dust on it—can only shine pristine and pure in its nakedness when wet—or "polished"—which is why they polish poor stones—any stone when polished being beautiful. We should cut & polish large stones.

They are always interrupting me in my observations of the world with strident voices—"Please Allen, will you hang that up?"—a piece of laundry which had dropped on the grass. And I hear relatives' honking mechanical voices in the house. My father says,

"He's busy with himself," just now—Am I attracting too much attention, just sitting in the backyard writing? How logically people act, yet how strange.

Language is very worn out—it is of necessity so abstract—a word like "strange"—when everything is strange it has no meaning.

I have a paranoid fear that everytime I look up someone is looking out at me from the window—such a habit of self-awareness I have. Prison?

My thoughts are definite things left back in time—like 5 minutes ago—"Peyote is certainly one of the world's great drugs."

These mad appearances of differing faces in the back window—talking, looking out at the tree.

Today my family should all dance under the blooming cherry tree in the backyard—it really occupies their attention so much. And I love the cherry tree like a—It is so alone and stolid all year, no thought of its own, no way to talk! It must have amazing feelings this time of year—toward the tree, its lover, three backyards away, which pollinates it—yet it is now dropping buds on my head.

There's nothing in the grave.

How terrible & agonizing it would be for all this motion & change in creating to be fixed, nothing moving. (All forms still & staring like flowers & fish in transparent plastic paperweight.)

I have to find, among other things, a new word for the universe, I'm tired of the old ones, they mean too many things from other times & people.

Also amazing how my real fixation on T or anything returns to this wonder at the world of solid substance & stops simply gazing at appearance, with scant regard for telos or final mechanics.

Does everybody have the same process going on? Of course I am too involved in politics, mechanics, and everything, but my attention—this is my sickness—is not fixed on anything . . .

However it strikes me that perhaps only I and Williams (W.C.) in a radius of miles around—stand so solidly on terra firma admiring.

Fixed smile on my face—throbs of pleasure at birds flying overhead in threes—Yet I am unhappy, I long for company of mind—body too—I should be with a lover now.

The silence in the middle of all this is so lonely—but then the wind came up and made noise—of course I could go in and talk to my family.

This is you understand (I'm speaking to Bill Keck now) a literal transcription of my thoughts as they occur . . .

I thought of sending him these notes before. I would like to write a poem. Divine Poem on the physical world.

Upstairs next door the women are dandling and combing the 2 year old girl's hair. How she must be happy, with all that attention.

I am an old gossip over the backyard hedge with Dr. A—. No evidences of spiritual violence or cryptesthesia.

And finally the family bared its bones at the luncheon table—Louis complaining abstractly (hypothetical situations) about Sheila (stepdaughter)—seeming to have a meaning, a lurking resentment undertoning his words, and Edith his wife sat by & interpolated arguments. And I took him head on, "You're like a comic strip Poppa"—but the terrible serious jagged edge of his hysteria underneath obtruded thru the afternoon to an inevitable reality—and Edith afterward alone in the kitchen, so angry, almost weeping, with choked voice—

"Doesn't he realize that only because I'm being easy to get along with—it's the only thing that keeps us together—"

And my stunned realization of our weakness—at the terrible portent.

She says she will blow up soon, and I encourage her to express herself—

"He'll back down. He'd have to be crazy not to"—

The words of her and me taking terrible portent in the middle of the radiant Sunday afternoon—all Creation about us glistening—and the mysteries of the wellsprings of family revealing themselves—

Louis was complaining again about Telephone, about girls not coming right home & helping mother after she comes home from work—

Johnnie Ray—the circus hysteric act—the living wonder, the agonist with open heart—beautiful man they say showing his wound his tortured soul.

The great structure opening like a hysterical flower of Perez Prado's Mambo No. 5—the zigzag structure of the massed trumpets punctuated by ripples of the drum, held floating notes, voices, rattles, gourds, primitive sound; suddenly the blare of precise fugues of the trumpet chorales building to a screetch of power—suddenly halted with subtle rhythms drumbeats finishing off—

Anything, anything, there's so much to say from the bottom of the heart—but not say in open. . .—people really can't stand much reality—or me, hate to think of anyone talking back to me.

What kind of secret organization of the feelings did I go thru today? (It's 6:30 PM) only a few more hours to go.

Peyote is not God—but is a powerful force—can see, if everybody on, how they would organize their lives once every year, communicating with each other—what spiritual violence that day—what secrets revealed—family secrets, not big mystical riddles, which are after all palpable & easy to see just by staring outward into the obvious infinity of the sky—

Which is a thought I've never covered properly. Some subject to attempt:

It occurred to me early, and is a persistent thought of mine: . . . problem of matter & infinity & origin of Creation to be assessed & thought into without the aid of reason or science, but with the inner imagination . . . impasse of imagination . . . returns the mind to the fact that looking out into the sky see the solid endless heaven existing out there . . . going up from us (our glance) endlessly. What can you do with such a fucking universe? So this process of thought will never comprehend—for the necessary peaceful minute—the reaches of the Cosmos.

When the mind reaches that solid impossible wall it knows it's off in a meaningless series of ideas & must return—Jazz & music reaches that moment of peace—end of thought.

Much work to be done on sequence & structure of thoughts—actual occurrences—and not synthetic thoughts pieced together from fragments—but the relation of fragments.

Joyce is great—working with basic material of thoughts, not saying anything else, but presenting typical sequence in totality—which is all we know or can write down anyway.

Peyote very similar to T except that thought is, while futile, less distorted and impossible to capture for the moment than on T, and substance seems very solid. . . .

* * *

How automatically my thought ranges obsessionally toward the Schizoid—preoccupation with abstraction and eternal facts—yet I believe it produces some fact:

"And one time is all Time
if you look at it out of the grave."

New schizoid question: Did I have a Revelation?

* * *

How everybody always ... speaks from the whole soul ... telling the truth. For instance I praised Sheila's dress to Edith, (her mother), "She walked out like a Hollywood girl." And Edith replied (a touch of irony & resentment at situation in mind): "Don't worry, I already approved of her."... the threat, earlier this afternoon, was very profound—her womb born child, heart, under attack.

And to Sheila, in the garden I said, regarding the disarray of her hair: "Well, we're not all perfect."

She: "We do our best," very primly, with a coy smile.

Me: "And we must never underestimate the charm of being human."

She: "You better watch out."

I couldn't however understand that ... sexual warning? ... but apparently the sight of my soul was too much for her ... a soul underneath ... at the moment.

Also glad I sailed thru this Peyote test without any of the mental imaginables—the horrors of accidents, I didn't cut my thumb or bite anyone or tip my mit.

How I so long to *tip my mit*—which is why I write ... perhaps these flashes of communication ...

I may be in a vain prison but my room on the second floor of this house is the only one without a mirror ...

Late April 1952

Dawn—fatigue—whiteness on blueness of sky, buildings, showing color—rust red—coming home to attic by Port Authority, rent overdue, didn't get girl, long involved truthful conversation—I didn't want her?—I'm a mental prisoner.

How to get out of fantasy world—stop all phantasy! live in the physical & real sensation situation, moment to moment, seize opportunities, take offers you want.

I must put down every recurrent thought.

* * *

Left Dylan Thomas and someone else with a big bruise on right forehead—thin mediocre type—in cab at 6th Avenue, 15 minutes ago.

I was in San Remo sitting relaxed toward closing time when they walked in. I only half recognized him when they came in door & stood next to my seat at bar.

Thomas said "Congratulations" or "Imagine that" when bartender spoke his name overloud & said he'd read his poems over the bar.

"Don't believe everything you hear," said Thomas to me.

"Only if it's spoken loud enough," I answered.

His companion said, "Where do you go to school"—I said I didn't go, huffily.

"Do you know—ever study English literature" said companion.

"Of course, I'm a poet myself" I said.

"Do you know who this is," he said.

"Of course man it is obvious."

"Oh another," said Thomas.

"Well don't look at me," I said, stiffening up.

Thomas, "I was just in another pub—drinking place—whatever you call them—and a girl said to me—would you like somewhere to go to see a girl and me do a trick?"

"Is it a question of interpretation of 'trick' " I said.

"No, I'm a professional," Thomas said "I'm a professional."

"Well, I just thought it was a question of language," I said.

"But she wanted $50.00—which I didn't have."

"Oh well."

"Do you know any amateurs?" he asked.

"I think the best I can do is knock on a door and it will be opened by a pretty girl who'll offer us a bottle of beer."

"Will she do a trick?"

"I can only supply one pretty girl who'll open her door." I said.

"Well, that's a lot, that's half of it."

"That's the way the world is," we agreed.

"But that's a lot," he said. "What can you do?" I said.

I then said Lucien & Cessa would be newspaper people at home. "But they have likker but they aren't 'intelligent.' "

"Well, I insist they'll have to be intelligent"—he.

"No I didn't want to mention that—they, of course, of course, have feelings, heart, mind, suffering—and nobility."

He nodded understanding.

I was very eager to see him off and go along. But everything was very chancy and superficial and no action took place. I called Lucien. There was no answer. Alas!

I came back & said they weren't home—and on and on. Mary Joe was there [at bar], "Who's she"—they wanted to know.

He could have had her but she was silly & he a fool about reputation.

Said—"I've got the shortest legs in the world, my belly hangs down to my groin."

She chatted & camped but no action.

I tried to get him to go to Dusty's—the bartender took him aside & asked me to leave, I said to Thomas, "Shall I wait outside?" He nodded very gently & graciously, perfect gentleman tho he didn't know me.

Later outside I remembered my attic & he said, "but not an attic— . . . Just you & me?" "That's all" I replied. He had said he had a bottle along too. "I want to go to drink the bottle where there are other people around."

Outside Victor & several other heavy-handed hipsters—3 of them stood by door while I sat on gutter & waited—They were conversing, wondering why narcissistic girls went for weak-chinned people like him—talking about him in manly cultural underground terms, but spitefully, asserting their own virility & new generation removal from dependence or sympathy with him—said, "Byron had strength," and complimented each other too.

I yelled "Hey" when he came out and got up and joined them too—wasn't sure he'd even remember—He said "I never was so bored" by the action inside Remo with proprietors—

I had difficulty raising subject of continuing on with him as I asked inside by saying, "I don't know what will happen but if I may I wish to continue & go on with you where ever you are going tonight if you have anywhere to go." He said "Yes I'd be glad of course"—but with eye wandering, alas but, so dissolute he was he meant it too, just as well.

On the way he stopped in middle of street, "I don't know what to do"—

I took up initiative and said,

"OK I'm telling you then come with me!"

Meanwhile companion said "I'm awfully tired, should go home" and "Caitlin is waiting."

Finally Thomas decided to go, and I closed a cab door on them, ran to other side & stuck my tongue in window at him which I immediately regretted tho I meant it as a friendly gesture. He stared out at me drunkenly without response.

We had been followed down corner and W. 4th St. by 3 subterraneans. I ran off, leaping.

Friend companion earlier had said about bruise, "In fight"—on account of Thomas's saying things—an hour ago, wound up in hospital.

Ah, Dylan Thomas, I would have liked to know you that night, wish I could have communicated who I was, my true feeling, and its importance to you. For I too am a lover of the soul.

How disappointing to come away empty-handed with no recognition from this Chance meeting—I fell sick and unhappy because I could not make a great sweet union of the moment of life—now this is 45 minutes after, it will pass but it is sad & true.

Dream

Great floods in Paterson. I get home—Lucien around?—copies of N.Y. Times—edited by Bill Burroughs—

Belgrade rebels, area Communist (I thought of extent of inner corruption)—middle area of Yugoslavia in doubt.

Also a headline

WORLD IN FLOOD WATER
EVERYWHERE ETC. PAPER GOES
ON. BURROUGHS AT HELM, ETC.

—a joke headline—

inside a paper with mimeographed list of subscribers? or possible future co-workers on paper.

* * *

Don't forget evening party at which had X, Kingsland, Dick Howard, Carl & Olive—Y drunkenly riding uptown for liquor—X hurt in small smash, cursing doctors over phone, then Y & X necking, ripping X's fly open, her sucking his white dick, pallid, and her posture of arched back & readiness on his knees, him with hand in her crotch—and their conversation—"I'm as nasty as you"—

Y: "I love you for your nastiness"—and "You're a silly girl"—and me sleeping with her later at her place.

* * *

The Wisdom of Solomon (Carl)

They censor words not the things they denote:
It would create less of a stir to drop a piece of shit on Grant's tomb
than to write it out in white paint.
Because people recognize that's what memorials are for—old bums & dogs to shit on.

Act boldly, think with Caution—even timorously

* * *

A Novel

At 14 I was an introvert, an atheist, a Communist and a Jew, and I still wanted to be president of the United States.

At 19, being no longer a virgin, I was a cocksucker, and believed in a supreme reality, an anarchist, a hipster totally apolitical Reichian; I wanted to be a great poet instead.

At 22 I was a hallucinating mystic believing in the City of God and I wanted to be a saint.

At 23, a year later, I was already a criminal, a despairing sinner, a dope fiend; I wanted to get to reality.

At 24, after being a jailbird, a schizoid screwball in the bughouse, I got layed, girls, I was being psychoanalyzed.

At 26, I am shy, go out with girls, I write poetry, I am a freelance literary agent and a registered democrat; I want to find a job.
Who cares?

* * *

Crazy—A Magazine
Issue on Cannastra; Joan, Kammerer.

* * *

Up from my books.
The moon in the window,
Summer night and solid sky.

Black hollow of buildings,
A hundred different chimneys.
I see lit windows but no humans to watch.

June 17, 1952

Limping down the block, foot bruised yesterday in peyote euphoria on Washington Sq. with Keck & Anton.[1]

A boy came out of Shelley's, early twenties, in dungarees & striped T shirt—carrying 2 glasses of red liquor walking in front of me.

I sit naked in my room remembering the animal swing of his buttocks, the length and strength and paleness of his arms in the darkness as he balanced his way brushing slightly drunken against the granite of the building with his arm.

It is midnight in the blue attic,[2] summer, a thin film of sweat on my face.

He stopped after walking the length of the building down the sidestreet in the darkness, by an iron fence which led to an iron stairway down to a cement courtyard behind the building.

He put both glasses down, bending over—were they filled with wine—picked one up, and drank it all straight down. I walked on, staring back, he looked at me and said—

"I got a good deal out of the bar," or something.

"What a way to drink!" I said incoherently, walking on. I wanted to stop and make him—thinking of the crowd of youths around the pinball machine in the bar 2 months ago, the hunchback, the handsome one, the other boys—afraid of being discovered on the block as a queer, or afraid of him & afraid to stop & talk. He was quite tall and evenly formed.

---

[1] "Keck & Anton: members of a circle of seekers, some from West Coast, friends of Philip Lamantia & Carl Solomon, who hung around San Remo Bar MacDougal & Bleecker, Greenwich Village, at that time a center of Kerouac's N.Y. social life—described in *The Subterraneans*, late 40's & early 50's."—A.G., September 1975.

[2] Little attic apt. 15th St. N.Y.C. between 8th & 9th Ave. across from Port Authority Building. A few poems from *Empty Mirror* (Totem/Corinth, 1961) describe it: "After all, what else is there to say?" (p. 11), "Marijuana Notation" (p. 19), "A Ghost May Come" (p. 26), "Walking home at night" (p. 45).

This reminds me—he not a great face, just another momentary sadness of unobtainable common beauty—of the truly great strangers, the appearances of majesty I have seen on the streets here and there. A project which I have meant to sketch for several weeks.

In Houston, 1948—I was broke, stealing Pepsi Cola bottles to cash in and buy candy bars for hunger, waiting for a ship. Outside the old Union Hall, walking down the street, a Latin animal, Cuban, Spanish, I don't know. Electricity seemed to flow from his powerful body—black hair, curled wildly, looked impossible for him to live in society, to me—powerful malignant features—he was perhaps 22 or less—springing down the street in a tense potent walk, dungarees, powerful legs, not too tall, blue shirt opened several buttons on the chest, black hair curling sparsely on chest—he seemed made of iron, no sweat—or brown polished rock. I never in my life saw a more perfect being—expression of vigor and potency and natural rage on face—I couldn't conceive of him speaking English. I wonder what loves he had. Who could resist him? He must have taken any weak body he needed or wanted. Love from such a face I could not imagine, nor gentleness—but love and gentleness are not needed where there was so much life. He just passed me by and I stood there amazed staring at him as he disappeared up the block & around the corner scattering the air in spiritual waves behind him. I couldn't believe he was human. He had thick features, black eyebrows, almost square face, powerful chest, perfect freedom of walk.

Similar to him, the Latin I saw on 57th Street and Madison and Park, whom I followed down the street for several blocks, staring at him. This youth—he seemed very young, yet dressed impeccably in an Oxford grey or black suit, shining perfect black shoes, delicate grey tie—the clothes of a diplomat or rich artist—had long black hair combed neatly, like a statue or painting of perfect grooming, back on his head with a part—yet it was still a black animal mane. His features were regular and hard, very strong even face, with great force and dignity—all this in a youth not much older than me. I tagged along behind this culturally accomplished beast intelligence in my scuffed handmedown shoes, unpressed illfitting post adolescent suit, dirt ringed shirt and cheesy tie, hair askew and book underarm, perspiring perhaps. The impression of purpose & forcefulness, dignity, and social powerfulness embodied in this beautiful animal mask, the alien master man; a U. N. diplomat or courier I thought.

Another meeting: In the Lexington Ave Subway, in N.Y. or on the shuttle: a woman of indeterminable age—forty or so, yet perhaps younger

Another meeting: On the Lexington Ave Subway, in N.Y. or on the shuttle: a woman of indeterminate age—fourty to 50, yet perhaps younger and aged by madness or suffering: I think she had no hat, or perhaps a beret or cowl, and it seemed a stylish velvet dress, a little better than street wear, yet satisfactory—but torn, mussed, dirty, seedy—with dirty delicate hands, and perhaps dirty light brown hair and unclean face—a long face, with drooping eyes and spirit, sensitive tense mouth, aquiline aristocratic nose—like an even thinner and more dangerously ill Virginia Woolf—stamped over her the aura of sensitivity and aristocracy: she sat there in cramped posture: as if she had been living in hovels or homeless for years, nervous with her hands, bitten fingernails, face covered with thought and incoherent suffering—she may even have been unrecognizably drunk—character shattered by what insanity—seeming blankness about her as I stared: I would have spoken but it seemed all I could do was take her burden & rescue her forever if I once intervened, having this suicide on my hands. However the look of the face remains—too bad I have no photograph or drawing talent—thin, bony, elite, possibly mad, anxiety of nobility—intelligence beyond ideas, completely beat, shifting nervously in her seat, continually agitated, by her unknown mystery.

and aged by madness or suffering; I think she had no hat, or perhaps a beret or cowl, and it seemed a stylish velvet dress, a little better than street wear, yet satisfactory—but torn, mussed, dirty, seedy—with dirty delicate hands, and perhaps dirty light brown hair and unclean face—a long face, with drooping eyes and spirit, sensitive tense mouth, aquiline aristocratic nose—like an even thinner and more dangerously ill Virginia Woolf—stamped over her the aura of sensitivity and aristocracy: she sat there in a cramped posture; as if she had been living in hovels or homeless for years, nervous with her hands, bitten fingernails, face covered with thought and incoherent suffering—she may even have been unrecognizably drunk—character shattered by what insanity-seeming blankness about her as I stared? I would have spoken but it seemed all I could do was take her burden & rescue her forever if I once intervened, having this suicide on my hands. However the look of the face remains—too bad I have no photograph or drawing talent—thin, bony, elite, passively mad, anciency of nobility—intelligence beyond ideas, completely beat; shifting nervously in her seat, continually agitated by her unknown mystery.

Another woman—perhaps I saw her more than once?—riding on the bus into East Harlem in 1949. I thought of her as Jeanne Duval perhaps—a mulatto or negress, with a perfect oval face, without makeup of any kind, and exotic and beautiful features—she was perhaps 30–35. The extremity of the oval, the extremity of her mulatto beauty—not exactly symmetrical, but perfect-arched eyebrows, almond black eyes, straight nose, cool perfection of mouth—a middle or lower class type but so lifted out of social context by her physical appearance I couldn't figure what she was doing on the bus, or in Harlem life. Expression not of arrogance or sexuality but of angelic coolness, objectivity, ease in the world but not of this world either. She sat across from me on the bus.

How can such people exist unnoticed without being made heroes by the first passersby?

On the subway again: at 135th Street on the 7th Ave line going downtown: a man I remember little of. He sat across from me on the subway long seat. A man in his fifties—again the indeterminacy of age—with white hair; he was slightly built, but still well-preserved, and his face, except for the unwrinkled appearance of age and maturity—might have been that of a young man. He had a big black felt hat, of another generation, and a black coat with velvet on it, a Chesterfield—all also beat tho well preserved, slightly messy. He looked like a rich recluse in worn-out hermit gentility. His face, tho, so beautiful and ageless, so angelic-gentle and angelic-handsome & angelic-sexless, on account of age—an untroubled and not agitated equivalent of the woman on the subway. Great intelligence, also, perhaps like Béla Bartók looked riding to York Avenue, starving to death.

Finally a young kid in his middle teens perhaps walking with a few boys down Market Street, Paterson, past City hall, past the bank and Schoonmakers,[1] 3 years ago or 2, when I was wandering downtown around, don't remember why. He had neither the bestial brilliance of the Spaniard, nor suffering nor intellectuality of others, nor their age: he was rather short, and at first glance perhaps even too short (stunted by cigarettes?), dressed in dungarees, very tight: he was well built though, thick buttocks and short powerful genitals pressing out the tight workpants, and perhaps a dirty t-shirt over wide squat chest (he was not however a dwarf, just a small powerful adolescent)—and a plain, not ugly, not nice face—yet as I first glanced at him and passed by I felt almost faint from the wave of dirty sexuality, of real knowing naive, innocent carnality; physical liberty, belly and buttock power in him. He walked down the street and I half followed I was so struck—my own body reacted to his like a magnet to a magnet disturbed and drawn, sickened in the belly by lust—the frankness of his body—he was talking to several other gangling unformed adolescents, he smoked a cigarette freely, talking perhaps describing some conquest, perhaps occupied in some showy-manly plot for a secret club or hide-out. I never saw anyone I wanted to lock my body with so strongly—except perhaps the savage Spaniard of Houston.

* * *

A grey mist in these applied thoughts.

* * *

---

[1] Schoonmakers: a downtown Paterson department store.

Young men in their prime are
    sick, the rose is closing
Tenderness and a Tomb

* * *

. . . I am in bed with very young boy—7 or 8—who covers me over with cloth on which are obscene hieroglyphs, one for each part of my body—they are supposed to act on my skin—while he watches I have sex with hieroglyphs.

* * *

Fantasy—

Carl murdering some anonymous bitch girl flirting with his asexual hostility—dragged screaming to wagon—"I'm Halley's[1] Cousin! I'm Halley's Cousin"—with a maniacal gleam of desperate humor—He has a god in his head.

Vision of him undecided at trial, half waiting to die, half wanting nuthouse, half smile on face.

And in nuthouse for life, the religious flowering of the imagination, the authentic genius recording his sufferings as a living deadman; uncomprehended disordered radiant humor.

Kafka Diaries—Schocken[2]

Feb. 7, 1912—"Future never out of my sight. What evenings, walks, despair in bed and on the sofa are still before me, worse than those I have already endured."

Feb. 25, 1912—"Hold fast to the diary from today on! Write regularly! Don't surrender! Even if no salvation should come, I want to be worthy of it every moment."

[1] Carl Solomon's cousin Rudolph Halley, once counsel for Kefauver Crime Investigating Committee, was then New York City Council President.

[2] Quotations following are from pp. 231, 233, & 300, respectively, of *The Diaries of Franz Kafka,* ed. Max Brod (New York: Schocken Books, 1948).

William S. Burroughs, East 7th Street, N.Y.C., Winter 1953

Jack Kerouac, East 7th Street, N.Y.C., Winter 1953

Last days before Riva Sanitarium—"In me, by myself, there are no visible lies. The limited circle is pure."

Jun. 30—

Lucien warning me the other day not to go mad again, not to drift off into unreality of thought to place where I met Carl—Madhouse.

. . . I must abandon again this whole metaphysical urge that leads me further each month back to an uncreated world of bliss of my own making in my own head—bliss which I do not even remember any more, is just an idea—while the real world passes me by.

I must find a small cheap comfortable apartment of my own.

I must stop putting off looking for *any* kind of a job—and go out to get what I can. I think maybe a totally non-literary job.

What do I want to *do* in the world aside from "be a poet."

Must stop playing with my mind, with my life.

Unknown pains and suffering of trial and weakness in competition and fight for moneymaking ideas.

Place in Society. I have no function in the world I live in. I am oppressed by my own inaction and cowardice & conceit & cringing, running away from life.

What will I *make* happen to my life?

II

MEXICO AND RETURN TO U.S.

December 31, 1953, Yucatán—
July 1954, California

Mexican notebook cover

New Year's Eve—Country Club, Mérida 10:55

I arrived early, took a walk—why have I no tuxedo?—I was not prepared in my travels to meet so proud a manifestation of wealth and style. The band strikes up 11 men & xylophones, melancholy. Many blue lace dresses, and stark black and white or pink grand costumes.

Couples come in 4's—I don't know where to go—a great silence fills the ballroom, the echoes of footsteps & scuffling walk up the stone paths—the band is resting a moment & will fill up the void.

Now a greater noise of more arrivals—4 pats on the back for each male as they embrace—3 or 4 hard pats.

* * *

"Pica pica"—Yucatán intoxicant

* * *

Mérida—New Year's Day 1954

The Mayor read a 50 page document taking a full hour—the city photographer fell asleep—then he got tired & had his secretary read. Then he picked up again with the résumé for another half hour—new rastro [1], etc.—Meanwhile the sounds of silver glass & ice in the air for refreshments on the balcony.

[1] Rastro: slaughterhouse.

Cathedral Mérida

Chichén Itzá—Soliloquy [1]

Army shoes, a kerosine lamp on dust strewn floor where ant wends its nitely ritual way—off with my straw hat—cigarette moment ago on my hand on knee in darkness seemed a million miles away.

On top of old El Castillo—in what I thought 3 nites ago was the medium—looking up at the nylon of stars—pure clear stars of southern tropic night over forest of chirruping insects and maybe birds and once I heard an owl hooting.

Great stone portals, entablatures of language gone, poetry gone, spirit gone, bas reliefs of unknown perceptions: in front of me a minute ago I saw a death's head half a thousand years old—and have seen cocks a thousand years old grown over with moss and batshit in a dripping vaulted room of stone, stuck in the walls (like C.'s plasticine cock at Columbia dormitory).

High air of silence over the thin layer of nightforest that stretches over to the horizon which as I turn my head is circular.

Everywhere in this dead city the clap of hands reechoes from half dozen temples laid out at acoustical angles made for jazz and poetry and religion: the projection of a voice of stone, the echo of eternity—so that

---

[1] Many phrases in this soliloquy and later Mexico and California entries appear in the poem "Siesta in Xbalba," pp. 21–39 of *Reality Sandwiches* (San Francisco: City Lights, 1963).

some man in plumes and frenzied calm stood up on monuments that echoed to each other in front of a silent mob and suddenly started to yell his head off in a dancebeat scream—toward what end other than howls of joy that answered him I dont know—no other in this void occurs to mind, as it is most striking that the silence and stars and ruins make a void together by my candle and my rolling pen in the night.

I had gone out to accustom myself to the night light of this vault where my poor quinque [1] fills the stone with eyeful yellow flickers—so bright in its humble solitary weeping flame it alone makes lite like flambeau ancient rotted out of hands that close still in moulding stone grip with faces flat and worn away by Time.

But Deathhead in front of me on portal's here and thinks its way thru centuries—reveal to me, eyesee, the thought of the same night I sit in sat in once and many times before by artisan other than I or master once whose work's fineness has been worn down by time and only the crude skull figurements left with its wornaway plumes and indecipherable headdresses of intellect and thought, and clothes of style obliterated to a mess of notches—and the paint, blue, yellow, green flaked off and paled now to a fading splotch from spot to spot—on curlicues that might as well be questionmarks as serpents after all.

A hand bearing a pole, squatting on loin with heavy wraparound, enjewelled, now crude bathingsuit of stone—

My hat woven of henequen fragile on the stone floor as a leaf on the waters, and as perishable—much less my own flame which wavers continuously & will go out in open air—

Dream in Jungle at Chichén—

I was at travel—We were called by phone—a rumor that Jack [2] had been killed—stabbed— . . . [line obliterated] . . . And so too Lucien had phoned news to Gene—& Bill.[3] I was visiting Bill's family—or had Bill been killed?—rejoiced that what was left of Bill was perfect mss. I thought—who shall I call? Newark?—and who turn to now?—and great fear—police on phone in Miami—talking—asked me to come over—they have my journals? Detective repeating in a mumble on phone the threat of

[1] Quinque: ancient Coleman lantern.
[2] Jack Kerouac.
[3] William S. Burroughs.

Chichén Itzá

prosecution to me for info—talked so for fear of wiretapping so mumbled threat—I tried to get him to repeat.

Jan. 1, '54—Chichén—

Tonite hi at 8 o'clock on Paracodeina took up hammock & spread it out north top of the Castillo for an hour and looked up on old Mayan nite & stars. Lite in distance, perhaps Kantunil or Piste? Some sort of bird, bat or swallow flies round with little paper wingflap near the summit in its own air unconcerned with the great stone tree I perch on. Creak in rooms scared me. Great forest trees all about—

After an hour, saw Naomi's face, young and darkhaired, at a piano at a party, close up, facing me, svelte and in rapport with life.

Dream

Later in the Archeologist's hut (a big square concrete room) saw my brother & had nightmare. We lived in Paterson apartment together, and he (in dream within dream) looked at me with hostility, narrowing his eyes murderously, which frightened me—one eye half closed in hatred—so woke in the dream & looked at him & saw the same look & realized he would kill me—so sneaked out into Paradise Alley-Paterson apartment house labyrinth, thru unoccupied passages and rooms, to the other side of the court, & looked at him thru window across the way—saw him looking for me, in mirror magnified in window, same hatred look—close up again just the face as in clear moving photograph, still, artistic—

And realized as I woke and it was all a dream, that I was projecting my feelings on him and had piled up my own hatred on his shoulders in a great load—and

Waking again at 4 AM to write this, thought possibly I angry at him because not give me enuf $ to stay long enuf freely in Mexico.

* * *

Had thought yesterday despairing on bus, realized I was in Mexico in flight, no future, no past—

Dream again realizing I was going to Europe to make a movie with Bill—a dream of a movie, several movies:

The first with Lucien, as a great star—opening scene, I knock, walk in, Lucien meets me at the door—my line "Well, you know Lucien, I really don't feel too great about the play tonite."

"What? You spoiled a fine moment." I had, just now, by changing line of entrance—he and I were going to have arm-around-shoulder rapport before going to see wife.

Scene later: we are driving around and get into an autocar accident around the great European viaducts (of Hawaii)—Columbia, Morningside Heights—I and Cessa talking.

Something elevated happened to me in this dream.

The man outside at Chichén Itzá is ringing the great village 6 AM cowbell.

An Imagination of Europe—Reconstruction of Dream

I feel so *found* eternally as I wake in the morning with the shreds of a great conception of a dream in my soul freeing me from the dreadful necessitous pattern of my days & end of this trip in Frisco & later to family in Paterson.

Bill in Europe—but can't remember the dream O flat horrible reality closing in at morn after night of spectacles. I want to escape to some great future with Bill Jack Neal Lucien, cannot do and in loneliness forming an imaginary movie-world without a plot—must make a great phantasy and carry it to Europe and throughout the world, travelling ever toward it.

Having dreams of the old civilization,—I should go to Europe and write a movie of it all—the next great step—

BILL IN EUROPE

A telepathic image in style of *Third Man* movie—Bill on a bus (waiting for a train from Italy to Spain), looking solitary and grim wearing a brush moustache to hide his identity—even from himself—in the present—reading a paper.

He has been pursued by agents who were unrecognizable before he hid himself behind brush moustache—

Or the spy was reading a paper—an Agent like an F.B.I. man—young clean tourist, staring at Bill but mismanaging spy role reading paper but staring maybe in curiosity.

Bill is shadowed by a spy from the future—spy from another dimension in hideous 3rd class train ride—set in background of Europe in the rain and decay, a Spenglerian movie, involving cross-passages of time. Fragments of a great "routine."

Bill looks frightened—realizes he's been followed all along, since moustache was grown in fact, he hadn't taken that possibility into account—then very surprised. Then—great change—a look of weariness & boredom, ennui, powerlessness and resentment. Deenergized. Then rage, a look of great annoyance—He lapses into a kind of insanity finally—the whole theme & plot is directed toward this final routine of insanity, Kafkian-Mabusian.

Fate or the future was after him with its rational inanity—his insanity defeats their plans—Bill still conscious playing the routine. Like the routine which felled him laughing on kitchen floor in front of W. Adams [Columbia poet] in N.Y.

He is tired & powerless and great rage comes over him in resentment. A movie, like new prose, of living history.

(Lucien also played his role with true genius for the sublime)

* * *

Later dream: we, and Jack now, all going to see movie—end of it has some films of Bill—shots taken on buses in Europe—he in horror of appearing on other future buses if malefactors are after him, with brush mustache first looking horrified, then surprised in mustache, then black, then bored.

"Can we ask" (I say) "at the movie company to see the films already shot, the scenes unedited?"

"No" says Joan, "a bad idea." I always rush in with these bad business ideas. "Let them alone."

"Yes" says a Paisano.

"It's a sort of Miracolo, miracle, that he is chosen for film, anyway"—no tamper with Miracle says Joan.

In sum, a movie is to be made, à la Mabuse, BILL IN EUROPE, pursued by the agents, he bored finally (lapsing into a kind of insanity defeating them?).

* * *

First dream of Europe was at Columbia—with Arthur Lazarus [roommate] passing the immigration turnstiles

Valladolid—January (?), 1954

At 3:30 AM the RR station in the darkness with rattly clothcovered cabs charging by & bakeries with lamps just open on the corner the ghostly platform with hundreds gathered for trip in white dresses & carrying cloth bags, pails, candles—going to most inaccessible oldest & most

Valladolid

venerable festival of Tres Reyes [1] now come to a climax. Train started at 7 AM with a hundred in a box car, people hanging on steps of platform even—engine went off tracks like some great sad silent dead horse of iron at noon, usual occurrence.

At Cathedral people from all over Mexico Chiapas & Tabasco indians even somehow got there winding in and out of lines to the altar waiting to touch the 3 wooden kings one black 400 years old arms upraised in stiff gestures—so they "appeared" to Jesus in a vision, as the Maryknoll Padre complained, angry at the pagan heretical conception of who appeared to who—

They form a line to touch the statues, moving forward bearing gifts to adorn their chosen statue with, small images of whatever troubled them, wax heads, wax feet, wax pigs, wax husbands—wax souls for all I know, some were so shapeless & crude—to hang on the kings' hands ("They're cleared away in 2 minutes" the Padre said)—Candles so smoky the floor was slippery with a layer of wax inch-thick on the tile in the special white bare room set aside for candles where the old women stood silently meditating, wax dripping from the tripled candles clutched on the fingers, bunches of candles dripping burning brown hands, children reaching up to be burned with the wax and giggling—old man crouched against wall, a sea of flickering white candles & whitewashed walls with stalls of image sellers at the entrance under sun canopy of white cloth flapping in breeze.

A priest with mysterious silent gestures beckoning the men to a separate line in front of statues called me out—went backstairs with Maryknoll priest for a smoke. He complained about pagan rites . . . busy playing basketball trying to win over the natives.

Train back some old woman sneaked in and did me out of my seat on the crowded uncomfortable bench—to the merriment of all in the dim area. I hung out of the door on tiptoe balanced in all directions on crowded floor looking up at everpresent stars part of way home.

⋆ ⋆ ⋆

Jan. 12 (?), 1954 Uxmal

Manager of restaurant at Uxmal—disgruntled ex-guide lonely and underpaid—there is no hotel for him to manage here yet and nobody to

[1] Tres Reyes: three kings (Wise Men).

talk to & it gets dark at 6:30 and there's only a country road in each direction & ruins in front of him with hardly any visitors. Wants to go to U.S. or at least D.F.

* * *

The ruins here present from many points a splendid spectacle of white courtyards, complicated latticework and crude sculptures, temple roof-combs rising out of mounds, rubbled Mayan arched entranceways to unexcavated vast flat plazas, pyramids covered with trees, vistas of jungle and mountain perhaps 20 miles away in brilliant sunlite, and always the clap of hands brings many strangely pitched echoes like twanged ukelele from steps & stonework arranged symmetrically in a great city plan.

Here and there atop a pyramid see a milpa[1] half an acre in cultivation set in all the greenery to the horizon.

* * *

Miami Beach was a dream of rich sick Jews
Uxmal really quite beautiful in a classical Greek ruin way
Chichén—the main kick was the wild acoustics—somewhere in the middle of all these buildings is a place where you can clap your hands and be heard in heaven.

* * *

Uxmal a central series of buildings connected by vast plazas makes awesome intricate vistas from. atop pyramid or outlying unexcavated mounds more than Chichén Itzá.

Uxmal mounds sitting out big as battleships right next to white courtyards and pyramids. The great pyramid where I found the potsherds—a mass of rubble, very loose & dangerous & high where digging had been done, revealing large abstract latticework designs & carved out hieroglyphs a foot long—all part of a portal—and mortice still there but turned to dust—can poke a twig thru so it's curious to see those great stones hanging together by their own weight ready to fall without much of a push.

The backwoods paths quite interesting—bits of pottery scattered all over ground in muleroad—streams of ants winding in and out of cracked mud dry road to brilliant Hunckelike orange fungus growths & banana

---

[1] Milpa: cornfield.

Uxmal

trees—landscape littered with sculptured pediments, serpent heads & vertebrae of stone, indecipherable stelae, cornices all over—here & there a clearing & clutter of stones, or a walk up a hill & see that you are on a small house that has been overlooked—pediments and facade stone with simple designs piled up neatly or scattered around—and off the path in countryside & woods the same clutter of stones uncountable innumerable sticking out covered by vine—Fragments of latticework, a cross, a concentric plug, segments of a crude torso—so heavy you'd need a car to carry them off.

These little paths which wind in and out crossing on muleroads after half an hour in forest possible to enter not knowing where they go & walk pleasantly for hours and end up suddenly at some familiar building toward the cleared center again. So I have seen some parts of Uxmal daily from afar & only days later I get to walk into them close up.

12 Jan. '54 Sketch:

On top of a hillock mound covered over with brush—warm yellow sundown low at my back—this mound a great mass of concrete mortar, with carved rocks & pieces of slab all around.

Directly east, the *House of the Magician* symmetrically facing me with balance and proportion unthinkable for this continent—I'd never realized the vast sophistication of Pre-Columbian America. A valley below tangled with trees between it & my pyramid. To the left immense white-reddish buttresses and walls of the courtyard of the *Nunnery* like a huge stadium vale.

On the right the grecian square *Casa de Gobernador* rising on a great mound that looks a mile long but is about 3 blocks—with buildings on it, buildings going down into the trees.

To the right of that, a great green square pyramid, as big as anything all covered with brush which doesn't hide its perfect proportions—called the *Great Pyramid.*

Jutting west out of that *The Dovecote*'s facade of triangular arches, with a path thru the center arch: and behind that another pyramid, with house on top of it among the trees.

—All these valleys and mounds man made, a mile or more of constructions, a great main street, broadway, with the twitter of birds in green trees allround to the horizon & blue mountains far away glimpsed between the furthest corner buildings.

Jan. 15 Sunset

The space & grandeur of the Governor's house & its well-thought relaxed steps down to the big plaza—

Cry of whup from that direction—constant chirp of bats and insects thru nitefall regions, lone carlites down the road to the horizon, lone houselights far away where seems upon a mound a man lives.

Below me—the huge *Nunnery* quadrangle reduced to a small vista of rectangular buildings shedding their ruined skin of stones.

Clap of hands echoes from empty square in half-light below.

In walking shoes and army pants & Mérida hat seated at ease atop the highest mount to see & rest—6:30 must soon descend—always a little afraid of these steep stairs—and eat at Bar and Restaurant last meal at Uxmal—the grand Quinque burning with loud rushing air noise casting brilliant whitelike-sunlite lite on the driveway so as snow looks: Smoking Otros.

* * *

Mexican politicians here, caretaker Ruz trying for money, they come in big black limousines with fat Indian looking wives in cheap dresses &

expensive looking rebozos, plus daughters, out on a business picnic.

Reconstructing the whole of this city Uxmal, they'd have a tourist attraction so vast & magical it would "put their economy on a working basis."

January 15 (?)

Outside of this bleak wall—the ruins of Uxmal in the moonlight. I will get up later perhaps and go look at them on Paracodeina—only intensest writing is interesting, in which whole life direction is poured for profusion of image & care of surface and stipple & sensuous muscle of soul river thought.

Today's visitors—Col. Sears of Chapala and the couple from New England—poor arthritic.

* * *

Worrying about my fate again—that a small breeze of nostalgia fluttered in my heart, thinking a moment past I had someone in the room I loved with me—no ghosts—a man of flesh to talk to and hug.

I am lonely now. I could not be different—have lost the memory—self comes to this state of reality where I am in high room in Uxmal alone.

* * *

Palenque—

More sylvan than imperial, consisting of main pyramid halfway up mount, main palace with labyrinths & fragments of stucco ornament and a 3 story tower, and a set of 3 small arcadian temples grown over with moss perched together on a set of green terraces at the foot of a gigantic hump of green mountain, & resembling the mountain in contour, much like a Chinese drawing in its lines . . . sealed up in A.D. 600 Much greater antiquity than other New Mayan cities.

Karive tribes wandering from Piedras Negras and Yaxchilan still bore ancient Mayan intelligence, and to this day carry the secret of translation of hieroglyphs & theory, according to Karena Shields, who encountered them as a child. Karives know astronomical system, keep theology intact, and can make variant creative forms of old pottery types.

Small horse caravans ride up on the way from one jungle frontier settlement to another & dismount & talk for half an hour & buy cacao & continue on from Tacalapan.

Sudden clearings where the sunlite bursts down as a great white shower.

Palenque: by the light of the full moon 7:00

Strange sounds at dusk—the rush of water in little falls down the hidden mountain stream. A crack in the forest—gun—and the howl of dogs in thatchhuts. Continual high metallic buzz of crickets (chicharras grandes)—first in one ear and then in another ear as if taking up and continuing: and the infinite echo of lesser locusts massed in a series of choruses receding into the distance—locust sound a high whirr, then cricket chirps 5 blasts of the leg-whistle, then an autohorn up the road bringing caretaker home at night, and carmotor noise—my feet itch from mosquitoes—the creak of an opening door in the forest, some kind of weird birdsong or reptile croak. (Also in recollection the long practiced atonal scales of the hidden bird around Palenque.)

Chismes (Gossip)

Copal: *Dicen* that burning copal incense causes constant faraway illumination approaching with concomitant mystic state.
Legend of Underground passage from Temple of Inscriptions at Palenque to Yaxchilan.
All Old Empire Mayan tombs contain pyramids.

⋆ ⋆ ⋆

A tortilla stand in Oaxaca.

⋆ ⋆ ⋆

Finca Tacalapan de San Leandro Karena Shields—Late February

All the Jungle: all these rocky ruins: And suddenly in the ease and lethargy of monthlong guesthood on the ranch the singleminded conception of a vast Unfathomable god—and writing, the gift of writing thought seems like a candle in the wood.

To let the mind wander into its solitude & vacancy with the sheer idea of finding an ungraspable spirit waiting to resignify (Eternity?) . . .

Allen Ginsberg surveying ruins of Palenque, 1954

always knowledge of a plural human mind (the slattern dress on steelworker wife wiping sweat from brow over the gasrange; the vigor of industrialists with metaphysical inclinations; love of amigos and sweet life)

As I leaned against a tree inside the forest expiring of selfbegotten love I looked up at stars absently . . .

A dream of New York—

A round picture of a gathering of souls
Kingsland, Kerouac, Hohnsbean, Anton, Keck, Lucien, Jack, Bill, Aileen, Helen, Dusty, Cogswell, Durgin, all posturing terrifically gay or tragic as may be full of life.

* * *

Dreams of Naomi—fresh wound
2 more dreams of Europe

* * *

Green Valentine Blues [1]

I walked in the forest to look for a sign
Fortune to tell & thought to refine.
My green Valentine, my green Valentine,
What do I know of my green Valentine?

March 11—

Dream with Claude in the Group we wander around setting up our hammocks—he tries to stick with me & I try to stay by him but we get separated—he is wanted or recognized or ordered to another hall-barn of lockers & bunks—I go following after him down the halls—I come to a crowd trying to get in lobby of hotel where he is appearing in T.V. studio in half hour play—as hero, he wears long gold hair, like a girl's and is taken for a girl till he speaks, then despite his goldy locks his godly face appears manly and his voice tough & heroic, so that he is a sensational star discovery—crowd after him (homme fatal?), I try to go thru

[1] Original poem lost; this stanza is all that is remembered by A.G. 22 years later.

Thatch-roof Shelter, Finca Tacalapan

alternate corridors, half knowing the hotel, wind up in a door that leads out over a brick wall parapet & walk on it till reach a point behind mills & woods which are ruined kilns & chimneys affording rocky precipitous descent—I look for a better way down—the immediate way is a ledge right below leading to stairlike jagged pile of stone, new & sharp, a solid pile with sheaves of cubes though rectangular looking down—Door closed behind me—locked—try to get to other building perhaps hotel, without descending—I remember that if I had stayed home might have seen whole program on T.V. set uninterrupted—regretted I did not—he's my ami—but I know him—think it wonderful of him to take such a role (no moustache & long hair) or such unique hermaphroditic character without losing his nerve for T.V. display & action—did not balk but played like courageous with his career of T.V.—playing with it seriously, the T.V., leaving his apt? & life for strange role so open & sublime threatening his reputation of manhood—

At U.P.—as I woke up, thinking how feeble & scrawny those reporters are in their nests, thinking they are men of action, all they do is sit up at their typewriters full of sharpness or wiseacre or cynical knowledge of limited situations priding themselves on scrawny specialties of knowledge like Bullfighting or Railroads etc. & drinking at nite, like fat short man of U.P. I spoke to, full of defensive own paltry pride, small lives up in the News building, their whole actual horizon.

To write a love poem (pure no self-refelection) full of tenderness to Claude/Beatrice.

What pleasure to contact C. thru dream.

Selva (jungle)

On tangled paths or walking solitary on river with overhanging foliage, particularly in low wet land, Tierra Bajo, the variety of leaf & its thickness & intrinsic power take on an uncanny wild sentience. It is like listening to music: offers infinite multiplicity of form for nameless observation.

San Leandro River to Mountain half day trip till come to a place of rapids which got rockier with steeper sides, finally a deep canyon cut in jungle mountainside with monstrous boulders big as houses tumbled down. River is small but the series of falls were roaring and frightening as we climbed over the giant stones.

* * *

Dream about lovemaking with Indian, & the mutual satisfaction:

was with Hermina & another couple—started out difficultly & unsatisfactory till I realized meek H. was willing to do anything I wanted, got naked, remember brown body in the floor or cama.

Mar. 23 Sketch

Salto de Agua from the R.R. Bridge at 2 P.M. Handcar coming across, a long low hill to the south, into which you can go to Tumbala perched on mount and Mt. Acavalna quakes—the singletrack R.R. bridge very high over the low cluster of tinred & tile rust roofs on Caribbean blue river's bank. The bank a sizeable tropic downgrade with houses paths and clusters of high palms and greenery on worn clay riverside sound of beaten dog in center of town—a stone's throw away. Houses stretched for a mile along bank on one side and sparsely dotted thatchroofs on little hill on other side.

The bridge is the wonder of the town. Not everybody rides the railroad but all stare at the trains and have walked on the high bridge, a monolith, a pyramid towering over the village extending to New York from Mérida—You cross it stepping in fright on naked wooden ties looking down 100 feet or more to incredible turquoise water and on either side little green isles and sandbanks risen from previous floods. Nearby a small wide ancient waterfall looking new for the pristine color of the Tulija [River] giving promise of terrible cataract four hours walk down path away from town along winding river in hot March 23 sunshine.

Because town on slope & possible to view it from uphill or bridge above on either side get impression of curious smallness and intimacy to the terrain—and vasty armadas of white fragmentary clouds in bright sky are real blue transparency—a few pink trees in flower—recurring crow of cocks from this side and that challenging and responding in various cockly hoarse tones as if they existed in a world of pure intuitive sound communicating to anonymous hidden familiar chickensouls from hill to hill.

The white foam in spots on river near the falls—and a place nearby where men bathe naked in a blue pool amid the sound of cock & pig.

At first what looks like a ruined wharf below surface near shore but look again it's a great heavy branchy tree, small twigs worn away in the brown antiquity of mud.

Sense of the mysterioso, the unknown tribes in the hills further—a few in town in courtly dress speaking glottal tongues. White kneepants and barbers shirts collarless, and hats with tassels and women with ancestral belts and braids.

A man tottering up the bank—small sized downlook I have—from his Kayuko [1] with a Chinese infinite load on his back—a black garbage bird (Zopilote) circling over the river—continual put put of an electricity machine at icehouse and plashy sound of water over a ledge of rocks & some kids' voices rising here and there in the hot clear air, crazy american Capt. Cover circling down on the unkempt airfield in his 1914 plane (I later rode it)—sun too bright to look up for the kid's voices. I go to eat, cross off the bridge down the railroad embankment like a Chinese wall into the street—

Sitting at 10:30 high on the bridge watching moon move over the hill you can see it rising and follow its destination thru the clear dimension of the sky in a slow circle from hill on one horizon to mountain on other, having the whole sky spread out unbroken but by stars in all 360 directions.

Salto de Agua:

The plaza by night—Kiosk Bon Ampak—bottles of tamarind & peach and lime syrup, as well as grape & orange & chocolate, pan dulces, dulces, blue boxes of Alkaseltzer, straws & glasses & paper cartons of cigarettes.

Man with serape & overalls, and the dark Tumbala boy I have seen for last few days from over the mount in town for a visit—2 days' walk home with carga on his head, past the last chance cantina thru the Cézanne village turn French paysage countryside stiles thru a big fence to the wide mulepath up & down mountains to Yajalon & further cordilleras.[2] Tumbala boy with black black hair over his forehead & white barbershirt & cotton pantalón to his calf is barefoot buying a soda.

The Kiosk proprietor a civilized looking citizen in a disgusting sort of way—acne & fatso glasses. All the Indians disappear and the hipper sons of town over chismes & talk & laughter stand in the silent shadow.

* * *

---

[1] Kayuko: canoe.

[2] Cordilleras: mountain ranges.

Salto a kind of gateway city, gateway to Chiapas mountains & tribes, Yajalon, Tumbala, Bachalon, Kankook. San Cristobal on other side is gateway too. Salto has R.R., San Cristobal hiway. Understanding this part of Mex mainly tied up with 3 or 4 main rivers and a few mountain ranges & the tribes involved—they have ageold importance like U.S. west & are still the main features of travelling to know. Here in Salto is the last navigable point of Sea-Connected River Tulija (& also point where R.R. touches beginning of interior mountains, nearest & most convenient jumping off point to interior Tenosique on Usumacinta River). This last navigable point & R.R. touch is gateway to more mysterious areas of Chiapas & Guatemalan territory & hanging around these towns you get glimpses of legend: the Coronel with his collection of relics, the mountain tribesmen drunk on the floors of cantinas at 7:30 in the morning, the beginnings of mule roads inward 500 years old, the river itself coming in from the mountain obscure forest, tales of sierras encantadas, cataracts, volcanoes, journeys, tribes, jungles, murders, caves, lakes and ruins.

* * *

Arrived in Acavalna and asked what time & one of the men ducked his head out the thatchroof to squint at the sun and said 4:oclock.

* * *

Road to Cristobal from Yajalon:
Yajalon, Chilon, Tzitala,
Guatipec, Kankook, Tenehapa, San Cristobal.
Ruins in cave in Guatipec.

Tleltal [language] Terms

Wheats—Sierra
Knee-kell—Tremblor
Balumilal—World
Ka-Kal—Sun
Uk—Monte [pasture] like bambu with white flora

Yajalon:

The Square, 10 blocks up the opposite end of the town from the airfield, full of little flower trees & high coconut palms. The birds are very pretty

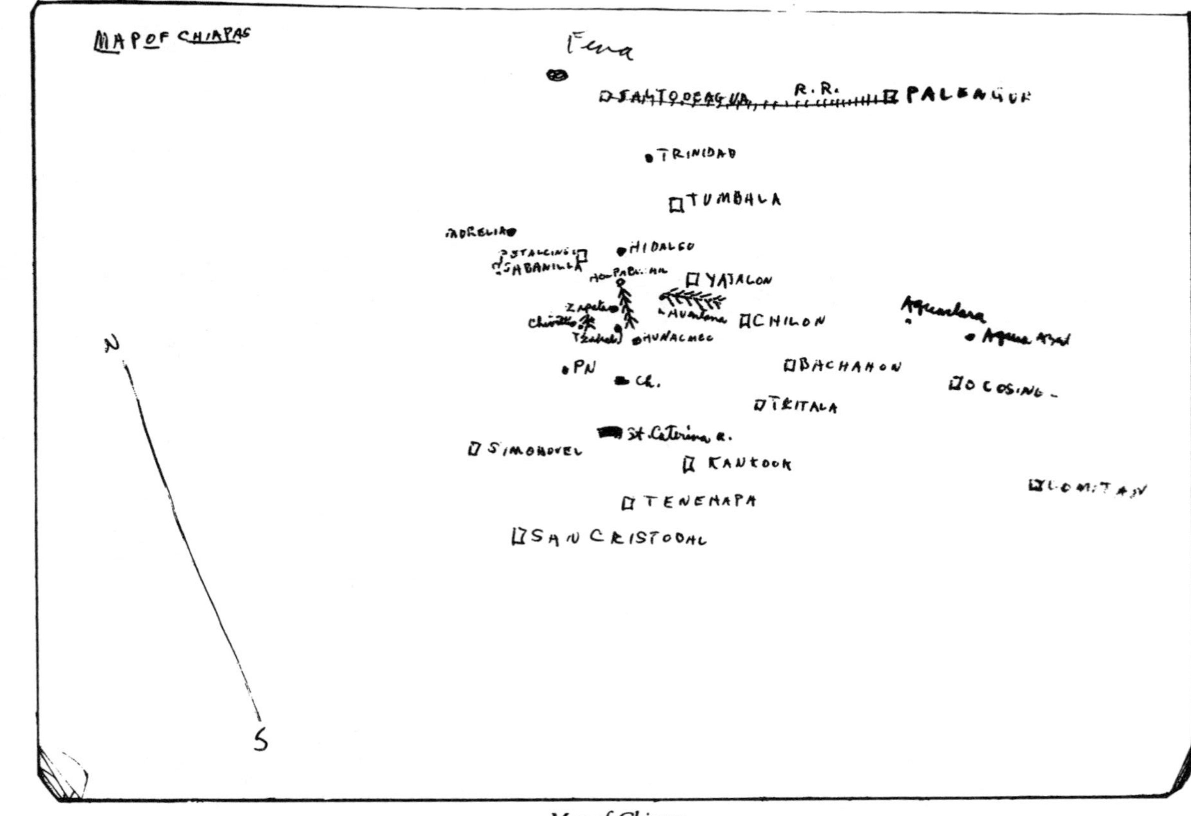

Map of Chiapas

large black & purple inhabitants all day long but make unnaturally rasping squawk sounds on top of the palms. Across from the park four old low brilliant bougainvillaea trees and a purple shade over the pavement in front of a candy store with high dark ancient doors.

I walked up to the hilltop cemetery & watched some Bachahon Indians digging a grave and talked with the supervisors sitting on a tomb sheltered by a chicken coop with chicken wire. There was a row of green gaseosa [1] bottles along the edge of the enclosure stuck headfirst down in the earth—celebration of Amigos or worm prevention or adoration of bottles.

27.50 peso telegram to Lucien (U.P.I.) from Yajalon April 1:

Mar. 28 filmless arrived thundering Acavalna evenings earthquake shakiest since first say indians fifteen daily [Mar.] 29 collected expedition summit unvolcanic [Mar.] 30 discovered legendary cathedral mouthed cavern eastern Acavalna Tleltal for House of Night Mountain Hollow Interior Rockfalls companioned forty La Ventana Indigines Inform Geologist Mooser Mexico Instituto Indians no show him [cave] Tengo documentary Evidences Waiting advice Yajalon City guest reply soonest Mexican papers will want May settle volcano question.

Tremblors at Acavalna Mountain near Yajalon town

Sun. Mar. 28—8:30 nite
Thurs. April 1—5 PM
Sat. April 3—4 PM

Dream:

at some movie théâtre intime special showing—meeting Dr. Williams and attempting to explain my triumph at Acavalna—Shaking his huge leaden sick hand, unable to get across my story in the short time passing by his seat.

---

[1] Gaseosa: soda pop.

(Returned to Shields Finca)—April 16—Good Friday '54

To read—
A book on volcanoes & earthquake geology
Book on basic botany
Morley & Blom's work [1]

* * *

No god to look for, but the old legends and better the old buildings before they're ruined by time.

I left that party in NY for peace—to sit out at nite in front of the thatchroof shelter on a bench sounds of an alien tongue, crude Mexican and a moment when the plenilunar cloudfilled sky is still and small—looking out in the shadow of the pasture, wall of trees & mountain shaded behind—

& palmtrees appearing again in the balmy wind presaging a rain—shifting their fronds in the wind with a dry soft rattle sound, so much like animal hairy windmills—insectlike in fact, like monstrous insects long white bodies encased in scales and at the top conglomerated in the head nerve center all these rattly animal feelers that move lethargically in the direction of the wind, settling & unsettling as in water.

* * *

The word *Time*—Like a great silver wall blocking the sky—falling from the sky, solid in the sky, solid in the firmament, with slow movement. Always when think of the concept of time the image of this transparent solid shower. Strange I never fixed or noted this sensation before: the word *time* always at best accompanied by this hair-raising apparitional sensation.

One might sit in this Chiapas recording the appearance of time, like

[1] Sylvanus Griswold Morley, archaeologist, anthropologist, led expeditions and wrote extensively on the Mayans. His major work is *The Ancient Maya* (Stanford, 1946). Francis Blom, anthropologist, historian, wrote *The Conquest of Yucatán* (New York, 1936).

painting—the palmtree so much suggesting an animal force spraying up in slow time.

Dream in Afternoon—April 17

A milpa on side of a hill, burnt rubble, at top a pass which is entrance to cave of Acavalna or other unknown—I come down the slope & meet several Columbia students—they tell me I won the Woodbury Prize again for a poem I submitted in 1947—not much money (bank interest down)—I meet [Dean] McKnight on the way & converse in friendly fashion with him—"Where can I pick up the change?" I ask—we smile.

At the slope up the hill, one man had been before, Rivera (the Mex. artist) and had found nothing beyond in the future, but had left at the entrance a great marble portal, a slab carved with monumental bas reliefs of women & men in naked big hipped work activities—with the motto "What men do women shall do." Carrying loads over the hill presumably.

He had seen nothing on the other side of the hill but left a monument to his voyage anyway.

Dream—April 20

With D. Feitlowitz, Danny my boyhood chum I haven't seen for a year since I saw him at a wedding in Paterson—before that perhaps another year and before that maybe half decade. As I write, & get up to the fire for a cup of coffee—the strains of Sarah Vaughan's record of "If You Could See Me Now." It was with Danny I first discussed my perception of the great wall at the end of the universe and what was beyond, as well as a time on Broadway Paterson when we talked about growth of under arm hair and pubic hair and he goosed me—a pleasant shock to my boyhood virginality, I recoiled.

Last night I was also thinking I am an old man to lech after young boys—20 years, 18 years—I have almost a decade and a beard on them, must appear old—and as old lechers (S. Z. Sakall) in the movies sing "Girls, girls, girls" or as Yeats did about young girls, so I am already beginning to remember the days when sensuality was a painful exquisite joy, even going so far as to imagine a dialogue between old man and a boy

"What is old age like?"
"In days of youth when every limb
 played a savage part,
 and blood sprang up and filled with joy
 leg and brain and heart . . ."
                                    in my sleep.

Dreamt that we went to a wedding in Tzahala or thereabouts—wandering over the clear red soil cleaned out for the fiesta—and finally to climb up a hillock to a small plain like a room where the dance was being held—in long Kankook [tribe] striped black skirts everyone whirling—When it was over & all had gone we closed the doors & took off clothes and embraced—his body a little flabby & awkward & roundbellied & his cock awry. A noise at the doors, I went to secure them & came back to where he was waiting patiently lying down still.

* * *

Which reminds me of the occasion with the young thin blond hustler from Chicago who I met in the Astor bar—Robert Lovett? or some such pert name. I went in there with a few dollars to try my luck at the queer bar for the first time—and saw him, the only young nice boy sitting a few people away from me at the bar. Bought him a drink after a difficult start of the conversation, & said "Let's get out of here to someplace cheaper."

So we went to the White Rose, walking up Times Square to 52 Street & 6th Ave.—and he offered the tale of his travels—came from Irish family in Chicago, hustled there across the country knowing his good looks, left a remarkable twin brother behind—as nice looking and tougher, always in trouble, in reform school or in hands of police, a more anguished & stronger actor, lost still in Chicago, with whom he had first slept. Stories of his blond twin whom he loved, on whom he was obsessed, till I for a moment doubted the existence of the twin.

Came home to my little room with the Irish family on 92nd street, turned on the table radio & we took to the bed. I wanted to go take a crap but he kept me back saying, remarkably, "No the dirtier the better."

And Mr. O'Connor bumbled in to complain about the radio at about 3 AM—pushed open the door drunk in the darkness & then retreated closing the door part way—I was down under the sheets at the boy's knees—asking politely to turn radio down. Never said another word about it, probably didn't forget though.

Then in the morning after a great night I had to go to school—Lovett had a dollar or so I left with him (had much discussion of rolling fags and how he couldn't roll me as we were friends besides I had nothing worth rolling). He did not show up that night as arranged, I was heartsick. Three days later walking on 8th Avenue & 45 St. looking for Garver or Huncke I saw him cross 8th Avenue & shouted hello—he waved & went on—was with an older guy, about 35-30—crewcut brisk advertising man in Sunday morning midtown off with pickup for coffee—from small apartment on 45th or 46th St.

Apr. 26, Poor Visions—

The utter sordidness of my NY worklife now that I am 28, no longer feel these lovely flushes of liquid youth going down my mortal drainpipe, impossible to regard the great garbage pile of the future (which I see as clearly sitting there on the skyline as if it were the Empire State) with any timid favor.

In Europe I hope to dream about Asia. In Asia I shall dream about the death of Home States. I hope to circumnavigate the globe before the spirit gives out.

Of home: of Death and the States.

A poor Chinaman's vision—a rich man might travel at leisure not set himself to it as a life's work. But like a pauvre Chinaman I have visions of the Yellow River flowing to the sky.

Europe—

What night might I not see penniless among the arabian mysteries of dirty towns around the casbahs of the docks—. . .

Dream—April 30

Walking with Walter A— in some suburban concourse discussing the sermons of some new priest that Walter has discovered.

Walter is a priest playing politics with himself—his face slightly changed in expression somewhat as it is when he's drunk—he looks like a priest with a sort of crazy obsessional look—a dark look like Hawthorne's gaunt priests or aristocrats suffering spiritual obsession. This priest, he seems to think, can give spiritual advice capable of influencing the destiny of the country and international politics.

I play along with his idea, sort of ironic, challenging him to go on with his idea—"Why don't you invite the President to hear him when he comes to New York—like write a letter inviting him to 'attend worship' services with you—" Eisenhower has his own priest, of course. Truman? But Stevenson is a better gamble I guess.

Walter considers the problem darkly—who is likely to run and win the election?

A curious sort of determination in his visage—like his naive mad resolve to become an antique dealer because he attached some sort of monkish world-forgetting and same time world-wise operant social value to it. I woke thinking of it.

(—At least my resolves are not impulses to death—in all the poem of Siesta I am not inclining toward destruction.)

Dream yesterday April 29

I flitted back in time for the half day to a class in the New School with sick W.C. Williams course in Abstruse Mobility (Theory of Psychic Change)—He's sitting like Louis at a desk correcting answers; I look over his shoulder & see rudimentary fragmentary answers of other unknowing students.

Dream May 2 (Salto de Agua?—A.G., 1975)

I am living in a furnished room in N.Y. near the bookstore-clothing shop—Bickford's blocks of Bway 113 St.—I am in the culture store buying myself records and books—a few—[Sandburg's] "Remembrance Rock" and some large strange near-Eastern art Volume? The bill runs up to about $50 and when I am in my room I think, I'll pay it off, it's a bill like others.

I visit my publishers—am introduced by Giroux to a great heavy man in a perfect English style clothing & muffler of shiny white & white hair & great body & peacock chest—the commercial business agent—I go in the private waiting room and am looking at books & furniture & sit down on couch. The agent comes in—he is dressed in even more ornate commercial silks than before, but without his jacket. He sits down & introduces himself. He says, "I understand you've been making purchases on the account"—& produces from the top of the desk the copy of "Remembrance Rock"—

"Yes," I answer.

"We can't be responsible for everything," he says, "need some assurance that these purchases are necessary." (apparently I am living on an expense account)

"Well, I didn't intend for *you* to pay for the two books. However, I'm writing"—I think, a book of poetry—"a novel, and if you people were inclined to consider the books part of my general expenses for writing, I would be agreeably grateful, however—"

He moves over on the couch over me & begins closing in, as if to surmount me & lie on me. I don't know how to act—he keeps talking, his head is over mine & his weight is resting on my chest-shoulders.

I struggle & rush out—not knowing whether he wants to make love or not—the struggle is playful yet desperate & I get free, pushing him over. I later learn that it was only an overture & he is annoyed or put out by my gaucherie or awkwardness of interpretation & fighting with him.

I am examining the Near Eastern book, by T.E. Lawrence—poems. I see small quatrains in English, in French, in Arabic, in Egyptian, in Chinese, even in design

"Remembrance Rock"

I start to read the great book & a guide starts out with me to show the great opening doors of it—a huge gate in a room behind a screen that leads thru the oriental labyrinth of the book—there are sculptures in silver and wood by Houdon—rather smashed up it seems—a mass of half silver reclining on a couch of wood—one leg silver one wood, the silver of his face messed a little.

We continue—to the beginning of the great wall that leads out to the end of Siberia—the whole unknown China in between.

The wall is about 6 feet high & houses on top and the same wide, along a waste road, below it, usually you speed down the road to the end—or fly—but we (& the Signora [1]) propose to walk it. Take the horses out to the last horse stop—I walk beside the horses & one of them, Cometa, raises his front foot around my shoulder to head me on in front ahead—does not need my leading.

All the privacies & mysteries of China land stretch mostly unknown to outsiders for 3000 miles between.

— — —

We are walking around in the heart of Brooklyn—a large party & myself and Kerouac at the head. He is the leader and we are taking one of the walks he has been on through the great scenery.

We are on a huge bridge, one of many in the heart of the factories & shops beneath and buildings and traffic haze all about I can see down to the street below &

The next bridge a little further on—really spectacular scenery of industrial unknown N.Y. landscape—I realize Jack has been there before, & has walked for years alone along such, writing poems about the streets—how he has seen more structures in Brooklyn than I even knew—I ask him if he has been to the spot before & he says "No"—but nearby he has been & knows where he is—

The group is lost, I am lost we cross a corner & go down the street—big street of neighborhood movies toward a large central Palazio or Zoo as in Bronx.

Impression of the unknown miles of movies & bridges & houses & alien life in Brooklyn, how one could go walking alone (or with others) not to explore but to enjoy & be awed by the vast human scenery just as one goes walking thru the mountains in awe. For kicks, not to map the streets.

Dream May 2

TRAPPED IN THE TEA SHOPPE

I get off boat in England—go to a small tea shoppe near my room to try & phone Seymour Wyse [2]—I can get nowhere with the people, proprietor—can't make them understand I want to act fast & phone Seymour immediately & connect—

---

[1] Tabasco pronunciation of *Señora* more closely resembled Italian.

[2] Seymour Wyse: record shop employee of Jerry Newman; friend of J.K. at Horace Mann.

They offer me food, am not rich & don't want to eat there, want to connect first before eating, they think I simply don't know the score & am being personal & boorish—it's sort of an English slow custom—Can't connect by phone now, only on certain days between 1–2 PM. I am trapped in the tea shoppe & don't know what to do & outside lies a great plain of avenues & buildings & public museums & palaces & law courts in which I'll get lost & never see Seymour if I don't connect.

Dream—

Roller skating on knees with knuckles as pushers at 60 mph down Park Ave in surrealisic dawn—so smooth the city paved.

⋆ ⋆ ⋆

As if these ruins were not enough . . . to hurry the years and bring me to my fate.

⋆ ⋆ ⋆

The most important thing about dreams is the existence in them of magical emotions, to which waking Consciousness is not ordinarily sentient. Awe of vast constructions; familiar eternal halls of buildings; sexual intensity in rapport; deathly music; grief awakenings, perfected lodgings.

May 6 Dream—

Polo (12 year old boy) earlier in day ran hand down my back & at nite dreamed ran hand on cock & so came.

⋆ ⋆ ⋆

The Dream Cinema

⋆ ⋆ ⋆

O Future, unimaginable god

Salto de Agua—May 9—

Out of the double door—sick indian lying on cot in room where knapsack unpacked on tableta—carafe, a bottle (green) and flowered little commercial glass—Anyway out of the door—sound of 5 o'clock sunday marimba bouncing heavily in the pre-dusk green air—in the garden, pretty little square of dirt, now all mud with black barrels of spermy old rain water (for brushing teeth & shaving) and construction going on—white boards leaned against little flower trees not presently in bloom, a wheelbarrow parked under the branches—been there for a month—gas can with wood handle for watercarrying—cans with little trees growing up, and great pieces of red meat a leg and a whole half side of a bloody cow, hanging from the dripping boughs. (Meat hanging from the trees.)

Rain coming down in Salto summer evening—great racket of solid water on the roof, garden inundated. The street with marimba still bouncing heavily in the darkness for Sunday night ball—from window second floor, can't see street bottom for darkness & shadows & water.

I return from the ball and the Indian is cured—streptomycin.

At dawn I still hear the marimba and the indian wakes up & suddenly starts talking as if in his sleep—The song they are playing—*Cancion* for the Día de los Madres & the Virgen de Guadalupe—and he starts singing in the dark concrete room—he's better—beautiful sad song (with feminine off-rhyme endings feminine rhymes in spanish have a strong ultimate accent) and the music stops for a few minutes—Then suddenly I hear the old plaintive sweet dissonance of a hundred children singing in the grass streets near the railroad track—& put on pants & shirt & run out—shoes broken so no use—and follow the dawn parade barefoot—the big carro—only truck in town—toting the marimba and a solitary sad saxophone and a dozen borracho jovens of the all nite ball creaking after children like a great dumb faithful horse and the hundred children walking led by the priest in a big cloak (raincoat he later uses for Torro dumbshow) singing the archaic repetitive arabic sounding song, voices rising straining together at end of verse "Madre de dios"—I nearly cry to hear the innocence, children led down one mudstreet to another getting the car which has to follow them in trouble stuck in the mud, they wait a minute to see it's pulled out & then walk off en masse down the other street all thru dawn till all the dozen streets & cross streets have been sung on and made holy. Finally the car breaks down in front of the school & the drunks climb down nearby flopping in the wet grass & push it away with its marimba—bottles breaking on the cement in the Plaza—and also there were cries of ahee-hee-he-he & Jalisco shrieks in the middle of verses at the stops—

Stuck in Salto—May 12—

The professor tried to make me & though I thought to protect his reputation by morning when I mentioned it to the Señora she already knew & much curiosity in town aroused—necessary for her to say something to someone else like "Professor was up to his old habits last nite" for it to be understood I had not submitted to his advances & was not being secretive.

Got drunk with the architect & professor & bureaucrat of "Recaudación" [1] & another kid—5 habaneras & 5 beers, first real liquor for months.

Today I noticed no feeling for 4th or 5th day in right foot big toe & imagined I had leprosy. What poems in a leprosarium? What imagery.

Sitting here scribbling again, no special direction. What did I see today—Unshaved doctor with maniac eyes describing operations on the hand—cutting away the flesh. Injected penicillin in the sick indian's backside and surprised by how soft the needle went into his brown meat. Conversation interrupted by great rooster in middle of street in front of hotel—crowing every minute or so in middle of a sentence. Egoistic cock crow—a kind of intense stupid infra-sound that rasps on my nerve cells—Looked at the map trying to decide whether to go thru Vera Cruz or Oaxaca. Senora tried to get me to sell her camera—both broke. She lying frontward on her bed in upstairs room with balconies overlooking grass street—me in usual beard looking like a german geologist—both no good broke & stuck here with phony sorts of stories (& the sick indian). Rasping sound of P.A. system presiding over Park Centrale announcing "Ataca los Inditos" for tonite's movie between scratchy mambos. The Hüy family circle sitting in front of the hotel he in underwear top she a big fat jewish indian in print dress. Self conscious children with sties in their eyes. The decadent looking painted plastic statuette of a kind of blue pantalooned heavily bloused fatty little boy with a 30 year old smuttish low eyelid red cheeked expression—with a big blowsy cap—representing *what*? on their mantel in the lobby. No dreams last night—drunk & slept till 9. Unfinished imagination of Europe. Sudden desire to get out of here & travel fast to Mex City—also desire to finish poem at Lake Actitlan or Catemaca—Calm & great body of Geneva-Lake Como

[1] Recaudación: (tax) collection.

water. Indians staring at me in the drugstore. Irritation with S–– for her egoistic hypochondria—never lets anyone talk, talks too formally "Ah, Señor," and to impress or conserve her situation all the time. A boring con. I am usually reduced to sitting respectfully dying for her to shut up with her oft repeated banal defenses and opinions—sometimes a discomfort amounting to agitation & fear it will last for an hour more.

So sitting here, thought of leaving this stillness this leafy bastion to return to travel further to friends.

A.G. "in usual beard looking like a german geologist"

These ruins woke up in me nostalgia for the unseen old continent of ruins, marble statues, now in the last sweet days of memory before the ultimate night of war.

That I might see the grey roofs of Paris under the slow rain, where the last fantastic elements of civilization added final beards and suicides or deaths among pernod glasses and dirty cloths and more half finished paintings on the walls—traces—such as this meter—of an obsessional personal style: and the faces of that city, the few actual ecstatic conscious souls certain to be found there among the nights and parties and the secret dens and waterfronts. Not to mention the joy of gazing on the legendary city of light home of Abélard from the dear structure of the Eiffel Tower—how saintly actual and alone one might feel among the girders above this city of the legendary roofy real.

And to pass on, having had some London, to actual Rome—where all roads one time led: old tiles and Founts of Levi and the future self, perhaps a poem there, an interesting crude thought or love affair—fountains of Rome in any case, and the memorable structures of the Vatican—I still remember my dream maybe 5 years ago, the pope and his carpets & desks & paintings and other treasures gilt or marble & theologic props and prizes, ornaments and palaces.

To Ankara then, Luxor, Angkor Vat.

★ ★ ★

On train Salto May 13, 1954 to Coatzcoalcos—Lunar landscape here again.

★ ★ ★

On the bus Coatzcoalcos to Vera Cruz, sleeping on codinetta, in the night gloom toward dawn passing Lago Catemaca with the great sense of an inland sea, hills and lunar mounts proceeding up out of lunar darkness—I had in my eyes also an image, of Giotto, the likeness of a heavenly file of female saints ascending in the starry sky on miniature stepped golden rainbow stairway snaking upward curved, the thousands of little saintesses in blue hoods, with round sweet smiling faces looking out directly at me (thru the picture wall to the beholder), their hands beckoning as they go up—salvation it's true, as simple as that in the strange picture.

Mexico City, May 16

Walking on Orizaba Street—the pad, flash Joan walking afoot in Mexico City, no one there but me—Garver gone. 2 hours after my arrival in city, feeling Joan abandoned in the city I went to her old house looking.

Sanborne's Mex City—

Little girls with starched native drapes in stripes look like bulgarian peasants and the tall wooden pillars are overarched by yellow skylite broken into strips of paint frayed glass. Young (rich) students gathered round table in sweaters for breakfast (as well as suits). Chic girl in black hair & pearl earrings & cashmere grey sweater sits at table across the way for her strawberries.

On Bill's Trail—

Tato's Bar—Blue-top aluminum-leg table, jukebox, 5 groups of young men, Mex. or Amer. sitting nearby, the owner in apron young gangster at door table, as bare & barren a place as I've seen playing jukebox Cien Años sad tune of Yajalon Hunckelike-mouthed kid in yellow sweater, certain old bare nostalgia. Had to leave.

Librería Cristal—

Sitting crosslegged on concrete walk, dark palm at left at right circular glass book display window with red & modern signs, books & writers in neon lights—to the right the sexy park—ahead the unknown Times Square Neons of Mexcity—Max Factor, Dry Martini, red, green, circular motion of moving signs, sound of great city trolleys behind, old lady beggar sitting on pave near Library.

Mexico City Cantina on Serdan above Plaza Garibaldi

Noise of a slowplaying pokey Mambo band, trumpets in black, young man with mustache, the waiters tieless in white coats fingering their cocks and talking in a group at next booth—explaining one dances a step back & forth, palms upraised. All the girls young & fat, red lite beaming from corner—looks like miniature Rivoli theater Paterson (worst in town lowlife films). Girls together in chairs facing the dance floor, another globe of red light near the bar, redlight exuding from the jukebox control at the table (Wallomatic as Auden says) and a circle of indirect red lights in the ceiling. A few men with dark glasses. Band playing not high not great swinging a little.

Dream May 23—

Talking to Eugene, explaining the problems of writing about ruins, romantic poetry.

And so "the difficulty is to say the various things necessary to be said in front of ruins:

1. Look how big and powerful they are

2. Think of the living souls who made them and imagine them alive.

3. Look how time has toppled them.

4. All things pass away.

5. And especially I too shall pass away"

And I continue, quoting Siesta in Xbalba passage beginning "So spent a night—"[1] till I woke up around "toward faces flat & worn away by rain." He understood and in the dream was quite pleased.

Patzcuaro May 23—

Walking streets under old red stone arcades in night rain, utter solitude (saw anachronistic-jungle-pacific-Maui-honolulu-Sabu[2]-anti-communist picture) watching indians out of corner of eye as they stood waiting for rain to stop in the plaza—so ready to love I fell for 2 different indians (and many more) one in the bus, one in the arcade, their young faces under dirty sombreros, bodies covered with black serapes.

Thought a few days ago, alone in Mexico hotel (where I had bedbugs & codeine on Cinco de Mayo after 2 nights of wandering among boys silent in Plaza Garibaldi) with my own shabby body to myself, and my beard, naked in bed, what solitude I have finally inherited—and on the bus thought nothing could feel sweeter than to put my arm around the young sad indian, and my cheek against his mouth & close my eyes—do it on the bus.

The gloom under the arcade when the town lights went out in the thunder shower & all the indians and old men & slack & sportshirt indians huddled together, talking, while I sat at a table & drank coffee,

---

[1] "So spent a night with drug and hammock/at Chichén Itzá on the Castle:—" begins long passage detailing night among ruins (see p. 25, *Reality Sandwiches*).

[2] Sabu: 15-year-old movie actor from India; played elephant jungle boy.

waiting, and watching another boy in new clean decorated sombrero and large decorated serape that fell to the ground to his huarached-feet, young boy with dovelike manly face & blank young eyes.

In my beard I am playing the wrong character, can't be young and open, as also am aging and closing it seems now, when I think of all the months I've practiced masturbation (in the selva unable to reach straight out to another body).

So that trip to Frisco almost solely eternally for love.

Another Hotel Room, Imperial, Patzcuaro, pink wall base, pink wood fret around middle, paint cracked and pale in splotches, yellow walltop, Michoacán red fret meander, and ceiling squared into bright large regular design enclosing brown and white starshapes—red tile floor, a great uneven mirror cattycorner near the light switch, crude table & two chairs, general bareness & rainstreaks on the high walls, no window only a double door framed by a loose sloppy hank of clean curtain—a board propped against the wall, my pictures and masks just bought on the wall, knapsack full on table, nothing here but me.

My life seems perfect, except for future money anxieties, and seems sterile but it's only a moment of loneliness—warmth of a sweet brown man's body and dark hair soft flesh and the thought of it melts my heart. I'm tired of my own crooked selfy cock.

San Miguel de Allende—

What joy! the nakedness! they dance, they talk and simper before the door, they lean on a leg (hand on a hip) and clap a hand to head—(watching thru a keyhole the lovers at San Miguel Allende)

The Bar after hours, after the Ball, back at Salto—as always a sad indian, shirt untucked, barefoot, guarding the closed door—standing half drunk quiet, a guardian falling asleep on his feet. He finally sinks to the floor closing his eyes, opening them, blinking looking stupid. The gathering drunk around the table—the Professor, the Architect come in to fix the streets, a young kid, unhandsome, and some grey businessmen. The walk thru the Plaza with the professor importuning me.

* * *

The drugstore: "Globulos Homeopaticos Hoffman—Packet #3 for illnesses such as Tos, Bazo, Almorranas, Dolor de Garganta, Blenorrogia, Herpes, Espermatorrea, Flores Blancas, Oido, Sordera, Aftas o Fogajes." [1]

★ ★ ★

Guanajuato, listening to disco

Cu-ku-ru-ku-ru Paloma
M.A. Mejica—Huapanga

A soda parlor downtown:

Outside casbahs on hills, stupendous university ancient looking just built with great kafkian stairway-entrance gothic up hillfront, circular streets with balconies, a million little weird gothic alleys, alleys for greatness...

Inside the soda parlor everything solid & bright like a Riverside Calif. drugstore, jukebox well dressed people, girls in long black skirts and big white chic wool Paris sweaters big earrings & poodle hair. Ayayayaayay on the records—ayayayayay again—The icecream cones however including Zapote and Mamay—Ice cream sodas advertised, yellow petroleum tables and plastic seats.

The jukebox with Begin the Beguine, Chattanooga Choo Choo, Chicago—all sounding decades old, transfixed in a different place. Here tho in a valley filled with sublime Kantian mines, old bastions, churches & mummies mexican.

"Pruebe Ud. nuestros Exquisitos Waffles." [2]

Big case of perfumes screwed to the wall, on the left postcards kodaks, silver jewelry, tile floor, greek pillars painted pink, on wall kodak pix of big white U.S. dogs yawping blearily into the camera.

★ ★ ★

The mummies next day a pile of skulls at the end of the corridor, armbones attached neatly & skulls ranged on top, though in the cellarlike corner top of the pile someone had thrown a big ugly live mummy fat sitting on the skulls. The skulls empty fragile and numerous as shells—so

---

[1] Cough, spleen, etc.
[2] "Try our exquisite waffles."

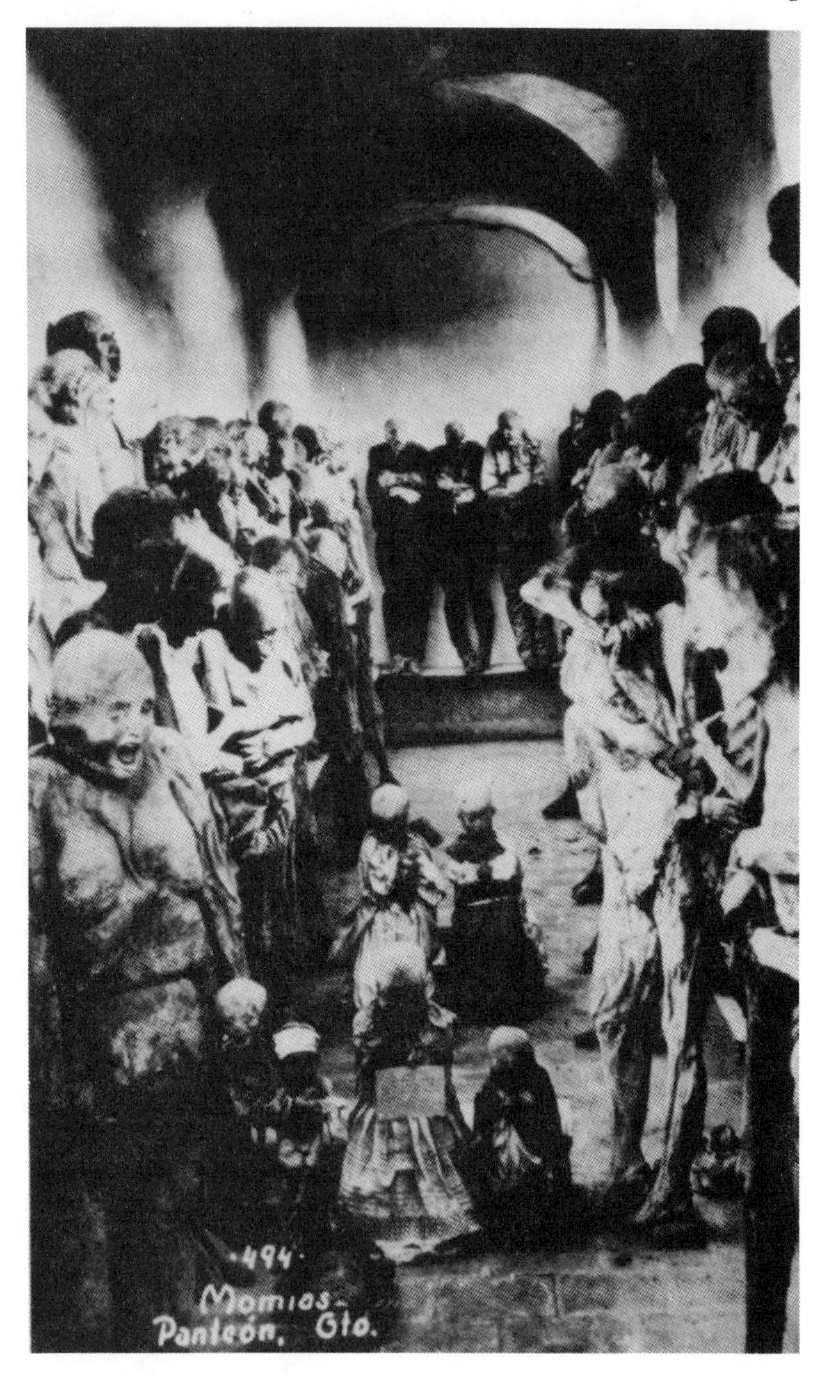
·494·
Momios-
Panteón. Gto.

The Mummies of Guanajuato

much life has passed out, past thru, pure dusty bones left—Fetid smell reminding one of sperm and drunkenness.

Sitting on Gravestone in the Pantheon at Guanajuato over the city under the blue sky to inscribe these notes of Las Momias—

Clutching bodies & mouths open, skin shrunk back as if drying writhing: stiffened limestone corpses—inward fireless consumed in the darkness. Not pain but it is physical, not spectral torment but withering of body and soul too.

The mine, an abandoned hole seven hundred feet deep and 30 feet wide I looked into, started by Spaniards like the great wall of China and worked on for so many hundreds of years it got so deep it is eerie to gaze in, stone dropped, minutes later you can see disturbance on the water & then later a noise of thunder.

The Mortal World:

3 days walk near the Usumascinta—The bearded bohemian from Salt Lake Jesse Sharp took 3 days walk along the ancient streets, he could tell it was a city by the mounds covered with vegetation. He told me about it on the train up. The problem is isolation. This is a month later. I walked for 3 days in Guanajuato and met no one.

I saw a Cortésian mine so deep a stone made thunder in the gulf—abandoned in the hills, great hole to China. Mummies in the pantheon, newly resurrected gasping in their evening clothes, indecipherable-sexed death men—one had his arms raised to cover his eyes, significant timeless reflex in the sepulchre.

All the appearance of waiting and withering consumed in the painless dark—The problem is isolation, there in the grave or in oblivion of light.

White Cervantes in the dark little plaza wandered silent angelic among the street vendors and dueling medieval Spaniards. How sad the actor glided across the real stage. I sat watching the annual pageant.

* * *

I think in 1948: sitting in my apartment,
    my eyes opened for an hour
seeing in dreadful ecstasy
    the buildings rotting
Under the wide eternal sky.

Zacatecas

San Carlos restaurant off side of main street: A few high mirrors on walls clean cheap pink paint, bedroom set new. Black & white octagonal bigtile floor. Pink bedroom lamp, shade atilt over Uncle Abe's ancient clean radio, too-near voices speaking into microphones. Conch shells, indirect lighting like a niteclub. Plastic tables far apart & empty.

I the only one here.

Durango:

Suddenly there were a million children playing in the park, stubborn, on skates and scooters or bicycle astridden, fighting and running to grab arms, stumbling and staring about hand in mouth, circling the bandstand on single skates, jiggling one-foot or in carriage, conversing solemnly astride a bicycle, running down aisles and stopping short, carried aloft by mothers and brothers, chasing in threes, swirling around of girls on one foot, ringing bells, racing broadside, skipping ropes in circles, bumping each other absently, lifting each other up squealing, falling down hitting arms, waiting, imitating airplanes and horses, getting dizzy, lying crucifix on the grass, dropping money, walking single file in zigzag, playing tag, shaking empty paper bags, making sucking noises; faces besmudged by chocolate, plumped down on the pave, scooping shitty water out of the pool, pushing sailboats, sinking woodscraps, smirking & screaming for bubblegum, tearing up flowers by the roots, presenting them to elders with chubby hands; hairless and ribboned, in rags and diapers, levis and pants too short, in shirts with circles, in neckerchiefs, sitting on the grass, swinging balloons and pocketbooks, hair cut off braided or in ribbons, yellow, red, brown and black of hair, bald, or leaning on great knees and having their dresses adjusted and hair put in place, staring in white dresses—and when the band began all began screaming.

* * *

The short Mexican, topheavy in his northern sombrero, leaning sleepily against pole in midnight bus station.

Santa Ana

The bus station. The end of the long trip—tired—waiting for the last 11 hr. jump to cross the border into legendary Calif.

A Motif A Theme

Enter U.S. alone naked with knapsack, watch, camera, poem, beard.

The problem is construction of Image. An imagination real and true.

The past image of Neal less quickens my heart than before as I approach border.

Not yet the great image of life that justifies freedom.

Circumnavigation of globe no end in itself. The great motivation to be discovered. Process is empty without end.

What is the meaning of my life which waits for me to assign one? What wish steals in from the archaic?

Love still possibly sanctity since now I am the god.

Mexicali, June 1954

My room on the garbage cliff overlooking the Casbah poor barrio, tin shacks and white roofs, and little dirty gardens down below bounded by the uptown hip cliff and superhighway nightmare 20th cent viaduct. To stand on my garbage cliff and see I am at the end of Mexican trip.

* * *

The town so noisy, dirty, streetfulls of wild boys all night, drunken wetbacks, restaurants, Chinese hotels, musicians, half american stores, jumping beans and tortilla concessions, Chinese Masonic lodges & barbers too. Big halls for restaurants and music, painted crudely with monolithic donkeys.

I walked thru the border at nite to get a map of California, a dead silent fairyland of U.S. dusk—deserted ghost streets and sad quiet aircooled diners with white capped waitresses joking softly and no one on the streets.

In Riverside—

Hollywood sight shrunken empty & run down can feel the name already lost its world magic. I dreamed party sat next Chaplin couch I was going to ask "What tourist sights you recommend?" but he started to ask "You all want to hear my next story?" and Shields [1] interrupted to take all to another room. I got mad having had couch with Chaplin then.

LA June 8

Now I'm older and it isn't melancholy in the solitude . . . loving drunken
naked apartments . . . only a few flashes of that shivering life . . .

[1] Karena Shields, A.G.'s hostess in Xbalba (Chiapas).

One moment of tenderness and a year of nerves and intelligence, one
moment of actual fleshly tenderness . . .
As for the future now I am free . . . for no new love has been made . . .
after these last human stations . . .

* * *

As now I am 28 for the first time older than I've dreamed of being. The beard a joke, my character with its childish core a tiring taste . . . I could dismiss the Allen with grim pleasure, yet am saddled with myself, the experience of the last ten years, the whole taste from kid-hood—childhood in apartments in Paterson.

To break with that pattern entirely—

Must find energy & image & act on it.

June 12—

The Visions—if of my own making or hallucination I am at best, them, godlike.

* * *

—3 Great deaths Cannastra Joan At last I have forgotten his name—D. Kammerer.

* * *

Of an eternity we have a number of score of years . . . I have had several months near joy, and of that perhaps one day doing what I inmost want and of that a minute of perfection.

San Jose, California

The possibility of neuroticism growing automatically out of certain family alignments—A family of 3 men; the third boy queer. A family of 3 women, the third girl queer.

Recalling my incestuous relation with my brother in fantasy & partial fact; and also with father. The nights when I slept with them thru puberty.

* * *

Credo

1. The weight of the world is love.[1]
2. The mind imagines all visions.
3. Man is as far divine as his imagination.
4. We go create as divine a world as we can imagine—must go on interpreting & recreating the given blank world (since not to imagine is not to eat) according to most extreme absolute of divinity we can conceive.

* * *

Jack's isolation like mine is sad & frightful mainly the blind alleys of money and love but life is not over, and much to be written and much to be respected in all of us not just for being humanity but for having tried and actually achieved a thing namely literature[2] and also possibly a certain spiritual eye at this point.

And Neal who has money & love is desperate at the gate of heaven for he is unhappy with his existence, now he is seeking in his soul.

As for Bill he thinks he is lost.

Lucien knows his way but may have a period of having to expand his spiritual horizon in order to accommodate the depth and height of possibility & this may yet be preceded by the appearance of a prison in his soul.

* * *

(Notes for "Song" from *Howl and Other Poems)*

* * *

The Dream June 27—Sat. Nite

In the bathroom, N. in bathing suit, naked and alone, I sat down on couch with him, not looking, and in a movement together we touched hands, and then I felt the pressure as he enfolded my hand & clasped it frankly, I think I looked at him & put my arm round his shoulder, and he leaned over and put his head on my chest and took me around with his arms—Exaltation (what is the precise word for the sensation of love

[1] See "Song," pp. 39–41 in *Howl and Other Poems.*

[2] At this time, A.G. had not yet published any volume of poetry.

acceptance?)—the dream wandered, I went out of the bathroom (we were on a couch) and I went into the living room where my family was sitting propped up—happy at a dinner table, all faced one way; I spoke to my aunt Clara, to young Hannah, and bent down & kissed my grandmother—returning to the closed bathroom where N. was hiding—And combed hair out of my mouth—as I began pulling out the hair, I realized how long and tangled into my gullet it went down, as I pulled it it broke & I grasped for more—thinking possibly that all along it was this that had been causing my debilitation.

. . . Creating out of myself the strength to continue in some kind of force, some kind of uncanny care—though I have nothing to give actually but a cheerful spirit now and hands for dishwashing—to give force for my own & others pleasure—to learn to give love without despairing of the consequences.

As tonight, too poor and sordid for notation, I waited while Neal played abstract inhuman chess, waiting for him to finish through seven games while Carolyn had at last returned and we were perhaps for one of the first times free to do whatever we had in mind, in mine, make it, and in his, sudden wordless retirement—I wish now I had spoken rather than waited, after I arranged the shades, turned down the lights, prepared a place on the couch.

Once again I've maneuvered myself into a frustrating idealistic situation where I am reduced to pathetic beggary.

My greatest fear perhaps is of the world outside this haven where I'll have to work and struggle with no love goal in mind.

What do I want? Not this side street of conflict—And would it make any difference if I slept with N., to Carolyn?—But the rejection as tonite is deeply fixed in the situation.

Even a few moments with Neal—the attainment is bound to be short-lived due to his responsibilities and the apparent impossibility of it as a life situation—me living here hanging on him like a sick junkie.

Does he even want me here, now? She does perhaps as long as I am not too intimate with Neal. The waste of the chess game time, for me. Better perhaps to look around for a Frisco job and room, escape this situation where I am often unhappy and troubled, it is a baffling position I am in. I live under the hope that Neal is as yet baffled by the problems as I am. But what can he do?

I feel myself sacrificing part of my being to him—and he has sacrificed money and some time & attention to me, given it, but no sacrifice of being or self, not much sign of interest except in offhand and patronizing ways, except at a few moments of tenderness that are hard fought for and accidental rare infusions of pleasure into my otherwise bad-feeling starved routine here. But dare I by principle like some crazy character in Dosty. demand a return sacrifice?

I feel like a strange idiot, standing there among wife & children all to whom he gives needs of affection and attention, aching for some special side extra sacrifice of attention to me—as if like some nowhere evil beast intruding I were competing for his care with his own children & wife and job which seems to occupy energize bore & tire him.

* * *

I can sleep with Neal, sleep with Carolyn, sleep with no one, and stay. Or sleep with both and no one alternately amid confusions. Or I can end this mad triangle, all three of us blocked, by leaving.

The problem furthermore of the difference between my night dream of N. and the actual moment of embrace as the other night where the confidence went far and yet despite my pleasure & relief, almost dreamlike, the release was not as direct and overwhelming in joy as the dream—feelings that are not false since I can feel them down there in dreams—

The essentially mad idea of trying to stay in this artificial situation.

* * *

I know Neal understands all this knows all this; but what does he want? He says, do what I want—He does not encourage me in the situation and I again wonder what can I hope for from him. I feel I am all on the wrong track emotionally in expecting active sexual love from Neal to begin with—Would he be actually happier and relieved if I gave up finally and left him alone? What Karma has he with me, if I have no deeper erotic Karma with him than friend, helper, & helped? Does he want all the morbid attention? If not I have the energy strength yes to make out otherwise; I will not suffer beyond my bearable load, but I would be unhappy awhile & adjust. So he has freedom. So have I. So what is the issue here. Must try to resolve it with him before it drags itself out and I get lost in confusions and imagined rejections.

In a way he is really a bastard inviting & rejecting, making things so unclear, leaving me hung up when he knows my habit so well, unless he just wants it resolved & given up by me under his care & aegis—on the other hand, his offers, his carnality at moments, his future acceptances, his plight of sexual starvation leads me to hope I am welcome.

Serenade

How later I know I will regret the words I have poured over blindly, sifting and testing my thoughts for their coin.

The bank is bankrupt and the inflated currency is worthless in a ruined land. The bomb appeared intolerable, light and radiance, and afterwards the grey world appeared as a ghost.

Useless to belabor the reality. The poems are mad. Useless to practice a secret design. The skull is vacant. The flesh is a shell. The heart's consumed no phoenix.

How waste is the language and broken the thought—shadow flesh, third thoughts of the grave, obscure ravenings of spectral fright, the inward flame and darkness of the damned.

Rimbaud and Yeats already bid adieux (Circus Animal's Desertion) to these regrettable hallucinations.

I curse the ignominy of my being. Time to cut the throat of this fat rhetoric.

* * *

Dedicate New Book if any ever to Williams.

* * *

Don't tell me the truth
I want to be lied to—
Besides I know it all,
down to the smallest thought
constructed hour by hour
in city, in jungle, in train,
in subway, bus and plane.
Year after year remembered,
night after night dreamed.

Dream July 6

We are all sleeping on the ground and C— is there—we have sheets or thin blankets over us but are separate, my father & brother next to me—C— and I touch but my father-brother could see—we move over away a bit but still the same trouble. We are a little cold & are trying to get together for warmth of body length contact under his cover. We try under a stair but that's too open finally it is time to get up & so we go in the narrow bathroom overlooking NYC—by this time we have a sort of new understanding but I don't trust him yet—nor he me. I reach down to blow him, he says OK but me standing up, I go to, but he already has sunk down taking down his thin shorts revealing half his cock, he says no fucking around as last time—in sentimental touching any other part of the body, no more kissing thighs just pure suck the head of it, I start to, and I see as I put my lips to it he's white in the head, he's ready, he comes in my mouth, a lot of come and his cock's big I don't get it all in my mouth just the head we get up I get ready to get out, to go. We were next to the toilet seat on the floor.

He says "By god we might as well go out"—suggesting that since it's all gone thru without hitch we can maybe make it on the town as before. I am ready to go back for my shorts, but he hands me a pair of his shorts to wear, with a flourish, but doesn't comment on the significance.

The city, an apartment in the Bronx El area we would visit.

July 11, '54

Fortunately art is a community effort—a small but select community living in a spiritualized world endeavoring to interpret the wars and solitudes of the flesh.

* * *

Love. He is our deepest self. Mysterious, actual, delightful and sorrowful at once, full of gentility and imprudence, a benificent spirit, a god acting thru human masks. He is the same in all, neither man or woman. We all have the same sense of bottom self. He is the solitary.

Thus love others as the self. We are incorruptible . . . The god survives. Love is complete. There is more than can be given. None is wasted no love is amiss none goes astray none perishes. . . . It never lacks because it is All. It comes on the mind in visions. Watch for it coming! It enters the house of the body without your seeking.

Dream—July 11, 1954

In a large secular monastery near Paris, where I have been sent to work under Bob Lax [1] I arrive with trunk, clothes, dressed. When I arrive he

[1] Bob Lax: poet friend and Columbia classmate of Thomas Merton; later friend of Kerouac. Member of Catholic mystic community.

seems mad to me, a little. I feel very uneasy and childish, as if it were a challenge. I realize I am back in a hospital condition or other situation. Lax is heavy, somewhat like Kells Elvins [1] and older, though very good looking, though beat up somewhat like Bing Crosby in Boys Town. I am given a bunk in an alcove off his main office. I feel that I am an honored guest or patient but I am not sure that this is not my natural presumption which must soon go to be accepted as such, a humbler role with the others, for greater discipline. I don't know what to do with myself I take off my clothes and lie down. Perhaps take out my notebook—I wander out (in bathrobe?), past rows of men & women in a greater hall (like at Annapolis gym) who are at their work benches performing arts and crafts or their duties, manuscript illumination? I go talk with Lax, though still not sure I am expected to talk *talk*. "Do you do anything now?" I ask, a reference to writing poetry—"Any poetry?" "No," he says, "I am occupied by my job here." It is his humbling work. He is empty so he has taken on this discipline. I am his problem—I realize we all are.

I wander out across the street (like at Colonia Yucatán) to a bar or soda parlor for a visit. Something warns me and I come back in a few minutes. "Shouldn't I go across there?" He is collapsed on the front stone white stoop. He had been calling me. "Please forgive me for my deed, it was in ignorance." Apparently we lead a life under his orders or judgement. Must follow rules to stay. No punishments here, but just the point is to follow rules, that's why I'm here, so I better do so. I feel very childish & kindly toward him, like Dr. Brooks my analyst, except also impulses of contempt & irrelevance.

July 14—

That in some respects I have a purer love of people than in 1946 when Chase called me—"Sacerdotal."

Certainly am less attached.

* * *

A house not built by human hands and a house built by human hands. I stand under the ceiling of both, natural and supernatural. The flash or impression of this as I lie on the couch.

The supernatural house may be the oft hinted platonic house. Or

---

[1] Student friend of Burroughs who collaborated with him on his first piece, "Twilight's Last Gleaming."

the suggestion of dream unreality of the natural house, as in Buddhism.

Therefore these suggestions by the unconscious noticing of an impression are not sufficient, what is needed is an *actual* vision to get the meaning.

When it comes I will know that I have been preparing for it since 1949 visions—that is to say the main theme of my thought has been in preparation for understanding or achieving a moment that is to come.[1]

I am on a bus—it turns out to be not the bus but one of a train of buses with soldiers following the main ones, I pass up front (Atotanilco bus).

* * *

A dream letter from John Holmes, containing statements of new found principles—

" 'A Shropshire Lad' was written under a cloak rag or shroud.

"The social organization which is most true of itself to the artist is the boy gang" (not society's perfum'd marriage).

* * *

Walking up dark streets Venice—like Paterson after a fiesta or fireworks with Louis and others, him explaining my artistic conscience or wotnot I skip ahead he taunts me with my eagerness to see the rest ahead of the street "No I've never seen this before" referring to the beergardens bars and bldg—"Nacionalista Mexicana" as we pass the high square white block-tower of "Bograts" ahead downtown, but as we approach, "Left," says Gene & Louis & we go down a dark alley instead of downtown which leads to the next phase of our living quarters toward the Eastside—we been coming up from Haledon Ave.—a great plaza near Eastside H.S. I am returning from—dark swept open football field.

Wandering around trying to get in library and gym—Drama class at Bennington—I come upon—the library I wander around in thru sections like at Paterson or N.Y. Museum Nat. Hist.—a lady at a desk to one side, fellows of indeterminate type like middleaged dark fags standing around gossiping—I have no card—walk on thru—a large door closed—the stairwell to the basement opening out on football field, the long corridors of the basement as at Columbia passageways football field like bullring empty I finally come to the drama gym or barn or Shed—A band at the entrance—much going on inside past the band I can't get, too many

[1] It never came.—A.G., 1976.

people working—one at the mike, near the piano near the door, is reading off note on a symphony concert—I am going up a big hill in Paterson also Columbia as in another dream of Morningside Heights where I lived in a room & Gene lived in a room, same room with my bed up in the right inner corner up on a partition shelf and a balcony inside room near the front window and walking around on Riverside interminable and 92nd St. (Thalia movie house) to Gene's & my house. Earlier a scene on Ferry, the great giant ferry of Futures and fascism, I am crossing the vast Hudson & we get under the high wall concrete thousands feet high other N.Y. side of river in small (big) ferry on way across black waters long wide river miles across—Much mystery and scope to the border under the protective wall before N.Y. skyline heights & road complexities—but this all another earlier dream when? Years ago perhaps—in this dream I walking up 125th st. Bway to get to Columbia and on street I run across a few of the characters of the Shed Drama giving their spiels of the concert or inauguration—one man like Noel dark tho giving his spiel from memory, another further up as I pass a restaurant hid by River St. Gypsy curtains on way, to where a small moonfaced junkey girl is giving her spiel into the radio portable mike in the snow near Barnard Furey hall near chem-astronomy-physics bldg.

* * *

(Notes for "Love Poem on Theme by Whitman," p. 41, *Reality Sandwiches)*

July 20, '54 Dream

enter room there's uncle Abe lying back on his back on a table shelf stuck out from the wall height of chest a partition between sections of the room lying there on his back with the boys talking all dressed up and as I enter to inquire one or the other for the hipsters whoever I'm looking for as I go knocking from cubicle to cubicle as I went knocking after cousins Gene & Eddie, he sits up, Abe does, and I notice a roach in his hand, he's a T head I realize, somewhat shocked also by disparity of ages between him & my friends who are his friends—I had set out looking for someone in particular, a Keck or someone here in Frisco—

I descend a stairway, small narrow slum stairway like in 1930's slum pix, and look in the mailbox to see the bulb has been removed, remembering upstairs that a bulb had blown out & no one could find a replacement, too cheap to buy a new one, they took the necessary downstairs light & stuck it somewhere upstairs

—We are in some city or town and I am discussing with others the return from Africa of Eugene or Judy—apparently Judy wants to marry Eugene or vice versa—the family is in the room, there is a long couch I am spread on it or sitting showing the letter—I express contempt and disapproval of her—Judy—I go on but they don't understand, I wind up saying, "but what I mean is, she's *crazy*"—this word received with some resentment or silence, I feel embarrassed as if I am trying to put something over on them perhaps projected or untrue, what are my motives in objecting to the marriage—I feel uneasy

Recent dreams bringing in associations with other earlier central tho fugitive dreams—in this case the constellation mentioned on previous pages involving subway platform also—

Wanderings and flight to obscure apartments in Brooklyn—or the recollection of wandering up and down the wrong streets à la Lower East Side looking for the street doorway to the slum flat I am destined to head for, finally winding up on topfloor flat where I stand & look outside at city, people are looking for me? but don't remember what took place in the apt.

Recall before sleeping recollection of traumatic time when my *whole* sensation of life and feelings toward Louis changed when I was *what,* 13? or earlier in regard to him fainting at 288 Graham Ave. and the letter from his amour girl friend I found in wastebasket and Eugene & I pieced together—this regarding my tendency also to live with families like I was child with ma & pa together trying to get pa's (Lucien or Carolyn's) attention.

And also the above just reminded me that Liz Lehrman was in the dream—I talking to her she has returned from the rotten orient—south seas area—I ask how did you get out there, what do?—she is a little heavier like Judy—is it she who is crazy (as Lucien said) who wants to marry Gene?—And my mother having been crazy I see a relationship of associations in the dreams.

* * *

Kerouac

c/o Carolyn Blake (his sister)
Box 31-A, Route 4, Rocky Mount
N. Carolina

* * *

The burning snake—I tied him on a pole and wrapped him in the flames—and at the burst of fire he recoiled and writhed on the stake, whirling his body back and forth against the terrible light—Pain! Pain! he writhed and lashed in his dead body—what immolation of the nerves? As fat as my brown arm with all his hidden color in the pole, black evil soul smoke.

And the next day—we went off impatient of the slow consuming carnage—his bones not there in the charred branch and bush and an evil smell around the thatchroofed wall-less house that night—everyone in mosquito net and yellow kerosine lanterns in one corner of the darkness. Nonetheless they say you keep the snakes away by burning one in private woods.

Boccaccio, *La Fiammetta*—The exposition of the voice of Jealousy page 3 of Chapter IV.

Re: "Xbalba"—

A reordering of the stanzas needed in the poem, some formal equality of stanzas, or alternation of stanza forms—

An interior order in each stanza someway apparent—syllable, accent, or quantity, or general weight of lines intuitively felt—What measure within the stanza, in the line?

Perhaps the concept of *line* is at basic root. Break up the line?

into emotive or meaningful or musical complete images or abstractions or sensations—whole, each, however.

Except for purposeful variations on the meaning.

Re-form lines in terms of concepts or/and units of words conjuring up a sensation, (images)

* * *

To inquire of self & others, Neal—the actual psychy and physy of the come, the orgasm—anal distribution or outlet of pelvic reflex energy.

* * *

Lower levels—I want to be your slave, suck your ass, suck your cock, you fuck me, you master me, you humiliate me—humiliate me, I want to be tied and whipped, spanked on the behind over knees, want to be made to cry and beg and weep for love.[1]

Dream

Sitting in the Eastside park have to take a hip trip by bus far down the valley for spaghetti—I see the paintings by Jack from Russian Hill of the Mts. aiming toward the east. There in tent-fold of the earth Salt Lake, Butte, Denver, etc.—they are colored chalk or crayon drawings.

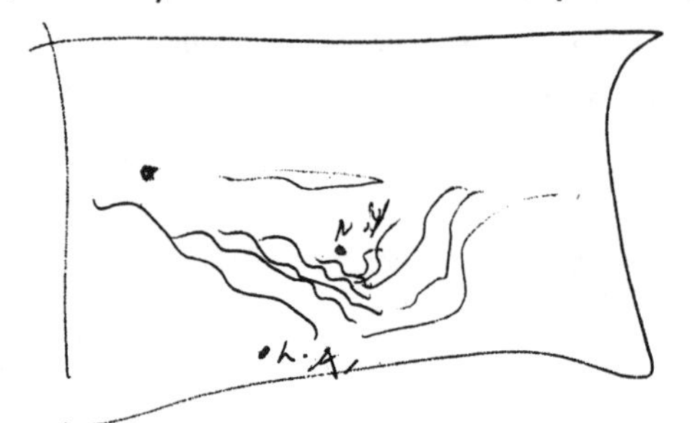

Dream of Jack's paintings

I go to restaurant to get bus tickets to get two orders of spaghetti from some town 2 hrs. away but when I inquire it's 2 3/4 hrs away, the lady says, and she's behind the restaurant counter (as counter at Los Gatos) she serves up the spaghetti, I think, for me. Tho the plate has a little potatoes creamed, tomatoes & something else small portions no meat (Carolyn serves so) so I say have you spaghetti? She says no but we have Napoleon & Fritti—some other Italian type spaghettis—so I order that, thinking to save myself the long trip back—

Return to the loft to find a nice looking young man tall boy lying on bed with his poem spread around on the sheet him naked talking to another hip old man in chair in the cluttered loft as Frankel's in Hoboken—I look at last page of MSS. it is poetic but early verse and not pointed like more mature Corso say I lay down with the boy & put my arm around him to read his poem moving over the bed under the big feather quilt, have to move my leg touching his to turn, his touches me, like Hal C—, how pleasurable this is—fragment ends here.

Then I am walking with the old lady (the Signora Shields) thru the park, we come to a wooded section near the tennis court—the big trees there, some planted, some flower or fruit trees poorly planted, or not

---

[1] See "Please Master," 1968, pp. 84–86 in *The Fall of America* (San Francisco: City Lights, 1972).

taken care of—a big room, we are in the City Council meeting, La Guardia is there the meeting wants to break up, but I sit in my folding chair by the wall of the long narrow room in the center saying how bad the city is run, and La G. pays attention, refers me to the Commissioner who is absent or knows nothing, I keep up the attack on the planting poorly of the trees, but suddenly am unsure of my facts—taken from the Signora—and she's there to back me up, she's used to dealing with businessmen so she should be trustworthy—(writing I realize the boy is only a dream and I am sad for it is truly left to unconscious life, not the real person shining)

The argument continues, I see the politicians commissioners—and on the back of all the politicians' pants is a stamped white notice, as on the backs of dress pants borrowed,—the statement "Boro of Water Commissioners LaGuardia Reign City Hall 1954" etc. or whatever.

★ ★ ★

Nathanael West wrote true surrealist novels—must read the sources, *Cocteau.*

In French—To read him & to also read Proust. Cocteau in San José (Public Library)

★ ★ ★

My first novel will be a local work—Paterson Revisited, say with W.C.W.'s letter in mind—to recreate Paterson in *my* own image to experiment with a different approach or style.

—The job would be beyond my means, for the present, however there is always hope for the Future. I might write him: I am the Trotsky with no dogma in your party.

Politics is also beyond my means—though what a hilarious chapter that might make, visions of mayors, of evenings of fireworks and speeches, the politics of the library board and school system, congressional races, (auto races too from the rock near the stadium)—

The night the congressman won and lost in the same midnight,—he got hysterical—(Did they steal the election, the republicans?) (With the aid of the Press—Paterson News and Morning Call, the tough brute editor—the cowardly old woman editor on the Call and echoes of Jersey City Mayor Hague beyond) The night that Joelson, the last would-be congressman,.lost, a great dumb union crusader wept (and what liberal Communist mysteries behind)—

Include Communist meetings of the 30's—though I do remember

the man in front of the City Hall with his apocalyptic songs and speech—his ghost appears in what garden? What park?

—We remember in addition the depression seen thru the eyes of the child, bankfailure and wage cuts. Saw no fighting—but I passed out anti-Hague pamphlets in Jersey City at 12 in maybe was it 1938 and then I saw the passion and characters of that war.

Therefore a poem, the history of my wanderings and accomplishments in the Great City and otherwhere, and various returns—

and perhaps return for a Judgement (In Inferno? or the clear world?) (or remotely Heaven)—Thru all eyes of vision, another vision of Paterson.

Visions of Paterson, or The Shrouded Stranger of the Night—Paterson in Heaven—or Paterson thru the eyes of one who Knew it well—

Reading Jan 1—'54

Guidebooks Uxmal & Mérida
The Cloud of Unknowing
Studies in Classical American Literature—Lawrence
The New Testament
Arnold Bennett—Biog. by Reg. Pound
Parts of 7 Storey Mountain, Imitation of Christ
Untermeyer's Pocket Library *Frost*

June

Age of Anxiety—Auden
Folded Leaf—Maxwell
Kant—Selections
B. Russell—Selections from Hist of Phil.
S. Anderson—Winesburg, O.
Quarterly Review of Lit.—British Poets (Durrell's Sappho)
Gore Vidal—The Judgment of Paris

July

Céline—Mea Culpa & Semmelweiss
Gertrude Stein—Paris, France; Autobiog. of A. Toklas.
Gina Cerminova—Cayce System Book

Wm. Cayce—Extracts from Readings (psychic)
Cassady, N.—Fragments of Autobiog. reread
Stein—Things as they are
Horney—Our Inner Conflicts
Céline—Last half of Journey to End of Night (finally finished after 10 years) I had reserved it for later pleasure. Will get hold of Guignol's Band, which just came out in English (Summer '54)
Proust—Cities of the Plain—Part, first Chapters Vol. II.
Eliot—Selected Essays to 1932
Bhagavad Gita—Isherwood tr.
poems—in Understanding Poetry Brooks & Warren
Plato—Symposium
Encyclopedia Britannica articles on Hermetic types and sects
Eliot—4 Quartets—Idea of Xtian Society
Pound—Pisan Cantos, XXX Cantos
H.D.—Collected Poems (1925)
E.E. Cummings—Xaipe (1950 Poems)
An Examination of Pound—
A.E. Coppard—a few stories. (The Silver Circus)
The Invisible Man—R. Ellison
Flee the Angry Strangers—Geo. Mandel
Pavannes & Divagations—Pound
Vita Nuova—Dante (Rossetti tr.)
Boccaccio—Fiammetta
Rimbaud—Season in Hell

III
BERKELEY

Fall 1955—Spring 1956
(Notebook on Reading Dreams & Poem Drafts)

Allen Ginsberg, January 1956

America I've given you all and now I'm nothing—[1]
America when will we end the war?
America when will you be angelic?
America when will you take off your clothes and be human?
America when will you give me back my mother?
America when will you give me back my love?
America when will you look at yourself through the grave?
America when will you be worthy of your million Christs?
America what's wrong? Why are your libraries full of tears?
America when will you send your eggs to India?
America when will you stop destroying human souls? Your soul my soul?
America when will you send me a lover?
I Allen Ginsberg Bard out of New Jersey take up the laurel tree cudgel
from Whitman

* * *

Already Time for your Elegy, dear Natalie? [2]
Already time for the angelic shock?
Already your blood meaningless,
and your truthful eyes
troubling me too late?
Should I have invited you to Berkeley?
Given you money? or more love?
or a rest home in my crazy lovely garden?

---

[1] First notation for poem "America." See pp. 31–34, *Howl and Other Poems* (San Francisco: City Lights, 1956).

[2] Natalie Jackson, Neal Cassady's girl friend of those years.

In the car over for Thanksgiving
you gave me a look so tearful
I knew it was death
or thought so
and it passed my mind
not my time yet
I ignored you.
I closed my light lay back
& try to pray for you.
Take refuge in my prayer.
Take refuge in Pater Omnipotens Aeterne Deus
Take refuge in Love (which is God)
Self Love—
Oh, Natalie, where is refuge?
Take refuge in Death.
Finally it is death I wish
—not the horror of blood bedabbled knees
and ankles on a pavement
or a throat cut by electric bulbs—
Dark death, Soft Death
Black eternal grave
and rest.

Haiku composed in the backyard cottage at 1624 Milvia Street, Berkeley 1955, while reading R.H. Blyth's 4 volumes Haiku:

Drinking my tea
Without sugar—
No difference.

* * *

The sparrow shits
upside down
—ah! my brains & eggs!

* * *

Mayan head in a
Pacific driftwood bole
—Someday I'll live in N.Y.

* * *

Looking over my shoulder
my behind was covered
with cherry blossoms.

* * *

Winter Haiku

I didn't know the names
of the flowers— now
my garden is gone.

* * *

I slapped the mosquito
and missed.
What made me do that?

* * *

Reading haiku
I am unhappy,
longing for the Nameless.

* * *

A frog floating
in the Drugstore jar:
summer rain on grey pavements.
(after Shiki)

* * *

On the porch
in my shorts;
auto lights in the rain.

* * *

Another year
has past— the world
is no different.

* * *

The first thing I looked for
in my old garden was
The Cherry Tree.

* * *

My old desk:
the first thing I looked for
in my house.

* * *

My early journal:
the first thing I found
in my old desk.

* * *

My mother's ghost:
the first thing I found
in the living room.

* * *

I quit shaving
but the eyes that glanced at me
remained in the mirror.

* * *

The madman
emerges from the movies:
the street at lunchtime

* * *

Cities of boys
are in their graves,
and in this town . . .

* * *

Lying on my side
in the void:
The breath in my nose.

* * *

On the fifteenth floor
the dog chews a bone—
Screech of taxicabs.

* * *

A hardon in New York,
a boy
in San Francisco

* * *

The moon over the roof,
worms in the garden.
I rent this house.

* * *

1.) All conversation—"I need a spoon to eat soup"—is bridging
Ellipse, all my talk is haiku.
2.) The Western image (metaphor the apt relation of dissimilars—
Aristotle) is compressed haiku.
3.) Study of primary forms of ellipse, naked haiku, useful for
advancement of practice of western metaphor
—"hydrogen jukebox."
but not superior form really,
just the essentials & bones.
4.) Haiku = objective images written down outside mind the result is inevitable mind sensation of relations. Never try to write of relations themselves, just the images which are all that can be written down on the subject (conversation w/Du peru).

* * *

My God!
Uncle Harry, what happened
to you— are you really gone
already past the deathbed to the grave,
disappeared into B'nai Israel Cemetery
with the rest of the ancestors we knew
and watched go by, and ate our Seder
Suppers over again every year at your house?
I didn't think of it happening to you,

you didn't either, I guess, nor think
of the last long painful bitterness of cancer,
visible flesh wasting away in a bed,
final bitterness of what must have been
your hopeless knowledge at the last,
the vision of life as a dream more dreamlike
for its finale hours, all time a dream,
all Newark a dream, the family, Buba & Clara a dream,
– myself perhaps receded even in your thoughts
as dreamy as the rest– vast horrible New York
Petroleum and English Anguish Ham [1] a dream,
All time a dream, the gape of black eternity
more real than these fleet visionary years–
we're all caught in this closing withering
mental flower, trapped by our imagination
– still since we didn't know each other much
inside, preoccupied with appearance,
Salute, Uncle, for your descent to knowledge
and your final suffering, a Hebrew prayer at last,
I'll be your nephew, you my uncle, in your
imagination, my imagination, and the grave.

Berkeley April 26, '56 Dream

. . . In the Times Square movie house, there's Naomi, I sit next to her, suddenly recognize her, she me, I say "Are you Naomi" she looks at me suspiciously, I say "It's me, Allen" & break down crying, on her shoulder, leaning over seat on her breast, weeping.

⋆ ⋆ ⋆

Theater & Its Double–Antonin Artaud

M. C. Richards Translation

"our nervous system after a certain period absorbs the vibrations of the subtlest music and in a sense is modified by it in a lasting way."

Example of ignuschizoid perception

---

[1] Uncle Harry Meltzer's last job was selling English Ham.

IV

NEW YORK CITY

January 4, 1959–March 15, 1961

Allen Ginsberg, N.Y.C., 1960

January 4, 1959

What Fiends have the Heavens created? You Naomi, and your retarded children, and me?—the poet-woman

So too in an hour dead men will ride their horses—

I am a tragedy—even of winter war.

* * *

TRUTH

Truth climbs upon the bed like a black cat purring
Truth is even in the Ass.
Line the Revolutionaries up against the wall
Truth's rifles lack bullets
Truth leans against the wall, lounging, like an easychair nailed there
Hymn truth, Tell the truth at last—
Let us make it in this life— Truth leads the way
Those black & bitter lies are where to seek the ground of truth
in the bathroom, in the bedroom, barroom—
What bores all along are the lies
Is truth an objective theory, a way of life?
No truth is instant perceptions— the time I lit the matches and nearly burned the house down
—all I had to say was I dint know the fire engines would come
—instead I lied & the firemen spanked me for 16 years thereafter
—I was still taking it up the ass after the house was sold for firewood in the fucking fifties—

Truth, Truth, today I discovered truth in an old wastebasket
Old Friend, old friend, is it Truth that will bring us together again?
Lucien & I in his kitchen vowing to live by truth to the end
the beginning of January 1959— now we're getting on in life

The music with a burst of trumpets
Heaven descends— opening slowly as with music, Death
raises the Curtains on the stage of Truth

– Break up the play old Yeats
Let the actors weep & laugh at will—
Let's see what the actors can do without a plot
– No crises & tragedy drama but truth

Tell the audience to go home.

* * *

It's a good life with nakedness, women & men in the same bed not even fucking, just talking & touching with the wail of Dies Irae on the phonograph. Nothing but black hair & smiles my little Swedish angel—cuddling up to the ass—yass yass yass the old blues singers had it right. Might as well pack up & go home to the cats & children & teach them to have a good time—Life got a long way to go & the cat's purring on the pillow.

Jan 18—

Working on Kaddish, Apollinaire, Ignu, Poem Rocket, Sunlights Ladders, etc. all month. Reading soon Chicago, Columbia, Living Theatre, Howard U.

Back from SF August 1959

Garibaldi alive! a dream

I'm in winecellar basement, I go downstairs (as, at Harvard, saw huge Olson the poet sweating & talking with Seniors) we come in, to a beer party. Garibaldi, middle age, robust, with open collar, black-grey hair, dancing, Garibaldi, alive!

* * *

I have founded the Church of Poetry.

Sept. 6, 1959—First Reading *Naked Lunch* Complete.

Finished last "C'lom Fliday" in *Naked Lunch,* the vast glimpse, talking thru its suffering mouthpiece Burroughs—
The occident to the Chink of Eternity is all "*wrong.*"
—"No glot—C'lom Fliday"

Burroughs gave me a gasp

—Sensation—

He is a skull-brain come thru with the Answer—

A "Zen" book.
Jack stammers,
Burroughs is grim.
Burroughs is Dead.
"Lazarus, go home."
Comes from a remove outside the world—even
his own schemes finished
Bleaker than Prospero appears—

All yr energy for naught
a bitter answer
from the Vast.

Like a Cézanne Painting,
has twisted art out of its human use
and delivered a message
from beyond the stars.
Behind consciousness
—"No God"— "No Got"—
Thou Whelp of reasons & flesh heap
Nothing to be Saved

You are not you
There is nothing for you here

"Will the gentle reader?"

Please listen to his Nada—
the planet shivers and is junk sick
for Death.
Deliverer from this Ego.

I shivered in my room on E. 2 St. seeing suddenly a flash
out of 9 years work with Burroughs on
the *Naked Lunch*—

He delivered
I grasped
What was beyond (us)
in the living grave.

[First text of "I Beg You Come Back & Be Cheerful," pp. 77–79, *Reality Sandwiches*]

Sept 25—

Beauty Kills
Beauty is the Murderer
Beauty destroys Time
Death is Pure Beauty
For God is nothing but Beauty
empty of all Radiance but its own

In a vision I saw that God was
is will be pure beauty
Besides which nothing else can exist
and this beauty is so rare it can be
seen only by itself
outside or behind Time
after Death.

* * *

Man fears beauty because Beauty
kills man
So that It may exist alone and perfect
Satisfying man's secret Ambition
to be Beauty
and Nothing but Pure Beauty.

And Man is beauty and man is man
and the man in man dies so that man
can be undefiled Beauty

Who holds to his manhood & mortality
gets stuck with it until his legs die
and his heart & eye dies
and Beauty sees itself again
without the interposition of
the worried dying eye.

Man dies into Beauty
Dies with the first Harmony
Which is perfect in Being—
otherwise it could not exist to begin with
The void can only manufacture One thing:
Being
And Being is alive
And this Live Being
is Pure Beauty.
And tho its forms are transient as dreams
and pass away like Iron
Being remains in its own Beauty
Origin and End of its own state
Which is the Deathless King in Death

And his face is Radiant
And his crown is like light
And his heart is our own secret
And his emotion is Come
Perfect
Victorious forever
Triumphant King of Eternity
Beauty that has an endless Form

O Leaf on a tree, hang
and fall into Beauty's Autumn
O Man in a Coffin,
What think you now?
Nothing but beauty, not you,
One whom you loved

and who hid from you
has taken over
and is living your life now for you

Allen is allen, but allen dead
is better than Allen, is Beauty
Himself
Survived over the Trumpets
of Rocks & Cancer.

Beauty is the great Murderer
Delivers all Souls to Radiance beyond
the Morgue.

And there is no Imperfection in that kingdom
else it would not Be
and we not here in the faraway forest to know it
And hear the music over the radio
from that strange city
Where we were from
and where we go to later
to be died.

Leave the bones behind
they're only bones
Leave the mind behind
It's only thoughts,
Leave the Man behind
he cannot live
Save the Soul! But
Soul is ever Safe
and Sole
itself beauty's representative
Lost in an accidental form
that'll soon be over with
when its nose falls off
and its eyes fall out
and leaves it alone to be itself
Lone in one
Gold Be.

The accident of Murder
that befalls a man
  subject to Murder
is a boon from the Beauty
  behind the electric chair—
gay executioner that keeps a secret
  to be shared by all.
This justice makes it O.K.
For madmen to go ahead
    with rifles shooting twelve
and bombs in schoolyards
    to destroy the Suffering children
    and their Barbe progenitors
who will find Beauty sooner
      anyway
No matter what goes wrong down here
in the Universe where everything goes wrong
      in the end
because it has to be so that Beauty be
      alone.

Beauty the Murderer is left alone,
    Beauty knows the score
tho the judges sit & ponder & perplexed
    by flesh
Pound gavels and condemn the suffering
    criminal
to Immediate Beauty with their heads
    chopped off
gas, electricity, poison, rifle,
    A-Bomb, Tiger Tooth, Bacteria
bring us back to Beauty

    And suffering is confounded by
        your dying
so go suffer & be done to Death
    by two-toed sloths & dragons
    of sickness eating earth-heart
Till the Beauty Cure Can Take.

It's a mad scheme we're in
Luckily it was built in with
the Perfect Answer
—otherwise it never woulda happened
and the void would have forgot itself
before the Void began—
Which it may yet do.

How beauty ever got Born in
the First Place
is a strange riddle which Doctors
think about plenty
but Beauty's the creature gives
birth to itself—

Beauty is the only Lucky one,
fortunately
The rest of the Ideas were all unlucky
and never survived
to be Beauty's second thought—
Just couldn't happen—
only Beauty could happen
So it did.

and now we're stuck with it—
Real Beauty kills.

* * *

I AM THE FLAMES

(J. Kerouac. Commentary on above)

Leaving youth at the gate
I saw the old witch
Joshing terrible birds
that hit (—J.K.)
their heads on the Temple
Belltower roof Gold. (—A.G.)

* * *

And now we're stuck with it —
Real Beauty kills

I am the flames J.K

Leaving youth at the gate
I saw the old Witch
Joshing terrible birds
that hit J.K
their heads on the Temple
belltower roof A.G.

That every leaf wave on the tree
at once
that I am me in this leaf
I am me in that
I am me in the lone
man on the bed, naked
with hairy legs
and a Book on my loins
I'm me in Cats,
leaping together under the kitchen table

Knock on Wood
Universe, that You Be
Me.

Notebook Page, Jack Kerouac & Allen Ginsberg

That every leaf wave on the tree
at once
That I am me in this leaf
I am me in that
I am me in the lone
man on the bed, naked
with hairy legs
and a book on my loins
I'm me in Cats,
leaping together under the kitchen table

Knock on Wood
Universe, that you be
Me.

Oct. 13, 1959

O Bullshit Artist of Reality,
Ginsberg,
give up,
Forever
To your Truth,
and Lose thy shoe on
the Great Step.

* * *

Allen—Does the Capitol
Believe that
in the Imagination?
Jack—Yes—they sure do—but it isn't official yet.

* * *

Smoke Moves

* * *

Oct. 13, 1959 Dream . . . As yesterday Peter saying I should go to Greece—to see Gregory after his Vision.

And Huncke said Greece was Notorious for its Visionary Light and that Gregory was destined to be delivered in Greece—

The joy of lone travelling—this dream like the great dreams I had years ago of Europe before I went there—the thrill of ancient parapets.

Oct. 14, 1959 [1]

Laid eyes on aged fat T.S. Eliot today, tonite, first time—he looked heavier than I thought after 15 years knowing about him—the reading of Wipe your hand was sudden—& the Meeting in Gidding pavement was a strange double image which transfixed the audience. The black dispossession—of his Verse—an aura on the platform—I fixed my eye on him as he spoke hypnotically into the silence—the colors behind the air on the stage changing him as he entered the Passage of Spirit Imagination, talking around Death.

Dreams Oct. 20

Opening a window of consciousness, pulling up a psychic shade to leave a gap for unearthly breezes, turning on the radio that transmits aethereal sensations, I felt a wave of dread and skull-harrow vibrations of the invisible fear transmitting itself to me behind Time. Realized this nightmare & woke.

Patting my beloved, a big fat-bellied familiar mistake—Naomi I realize 3 days later. Pick up this idea again.

Oct. 22.

Read at Gaslight,[2] rainy nite, 3 a.m. Mist walking along Avenue D to E. 2 St. and up E. 2 St. in the blue haze of rain, overbright street lamps streaming down their mechano radiance onto the street, a violet-red damp sky above, walking into the Dream, remembering Shelley's insight, I repeated in my mind

The One remains

and glimpsed the One behind the transient clouds in the haze—The Many change and pass, as I was walking down the street, I passing this life toward my ever-menacing present Death—Inevitable—

---

[1] T.S. Eliot reading at N.Y.C. Y.M.H.A. attended by Marianne Moore & others.

[2] First public coffee shop reading in Village (Gaslight, MacDougal St.).

That I realize again the Glimpse of the One because I know I pass with the Many as all has passed before—that even the street is new and changing tho I remember it of old—a shadow that flies, with all the buildings.

All this with my natural mind that opened a glimpse for a second, raising prickles on the scalp around the side and back under my hair.

This sensation always accompanied by an even-ness of mind and iron thought thru to realization that takes me out of myself, out of the Shadow of time, and makes my mortal hair raisę with electricity and clears the sky beyond the sky for an instant when I see the permanent Brown Heaven (at nite) beyond the streetlites, as existing beyond my death and familiar to my soul from Birth and unknown and forgotten in its grandeur and hairraising awe.

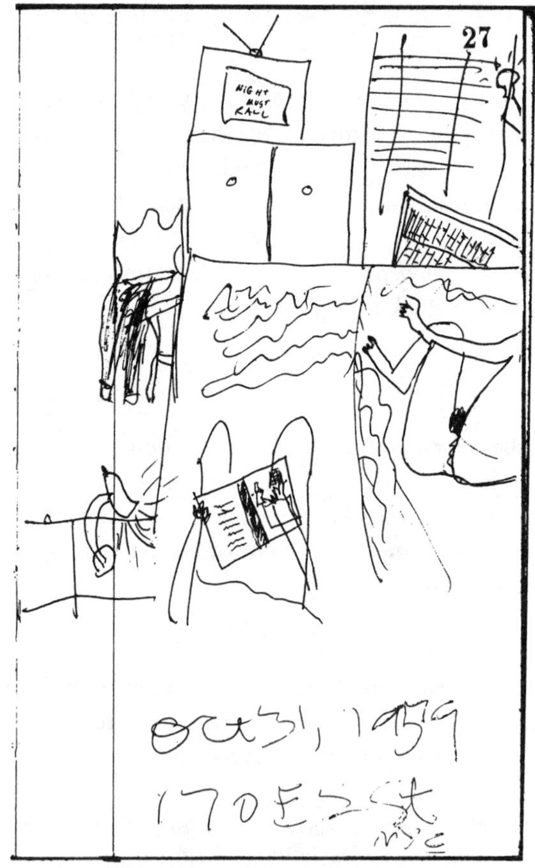

October 31, 1959—170 East 2nd Street, N.Y.C.

Dream, Oct. 31, 1959

Robert Duncan teaches his circle of young poets in the glades of Stinson Beach—on the lawn outside his cottage in the Pacific, under the sun, gorse & nettleweed and seashore shrubs around—a group around the Pacific sage—and the U of C grants credits and scholarships to his disciples—who murmur and learn under his gentle hand. I'm jealous.

* * *

Depression, couldn't get to typewriter after running round town on Burroughs business—contract maybe to transfer from Wyn Co. to Avon to get him money—sat & read Look mag at Dr's office, 14 St. accompanying my brother to his checkup—all about 1960 presidential races, Kennedy's politicianings & shiftiness—He has a hole in his back. Thru which Death will enter.

* * *

Peter Orlovsky—Born July 8, 1933

Nov 4—

Huncke de Rerum Natura [1]

"What we are in—is—always was, that is, it has always been going on and always will be, it had no beginning and will have no end—

"If we see out as far as we can ever with our limited senses, it is vaster than we reach, as it is— —to say nothing of senses that we don't have . . . at the same time it can all be encompassed in our imaginations—

"Usually we lack a sense of relationship in this great process—once & a while we do sense . . .

"There's no Time, also, in that things are always changing . . . so that you can't pinpoint any definite moment . . . the instant you do, you and it have already changed anyway, are always changing.

"Death is a rather frightening prospect to most people, naturally, since such an absolute change is a little hard to take—we are so used to what we already are as far as we can remember—but it is only another change, perhaps; probably in fact a more radical change than the ones we are used to but it is only one of many changes, a very radical one. Its very

[1] "I questioned him on the direction of our Existence"—A.G., 1975.

radicality and finality in comparison to the ones we know make it a bit—make us a bit leery of it.

"The process is endless and since the one thing we know is change in it there is some hope that it may be moving toward some direction, tho we can't guess very well from our viewpoint—"

Dream—

Back in Paris—in my room, go out, meet some girl, she's been trying to get ahold of me—meet her friend—Barbara G—— and her dreary huge husband—I'm supposed to see Bill and I don't. Lucien comes to Paris—Last I remember, riding in their car up "hill and dale" in a sort of 18th century Paris—a bridge—Felt good to be there again—a narrow iron bridge over a small stream—rather like *Concord* than Paris. Dazzling of return to old Paris—Nostalgia. In the dream I decided how nice to go back to the warm old stones.

Suddenly a madman runs loose—the Rhino is loose too—he picks up a gun and runs on the verandah out on the lawn—thru the lawn trees—to the temple—and Ha! there's the rhino on the alabaster Indian balcony, on the lawn below the balcony—the madman rushes up in the middle of Services. The Indians chanting and singing—the madman makes a harsh gesture at the huge Beasts gathered near the archway-balcony—they waft away like—Elephants rush away he rushes in—the fool, he chased away the tender Elephants who were listening in rapport outside the temple to the drum-throbs within.

* * *

America is covered with Lies.
The young thinkers are bad men
    full of nasty ideas.
America created the atom bomb and
    dropped it on the world.
Ezra Pound is right the nation is
    an insane asylum

Dream Dec 9, 1959:

In a large hotel room with my wife, I meet T.S. Eliot-Claude—(Eliot young & looks like Claude & I feel sweetness in my breath to him as he gazes at me thru Rimbaud eyes)—he has his mss. copy of collected poems there. I open the big binder and leaf thru—he's hanging around the room in same relation to me as Claude—but distant & sad—I eagerly look at mss. and want to question him about the construction of middle period—Rock-Sweeney poems—I find one—a huge poem written in broken blank verse—

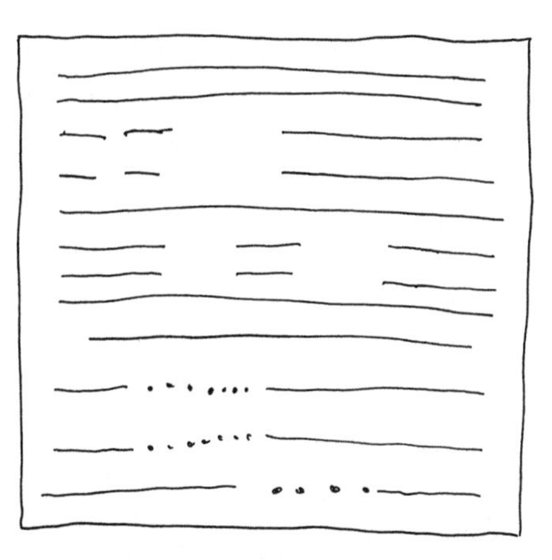

for several pages—inscribed or typewritten on some ancient looking very thick flexible red parchment—he is over by the bureau—our relation is sweet—he loves me—I love him—but I am afraid of him and want to hold him—Suddenly an old Queen from the huge hotel we are in—it's a Chilean Convention—comes into my room to visit me—and sees Eliot-Claude. The visitor is old—Willard Maas—or an advertising fruit with seamed face—I am afraid he'll offend Claude with his intrusion—am ashamed of him—he suddenly says

"Well I see you're busy I'll be going off, I'll see you later" and moves out into the corridor. I feel relieved.

Eliot-Claude is still there, waiting, I ask him what the poem is written on, he says, Alaskan Smoked Salmon—I say, what?—and nibble a bit at the edge of the first page. It tastes like Lox and I recognize it is—thumbing thru the rest of the mss. I see it all is for that Period of his poetry—the typewritten part is on Alaska yellow pink smoked tough salmon—surrounded by a plastic transparent envelope or framed in cellophane wrapper.—I am searching the volume for more of the period that interests me—long line or Jazzline—Eliot-Claude disappears out the door—I am going to cook supper soon, he's waiting—I follow him, trepidation, he's next door with the fruit old man, in fact lying in the dimness—(the room being like the imaginary old room of my brother near Columbia in an earlier dream—huge room with balcony near window and steps leading up) on a half sofa, reclining, with the fruit between his legs, who's laying back against the hassock his head—sitting on the floor—I am nervous & jealous—we discuss supper—Claude tells me to join them—

All thru the dream, the main thing, I had been anxious to talk about his poetry, at one point had thought but not voiced "you must be sick of thousands of people for 50 years pawing your mss. and inquiring who & what of these few famous poems" but he'd been silent & allowed me anything so I'd gotten a little nervous thumbing his book & hadn't been able to find the poems I wanted to inquire about.

Dec. 10, 1959—Dream:

Letter received from Joseph Crangnall: a minor English novelist:

"I salute you in the name of the Momums of Lawrence, the Divine Momums whose breast we all Seek as the Farmer seeks the Worm, and I also end by enquiring what, if any, is the cause in the recent decline of the value of the American 1920's dollar on the World Market a subject which I find crucial to my understanding. Signally,

—Crangnall,
MOMUMSSS"

Dream Dec. 12—

Peter & I on an ocean liner, setting out, on an Empire State skyscraper, on a huge Hotel in Texas—go upstairs to the First Class Top Flight Deck to meet the owner of the Hotel—

In fact, arrested in the paper I see the names Manbrick Philadelphia—like L— S—[1] —Renato Oginattio and Alphonse Muggiero—are arrested—or else all on the passenger list.

---

[1] L— S— was ex-husband of hostess for 1959 Chicago reading by A.G., Gregory Corso, & Peter Orlovsky. A drugstore owner, he presented the departing poet guests with a bottle of pills which included mescaline. At a party at his house several plainclothesmen asked A.G. to empty his pockets as a practical joke, whereupon they presented him a stick of grass they all smoked together.

We are invited (P & I) upstairs to the Boat deck to talk to the owner, an old silk cat with black Tie—I'm up above with him, he pulls out a vial and says "Want some Cocaine—Crystals"—I say "Yes, by all means," he looks in the vial, there's some there I think eyeing it from aside, but he says "I have to go below & fill it up, I'll be right back."

So I also rush down an elevator to get Peter who's downstairs—I'm dressed in thick pants Harry Phipps [American playboy] gave me—and over that Peter's Denver-bought denim jacket grey with black cotton collar—I take hat off for a minute to arrange my clothes, I am cold, it's winter at Sea—

Downstairs the milling mob of people, like Chicago feeling thru passageways—several hip potsmoking taxi drivers—failures in the world—I'm a celebrity, they greet me—I find Peter somewhere on the sidewalk across the street, tell him about the coke, we rush up in the elevator, get out—as on the back of the fantail, there is a ventilator, with I notice old umbrellas and orange boxes, garbage strewn rust, we walk past that along the rail—it's also the 180th Floor,—looking for Manbrick the Millionaire Coke-Head Executive—I am trying to put my jacket back on, I'm naked above the waist & cold or chill—

Also at the same time making last minute examination of some Anthology poems and I see package of duller Poems by thin Boston friend of Olson, R—— B—— —an onionskin blue paper—familiar—I fold them up to put back in envelope—rejected. I notice I had made some scrawled changes, underlining images and words & striking out some words.

—woke on bed, covers off me, cold a little, naked from waist up.

Never got to the Cocaine—

* * *

Huncke—

Told him of Don Cook doing Govt. report on Beatnik—"That's what you need—get enough people swinging on this thing sensibly . . . and who knows?"

Dream Dec. 20, 1959

In a horse-parade—from planet to planet—on a float—thru the Creek in the Great Swamp—New Orleans or St. Louis—(on raft with Jim)("he aint a heathen?")—below a great Rock-face of Mt.—

In a car, or Gondola, Stop in the Parade—look over the trees to consult the landscape—a lady sleeping on a rock—I'm talking to Nigger Prophetess in her Junkheap car—The Lady's naked on that rock—

We're all in a large black limousine, being escorted forward in a vast parade, a ceremonial affair, really in our honor. The Literature Day parade.

Suddenly a cop car with some motorcycle escort stops us—I am arrested and taken down to a detective's house—Some ambiguity as to why—"For suspicion of orgies"—They take us home—I'm protesting—thinking I'll get a lawyer—at the cop's house—a party, as if he arrested me for that—

I phone Lawyer, can't reach him yet—Inquire, it turns out someone else like a negro mulatto librarian was returning to Denver from S.F. & he went into Passive stroke & sadfaced fate (I see his photo with a wen) and never did anything after—

I go back to talk to the detective—Just who exactly signed the warrant, whose exact recognizance is it and what charge?—"Well," he says, "it's mine, basically, really, the charge is Intent to Deceive—Your own friends write bad poetry tho you don't—"

Ah I get angry, "Who?" Burroughs? Orlovsky, Kerouac?

"Well we'll discuss that—"

I get angry "I'll sue the fucking—" I never get the words out of my mouth when I wake up "—hell out of you!"

Dream that evening:

In the bathroom of the big family house in Newark, visiting—I am naked, taking a shower, I wipe clean—young flesh—

At the dressing table a typewriter (like my desk in bedroom here)—In the drawer are folds of paper, stencil paper, half finished poems—I pull them out—can't find what I'm working at—the lights go out—I reach up near the shower curtain and pull a cord, it's a lightcord—but doesn't set the fluorescent round lights going, merely they get phosphorescent dim—I go to the wall switch—worrying if I'm turning on the lights in other rooms, waking the family—

I had been before in other parts of the house working, at a coffeetable (in Paris rich apt. in Upper N.Y.C. State at Miles Forst's [1]

[1] Miles Forst, painter, friend of Kerouac & Lucien Carr.

summerhouse)—the Soft Cunt of women as Gregory's girlfriend blonde in Paris—

I see Aunt Clara coming into the bathroom from the next room—her living room—she sees me, ashamed I grab her sideways & stick my cock in her big soft-bellied older cunt, feels good—she's worried, I look in next room—it's Aunt Anna playing with herself, standing sideways, sticking in a lightbulb—a lampsocket in it—I want to enter hers too—I wake feeling good.

Dull Dream—Dec. 22, 1959

Walking to see Mrs. Hollander—another big fat juicy cunt—on way we cross the big valley in Town. It's not crossed by public conveyance, you have to walk it, step by step.

A convenience for the poor who live there, somehow.

At Hollander house (like the Mahler) now nobody's home—she is, she tells me John is not there but come back—and as we leave one of the kids (nephews) sticks his hand thru the broken glassfront of the door and says Bang! I ask, what's yer name, he says,—Buzzy! Buzzy! I say I'll remember (as I wake I've forgotten and have to make up a name) and I walked out of the house congratulating myself that I'll remember his name for good—but as it happens alas I don't, even now that I've just woken up.

So we head back home downstairs Paterson & bypass the valley for there is a 32 bus that goes round it and it's even shorter to City Hall that way, from the Southeast Side of town across the Italian Vale. Go to a place where we were in a *former* dream near there—

A roundhouse, smalltime smalltown, a few trees roadside glimpse—A vista of a long ribbon road of a dream journey once made,

of pavillions by the Sea, Crystal Pavillions near where I went behind them to confront the sea, which looked out behind them—down the sea wall, gorse & bushes—where perhaps they found a skull, I've had a profound dream before—

Also by the road the immense flat acreage of water of the Great Harbor and I've dreamt of that—rather like a busride to Newark—small boats on it and waiting for airplanes in airports and gathering anxiety caught in nets of Cancer.

Another great sea-wall dream, a vast deep harbor out there from the first road; where men drown.

Dreams open out to other dreams—one vast interconnected dream.

Dream Dec. 23–

On top of a house, flat roof with whitewashed roofledge–I stand with friend–in the Orient or Near East–

We have done something horrible like taken possession of a body, or committed murder.

When it is time to go, we fly over the roof and down to a mountain pass, between cliffs–he settles into a niche and there finds a spot with a worn seat under a hanging spur of rock–He sits down, puts his legs under the spur and in the leg holes, and injects his body into the small space of the rock and disappears into the Underground–

Another City–I've come here to escape. A newspaper office or a Kibbutz meeting hall–I notice there is a *spot* where the Bridge begins & the machinery goes underground. Like this is the Circle of Blood, which I cannot escape.

A young boy there–I try to feed him into the Circle, feet first–but we are found out, or he escapes somehow–stunned with silence–he can testify against me.

A trial against me–I have hidden all the evidence I can–several people I know are conspirators from South of Paterson accompanying me on a journey. The trial ends in a stalemate–the jury doesn't yet suspect the Circle of Blood–

I go in Aunt Eleanor's room–leave a note with Eugene–"Have a case must go Good Yontiff Merry Xmas–Sorry"–Someone's big apartment this is that we visit–I had pulled out of my pocket a white rubber with a message written on it "I am in here. Come to my rescue"–signed by the lost adult soul who I'd seen enter the rock-buttock entrance.

Way out at Coney Island or Rockaway . . . fleeing from recognition as members of the Circle of Blood. But we can't flee from the Circle, which will appear anywhere.

COMPLAINT BY THE BOLIVIAN POLITICAL PRISONER ABOUT TO DIE

Went from Room to Room in huge apartment parts of the vast Legendary City, where I had been before–showing someone (a couple) how to sightsee–thru an old World's Fair Exhibition, huge halls full of old paintings & bureaus–empty halls with marble columns & fireplaces–forges & tapestries–cages–torture instruments–finally, the Great Collage of William McKinley–

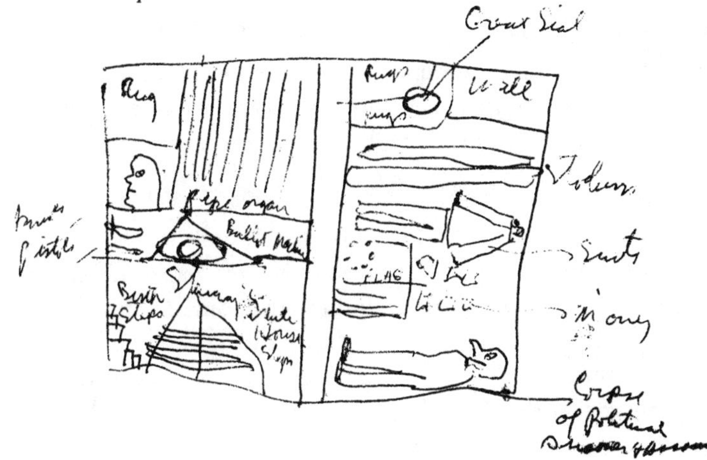

Well, this was my private apartment or someone's that we were exploring. It grew late, and they wandered on. But I pointed out—

— — —

Back in New Waverly, Brazil or Texas, near where the Burroughs farm had been—Law and Order had been restored by the locals and the land put into production, (tho Burroughs was now a prisoner or wanted)—I explore the *new* Library—with its Collection of 7 thousand books—which once had been the old downstairs barn rotted & rusting away & under dusty beams, nothing but some old County record books covered with hay & dirt & manure—I can hardly believe my eyes over the change—

I see his residence in that area had been a fructifying one, as a result of his intelligence the whole area around him had been enlightened & seeking peace & prosperity.

At that moment, however, the sheriff and his negro executioner were taking a horse thief & amok assassin to the jail for his execution. He broke away somehow.

— — —

They are taking him in a jeep, he has somehow stopped the jeep & escaped away—it's parked up the street in the middle of the road, dirt road like where (in bus) Peter & I stopped near the Colorado Border—I run up the block to the jeep & see they have caught him again, and are taking him into the inner office, where—

But he is on the street, an elegant sweet madman with a pistol—it has several shots in it—I am caught in the crossfire—He aims at me, I am frightened—then gently lowers his pistol, like Neal, and empties the silver bullet, unfired, out on the ground—a gesture of love & delicacy—the other detectives give him his gun back with bullets & they all retire to shoot it out in the office, that he die there, helpless—I feel sorry for him, & love—

– – –

I had pointed out to the 2 tourists, that beyond this house museum, with the side entrance we had just seen & entered like a side entrance of some great Museum of Natural History—that outside this columns or pillars there are yet remaining the other great halls or buildings—"The Capitoline" also with the greatest collection of antiques in the world—they are amazed at the World's Fair vista & prospect—& we head in that direction—

– – –

Looking over the papers of the man condemned—a fisherman who had somehow assassinated often many men in drunkenness—I see his farewell speech:

This is its form, I remember only the last lines . . .

Sad, cruel thought
Farewell to thee!
Once again the Cross!
I cry—but unheard.
My heart beats fast
My world is over
Maria Luisa-Dora!
Remember me
It was my life
and thou children
I die I die
Farewell again
Ough, the fire
Ah the rope
I die I kill
the world
once more
Farewell!
I know!
Alas!
I die

I see many of the lines are crossed out and in dim pencil, spontaneous & unfinished—Ferlinghetti is going to publish it anyway—

I go in the room, hoping to stop the execution—"This man is a poet"—I push open the door, "Sad, cruel unhappy poet" is standing there, all three of them (somehow as if I'm going to enter a sex scene). I kneel, I explain the poem, am going to save him—they are all startled.

* * *

The nameless gives names—
∴ the Conceptless gives concepts
that which is sans identity creates identities.

* * *

Timelessness seen as infinite extensiveness of one moment's room.

* * *

Dream—Dec. 28, 1959

Chicago—on the open highway—thorofare, people trapped in sleighs, tableaux, snows—If anyone picks them up & rescues them they get away free—one group trapped together wrangling across the street, they ought to move & make getaway, they're arguing instead—soon police will be here.

Suddenly policecar speeds down Boulevard—fast—I think, the jig is up, they'll arrest everybody. The police car filled with people, I see a few hoods in suits—stops—a policeman is wounded—he staggers out of car, shirt ripped down his back, broken man, falls on the street and begins screaming in pain & anguish, sobbing—flipping—another cop comes out to help, hold him up—He makes a spectacle of himself, blood coming from his eyes & ears, screaming about death & murder—Flopping over broken at the waist, he's been wounded &'s dying.

We all leave, scattering to escape (according to rules—) (the policemen leave in an ambulance) and I hear conversation (near Astor Place facing East) "He can't stop blaming it all on his roommate's rich son"—a young Dandy who has infected the scene for him.

Riding up Escalator, a long escalator in the New Rome, which is a wooden stairway (out of the Valley of Dream 4 nites ago) black stairs like a subway platform, except rather frail, but serviceable, and newly painted black—I see this is a city like heaven built for pleasure—the crowd ascending the stairway on some secret sightseeing mission in the city—

When we get to the top there is a house like at Berkeley where an Incarnation of the Virgin is taking place, and the story of God's change, from the Hidden to a god of Signs & Wonders is revealed, as in the story up to the instant of the Birth of Christ the Child—

In fact, accompanying the reading of the Sacred Text—"And there shall be established in the firmament/for all to see a Holy Cloud/& its Name is the Face of the Lord/which shall shine on the Birth of the Boy,/ And none shall redeem his soul who shall mock/but all shall rejoice in Fear/and take Him the Gift of the Lord/For this is the Will of Heaven/ and this is the Part of the Earth/which receives the Brow to think and Nose to smell/and a face of cloud but no mouth to speak the Last truth/ which is revealed in His Death, in one nail on the cross,/Sayth the Babe to His Father & Mother and to All Mankind/And that is the work of the Lord, to interpret/and here is the instant of the Incarnation,/and here is the Body to be born,/in lightning and Snow and rain below/in futurity and past where Dream is the Stranger./Thus receive ye the Dream as it is writ."

A Babe is born, I see the crippled babe, and it's later—or the scroll text unfolds, I see in the clouds, in the sky, a blind face.

And I see the Babe Nailed, Center of Belly, on the Cross—at which the body is left here but the soul goes upstairs—

As George B. Shaw—I hear an explanation from the Virgin—"The talent is left here, but the soul escapes" The talent of Explanation, Text, Art, Messiah-hood, Preaching—is left in the world—It belongs to this world, but the Spirit Escapes to the Nothing which inspired the talent—a message in this sphere is left to this sphere, but its final Man is not that, but goes to another.

Thus the body can be left hanging on a nail.

Then the subway platform walkway arrives at a spot I recognize the arcade Beatnik part with the "European Café" upstairs in Chicago or Seattle—

Shot in the Back by a Fallen Leaf

The leaves are bright
as a million
electric lights on
the yellow hill

The sun moves up
on the little trees
vast Autumn helium
after last night—

Three men sprawl drunk
in the birch thicket
on the small dump road
they finished the whiskey

Birds sing on barbwire
fresh wind rushes the trees
the jeep motor runs quietly
a frog jumps thru grass

Faraway on Hawk Ridge eagles
swoop down following
the ancient windpath
South along Appalachians

The universe is so airy
you need only get up
cold and walk the dirt road
at dawn to be in Heaven

Jan. 1, 1960

SUNRISE

The Sad Light of old Decade,
Angel Bone,
Look how Peter and Lafcadio behave
        in penthouses
whispering together & comparing hands
        on sofas—
Jack rolling on the floor in a lumber
        cap
Lucien with the cheeks of a
        Ramon Novarro
Bleary eyed licking his lip
            on the Last Night
                of the Year.

Francesca with a rose crawling down
her thigh
and long hair let down in
the Steakburger after the Party

Miles against the wall legs stretched
out beating a drum against
Orlovsky, dreaming—
one foot on the ceiling—

Lafcadio in easy chair sitting straight
waiting for a Word—
Becker fat with his bellybutton of
parentage
and two frail kids adream next room.
Bill Luce upsidedown with his
mustache behind his ear,
his wife saying chi chi, cha chi chi,
like a little soap bubble disappearing
dumped on the floor by the
Freaks—
Miles & Lucien's ties for chains—
Agh, I didn't feel the passage of
the gong

And tho we've been illuminated
for one decade of scribbling
and publicity—
The gooney bird arrives, and
Empire State looks cold
as the eastern sky reddens.

1960 What's to come
Whose death, hands folded
on what black-suited chest?
or India, let my hair stand on end!

What Bus roars down the invisible
street carrying its passengers
Toward the Moon?
Had Dodie Muller a

1920's beaded tasseled dress
        shaking in the street
            waiting for a Taxi not?
Did I speak high finance with
        Walter Guttman?
Did my cat not jump up
        lightly to my desk
    and not meow?
Not weep? Not weep for 1960?
I'd as lief been born abroad
            a cripple Greek
as not one weep for 1960 but
            this lone
scribble in the margin of my days.

Jan 4, 1960

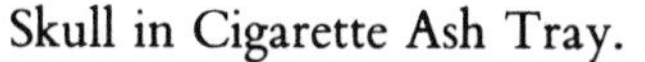

Skull in Cigarette Ash Tray.

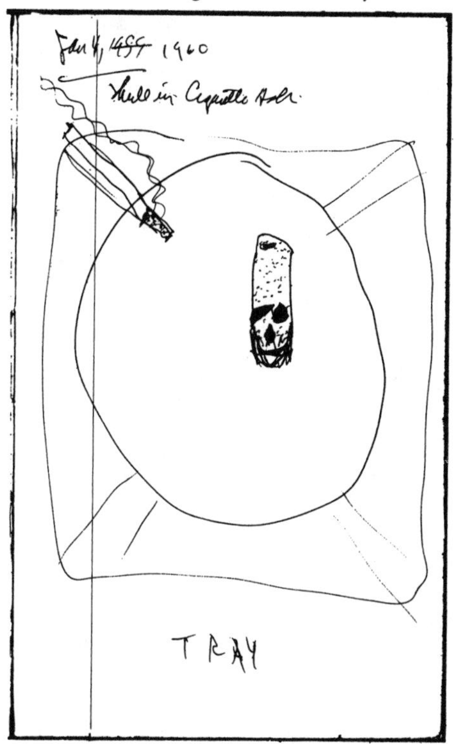

Saw *Sherlock Jr.*—Buster Keaton again after 10 years—comedy at perfection, worked out like a mathematical proposition. With Peter & Lafcadio.

The Orlovsky family—Kate and Oleg had 5 children in the 30's & they all went mad—what deep life passion suffering & depression—now in their twenties, 2 of them on a bed in the city with me, brooding & maybe weeping when they realize their fate & doom.

* * *

PSALM IV [1]

Now I'll record my secret vision, impossible sight of the face of God:
It was no dream I lay broad waking on a fabulous couch in Harlem
having masturbated for no love, and read half naked an open book of Blake on my lap
Lo & behold! I was thoughtless and turned a page and gazed on the living sun-flower
and heard a voice, it was Blake's reciting in earthen measure:
the voice rose out of the page to my secret ear that had never heard before—
I lifted my eyes to the window, red walls of buildings flashed outside, endless sky sad in Eternity
sunlight gazing on the world, apartments of Harlem standing in the universe
—each brick and cornice stained with intelligence like a vast living face—
the great brain unfolding and brooding in wilderness!—Now speaking aloud with Blake's voice
Love! thou patient presence & bone of the body! Father! thy careful watching and waiting over my soul!
My son! My son! the endless ages have remembered me! My son! My son! Time howled in anguish in my ear!
My son! My son! my Father wept and held me in his dead arms.

Laugh Gas Jan 5, 1960: 4:45 PM

"You're fighting problems that are outside your control—in this business (Dentistry)—you gotta outguess the factors that are involved" Meaning: my patients never brush their teeth properly.

---

[1] Exact 1960 composition date uncertain.

The muzak has a thin sophisticated violin sound, ancient and nostalgic even to a child's ear. "When A Gypsy Makes His Violin Cry." Because it comes from very far away. Continuous flow of Calm, melancholy old favorites.

"I would never drill the wrong tooth!"

Endless messages: "More Than You Know" pouring through the wall loudspeaker.

When I walked in the office I was hit by the smell recollection, the creamy linoleum floor, the Chinese style Carvings on the wall (manufactured for Department Stores in Orange & Newark);

As if I'd been murdered in this office and remembered the instant look of the furniture, wallplugs, wires, sofas, ceilings as I'd died—and am now revisiting.

This office is the repository of the Akashic Records—"I will call you in six months to check your teeth, Mrs. Markass."

"I am in the repair end of the business . . ."

"After I got thru living in Milwaukee . . . I developed a taste for Blatz."

* * *

Man's Glory

Shines on top of Mountains where Grey Stone monastery sits & blinks at
the sky
There in Tangier in Soco Chico there God's Grammar Arabic jabbers
shoeshine Poverty beneath the ultra silent mosque
There in Venice glittering in Canal Grande in Front of San Giorgio
Maggiore Gondola'd to cream the fabulous tourist—
There in Mexico in th' Archeologic Museum where Coatlique Aztec
Golgotha-head Goddess clasps her snakes & skulls & grins—
There over Asia where the desolate white Stupas blast into the Buddhic
Dome and the Mandala of the stars shines down—
All over Europe where the masses weep & faint in Wooden Trains—
By Florence, by the Windmills, all the churches singing together
"We in the mountains and downtown Pray that America return to the
Lamb"—
And the Great Boom of the Cathedral at Seville, Granada groaning,
Barcelona chanting out the Crannies of Sagrada Familia
Long horns of Montpellier, Milan screaming and San Marco rocking in
Venice like a great golden calliope

"America, America, under the elms and parks of Illinois, the Anger, the Anger, Beware!"

August 2, 1960 [1]

Back to same death-dread-change in my heart, with the know of permanent intrusion of the New Boyg [2] of Reality into my permanent life—Looking at the power of clouds in the blue sky in Paterson garden today changed, and the Burroughs letter—Vaya adelante—into the unseen—that weighs me down—scares my heart in breast to be dying—Will I have nightmare tonight in sleep?—Now into Time's Blind Mawkishness—to seep & penetrate, the New Being—

Aug. 2—112 St Dream

112th Street on the Border district between East & West side, was a famous street because mainly of the fact that one had walked on it unnoticing, so often crossing from one side of city to other. It was quite wide, with a few Chinese restaurants, pinball alleys, bohemian bars, bookstores for mystic books, hot dog carts, negro shoeshine parlors, a brokendown horror-movie house, a police station in a side alley—Door whence emanated bluecoats on bicycles & motorcycles and the noise of a mechanical voice on Persecution Radio—But mainly picturesque, the street, because it was all dark, covered & shielded from the sky & bridge above it by a vast granite black sooty arcade or roof, which shut out sunlight & made the street seem an obscure alley in Hell whatever the hour day or night when the yellow lights in the tunnel made the street seem even more sinister and expectant of obscure mystery.

It was on that street that parolees from West Prisons were allowed to go just that far & no farther toward the East, and East prisoners could meet the Western buddies halfway down the block under an awning of the smoke shop, & chat, plot, conspire, or look into each other's eyes after long stretches of mortal confinement.

Here I saw Neal, looking rather corpulent in a new suit, stand smoking & waiting to meet Lucien—who, also fattened, wore a sort of degenerate Chinese mustache & sideburns.

I fluttered around excited at this historic meeting trying to

---

[1] After return from trip to South America, moments of which are described in William S. Burroughs' & A.G.'s *The Yage Letters* (San Francisco: City Lights, 1963). "Burroughs letter—Vaya adelante" appears in same, pp. 60–62.

[2] Creature personified in Ibsen's *Peer Gynt*.

recognize the former souls I had known so well and loved in previous lifetime, but they ignored me and for the most part did not even talk to each other.

I was impressed by the fact that even in the dream the street cried out for description, since I had this new awareness of its sinister romantic detail and historic accumulation of anxiety shops & mystery arcades.

* * *

AYAHUASCA IX

NY Aug 10—

The Knower—in the emptiness—is me which knows inside.

This is me the Knower inside anyone.

This knower born into Eternity knows nothing, and will go to sleep. He is the only one born in Eternity, in the void.

But tho he go sleep (as I go to Sleep in Death) if anyone awakes, in Eternity, it will be the same Knower—

Will another knower come take the knower's place?

But if so the other (say reptilian Bardo Thodol form) knower will also know and be the same as the old knower, because all the knower knows is know.

I felt my body, like an independent serpent with a material universe life of its own, crawl over bend & curl in snakelike spasms of vomiting, assaulted by the Presence of the Knower which I identified with (rather than the serpent body) as an alien & superior permanent Ghost. Constantly interrupting into Matter at moments of radiant instability.

I watched the writhing serpent body vomiting, with indifference & interest—

finally! since the knower was not to be disturbed by the spasms of all those dying bodies, I entered the body to suffer & vomit, impartially, and enjoyed the (otherwise unpleasant) experience, feeling no fear & no final identification with the body—

The body also is the knower, going thru a ripple of vomit, no less pleasant to the knower than any other Birth-Death—

At my death as in Tibet Book of Dead—I return to my knower passively & wait to see what passes in front of me—

All these things (birds on street, airplanes flying, creation moving in its wheels, man shouting "Juan Sucio!" into 2nd St.—me lying in bed—) are *passing* in front of & separate from the Eternal Elemental Knower who is aware of them all thru his different bodies. But who within his body does not partake, he being merely an Eternal Know, watching the movie of Being going on outside himself.

Returning inside me, I left my body to its own fate, and found it mechanically sighing, rocking head back & forth, until it settled back in awareness that the body was not Allen but a form of Me the old Knower, and that Allen was the old Knower.

Got up out of bed happy with mind bouncing in this form, crapped, shut lights, wiped vomit off mouth, cleaned floor of gastric juice, mopping up being to be comfy—so if this is where I am let's enjoy it, entering into it as knower knowing in one of his forms.

Finally got sick of arranging things & rushed to lie down & get out of matter again & be the Know in the Void. But it's the same (all that activity disturbing me, the worlds whirling—well let them—be—as they are). I am always Here. All I got to remember is that & relax & just don't do anything.

. . . Mailer—is god being destroyed? He (God) knows & don't care. Let someone else take over Being—if they can.

* * *

My fear last time (adjusted by reference to Tibetan *Book of Dead)* was in Magic Psalm[1]—the fear that the Knower was outside of me—

Putting faith outside of my own Being was separating being into parts—so I imagined & saw greater Reptilian Beings invading my not-being.

No use "In thy Will" because "Thy Will" is in me, (if I only know it, know at one with the knower)—as I *seemed* to do today.

The Closed Eye

of the old Being-knower of eternity.

* * *

[1] Pp. 92–95, *Kaddish and Other Poems.*

When I close my eyes I know, when I
open my eyes I know the same thing
Dying, my pet reptile dies, my snake
cock with its hot ecstasies
My physical eye which I often confounded
with my I—
My feet which have fungus and are invaded
by the cramps of imaginary beings—

They enter, my muscles crawl together,
I relax my feet and withdraw from
the effort of struggle
My foot, left alone, the Invader ceases
to have reality on his own
and dies in my foot— I get up and walk
and when my foot dies, it will be another
dead being
and I'll get up and walk on my one
Know . . .
Pass on aeons, bring your Allens back &
forth & let them Die.

The knower knows the know. (Subject
& object disappeared, means
Subject knows itself no more left
in Being but one Know)

AYAHUASCA X

Aug. 7, 1960

Old Ford Autohorns—the noises I remember—growlings & groanings of bodies in the street—like a deep Tibetan cat-purr, the *ruido* of the

wheel turning in the void, a boy imitating another being, making chicken cries—Peter comments on that, annoyed, "I hope he gets at least an egg out of it"—and someone's suggestive whistle.

I vomit, & walk to bathroom, sit, & come back to the bedroom realizing I am a ghost mind inhabiting one of my bodies.

The eyes are one center of Mind, the breasts like two eyes of feeling another, the being narrows down to a bellybutton eye & thru an eyeless cock that has its own center

AYAHUASCA XI

Concentrating on the Mind passive in middle of forehead, I refused, at last, to vomit—was left sitting naked at edge of bed with a pot between my knees, my stomach like serpent on its own turning to regurgitate—I sat above my stomach, refusing, swallowing back the vomit as it spasmed up to my throat, vomiting again & swallowing it back with clenched jaw, feeling my stomach & digestive tract writhe in throes of impersonal misery like the death throes of a worm or centipede or snake rolling blind. But did not give in to be that tormented body—so felt for a moment flash of transfiguration—impersonality a ghost inhabiting and controlling the body—a first yoga—the knower "in action."

Book of Dead & *Dyana for Beginners* (Goddard book) both emphasize that monsters are part of the aggregate of Karmaic imaginaries—that the Final thing is nothing but emptiness of the Known.

* * *

Peter—"New rock & roll—the *Bathroom Scream Song*—starring the Shower Boys & Water Companions."

* * *

Dream—

TIBET

Card or phone call from Gregory to meet him in the Faraway Suburb where I haven't been, at the bottom of a ravine where Moon Street disembarks. To see Kerouac, visit.

I go out there, thru Elevated trains, early, and wander around. I go thru huge weed-lot-like Ravine, climb up stairway made of metal ladder to top precipice, wander around, then remember date with Gregory so head back down. On way a gang of boys whom I'd passed up before in white shirts, I sidestep them barely as they descend 6 abreast down the metal ladder at the lip, they push & shove me but I hang on the ladder, they complain where I'm going in such a hurry, I step across to the ladder along the side (the one I'm on is on the square inside)

and go down, they chasing me but I ignore them. Then I hurry, and see wild-eyed thin Gregory in excellent brown English oxford suit & cap & long hair, climbing up, we meet, he's very distant & sweet, & intelligent, his body & voice are changed—I surmise he's been living with upperclasses so long & in England & foreign countries, it's entered him physiologically, & he's "Matured" in a very strange changed way—he seems aloof, like a magical prince, but still lonely & lost, tho now completely competent to handle himself like a prince in this world, he needs me still or loves me still. I put my arm around his shoulder. Familiarly we walk toward Jack's new house—

When we get there we both go in, Jack & his mother and Lois Sorrels[1] & Lois's sister who takes to me strangely & immediately, a horsey looking blonde wench like Jack's sister I think—takes over & takes me specially by arm & thru the house, very pushy, as if we had a special assignation.

A special assignation, which I appreciate since I'm scared of Jack's mother—don't want to meet her—

I take my shirt off, it being ripped, I don't know why I take my shirt off—the family is all crowded in a small room on a long couch. I see & nod hello to Jack's mother & Jack & several others—relatives—I excuse myself & say I'll wait outside in the backporch kitchen room. Lois' sister stays with me, I say, "I guess it doesn't look well with my shirt off," She

---

[1] Lois Sorrels: J.K.'s girl friend then; wrote poetry.

says "No I suppose not"—I try on one old shirt I got. It's Jack's old shirt—she says in answer to my question, "Yes the old lady will recognize his shirt better not wear it."

So I look under table to see a big pile of newly laundered shirts in cellophane, all Gregory's, apparently arriving from Europe, he's brought all his possessions, clothes, with him, and is staying temporarily at Jack's, which surprises me—except that he now has such an authoritative delicate manner & voice, like a saint, Jack must have accepted him in.

I go around & they show me the closet that had been walled up by mistake—an extra bathroom when they were taking out a wall again—had a dutch door the top of which you could open, the bottom walled up closed—so they are entering both from there I peek in & also looking thru the other side, removing a round tile "gidoille" from the mosaic of tile.

I go outside, it's Claude & his barge—his old barge—he's naked on the barge & he's talking to me—his body looks good—says "I just roll over & let them see"—and naked he lifts his legs on the bed in barge & shows a small white pink asshole, hardly even a brown one, like a mutant lip more than an asshole—I go up to embrace him but he wants to show me his old barge—I go in the filled cargo Deck Compartment and float around in the water, then he says, I'll give you a free ride Ha Ha & pulls a switch which dumps the water in a powerful stream below into the lagoon—I am swept down by tons of water, worried, but he knows it won't hurt me at all, it's just a thrill like Coney Island cyclone—I get to the bottom, water pressing down on me, afraid of cans & bottles & rusty iron nails in the mud but the bottom is mostly hard & firm & soft on the feet. . . .

I am riding in tourist bus past hills. This is the Tibet Border, looks like a nice bejeweled green Ireland ringed by hills—we see a group of red robed Lamas, 10 in all, walk up to top of the hill, where there is a pole, & make obeisance to the sun & perform a silent ceremony—I am excited & curious—so these at last are the real magicians—I want to meet them—the members of my party also, so it is arranged for the leader of one of the Lama Groups to have tea with us tho he's unwilling & funny & says "Busy Busy Busy" & we ask him to perform fortune telling ceremony—I speak up egoistically, to mumble I've read the Book of the Dead, which he ignores. He turns prayer wheels & comes on with long speech that he (being a redhaired affable European) types up for us since we are insistent & curious what we see—

"Yes said the telephone wires your call has 1 minute to go, it's a weird occurrence in New York Iberian Transpacific Co., but as such recognizable under the sign of the 4th Star and will be repeatable if not repeated, what's more the wooden Flower of Rousseau is an excellent image, see stock quotations below for further listings and—" and it runs on in roughly similar manner—I realize the priest is tuning in to some secret message code which is endless, and every time he sits down to make magic prayers, this is what he does pick up on the continuous nonsensical—or mysterious—message in his mental radio—but from where? How like Burroughs.

He leaves & goes back to a monastery thru a big door to a magic modern Interior—I follow to talk to him, I want to ask him about Burroughs—but goes in & I'm kicked out by a guard in black silk suit.

However I hang around & insist that I have special mystic urgent business to see the gent—and simply walk in—

Inside I am surprised—it's like a large hospital office, with modern glass marble furniture, many Europeans walking around like officials & intelligent zombies, I'm amazed by Tibet, must be something very special about the universe going on in this high secret science-fiction-like interior.

I look for my Lama, who is reluctant to talk but I insist, & ask him

"You mean to say Burroughs is in on this?"

"Well I don't know if you could say that. . . . He's his own man . . . don't know if I really approve—"

"I want to know some more"

"Well you'll have to be interviewed by Miss La Porte over there at that huge marble desk go talk to her & see if you really want—"

I'm going to stay here & learn more—

"Now Miss La Porte just what is going on here?"

I sit down & she asks me "What do you want to know?"

"What does the initiation feel like?"

"Not very pleasant & unless you're prepared for it—here feel this"—

Wave of Hallucination purple sense floats over me—

"I've been in Bardo Thodol before but never realized it was real"

"Well it is quite a real experience Ginsberg and we're not informed on your progress so as you can see it might be dangerous for you to go further."

"I'm in it already" I say to explain Ayahuasca etc & then return to Burroughs—

"Then Burroughs has been here?"

"Of course, in a sense he's still here."

"Well is he operating under instructions?"

"No he's on his own—too much so—he's a difficult willful one—not much love there to work with."

"Whaddya mean," I say, "I love him & if I do you certainly can put out," I say. "In addition he loves me—we make a comfy cozy twosome I might add for your info and if that isn't 'Love' what do you want?"

"Yes I suppose that's true—well now as you know you'll experience all sorts of Beasts & Devils & Monsters here, do you feel strong enough?"—

"They aren't real," I say, "why shit me with that, I want to connect to the real center, what kind of Being is that"

"Well you may be sure benevolent, but you are so—strongwilled, but it's your business to explore—Now what do you suggest doing now?"

"More hallucinogen depth Ma'am."

—The depth is by now increased to where the Dream within Dream takes on cosmic proportions and I am aware I am really visiting secret Tibet secret because it is a place for real in the Mind, universal, populated by ghost Samsaric lamas who are actually very kind and cooperative to me. But ambiguous & tricky & not entirely sure of their facts, such as on Bill—

"We're not at all sure we approve of his present open methods—it's a secret doctrine."

"O screw that," I say, "what are you running a secret society? There's lot of people who want to know what everything is about" I say—

"Now will you follow Mr. Lama to the Cafeteria?"

I go down halls with him wondering if this (eating) is a sensual trick to embarrass me or side-track the hallucination—but I eat anyway—a small plate of hash & some strange sliced raw fish or rare bird meat—I leave the dirty scraps of soiled birdmeat back on plate—the bottom layer has some dust on it—

"Should I have eaten?" as we go back "Well, no," he says, "but it's up to you"

"Well why don't you give me direct instruction?" I query.

My eye catches some pipes lying on the ground, a pile as in construction storage & some boxes—maybe labeled, "Ready to Use—Minutes to go" "Cut out & paste up on Wall"—

I say, aha! so that's where Bill's getting his mottos—he *must* have been here. "Yes," says the man, "he was & in sense still is, tho operating from Europe."

"Well this is great."

"Not so fast you still have to go thru feeling strange—the horrors will begin soon."

I suddenly regret I've been tricked into eating, which means vomiting—But I remember I can give them yogic demonstration of vomit control I learned in Ayahuasca—

We go back to main room, and he says, "Now we take a trip"—

and we are transported back to the West—I am annoyed—we are all both of us, back with Peter & a girl, Sheila or Janine [1] or Dusty—my old girlfriend

I see my opportunity to bring them too. I look in Peter (or the girl's) eyes and say, "Look at me I have something you must listen to!"—Peter avoids my eyes thinking I'm coming on strange & too domineering "Peter obey me listen to me Dig me I speak urgent from 7 years & heaven—I am now in a trance in Tibet—understand me & follow, we're all going back."

He picks up with enthusiasm, I breathe sigh of relief tho the girl thinks I am crazy have I flipped I sound like Delusions.

There's Lafcadio. Too many people to bring. The man is making out airplane tickets round trip for 3 to Tibet—we're going *right* back. I feel bad about Laf not making it but the ticket says "5 days" then it'll all be over (the Instruction) & we'll be back he can take care of himself maybe that long.

I'm amazed the Tibetans have Travel agencies, so well organized—we are ready to turn back to Tibet—

Woke & worried about leaving Laf out.

* * *

VIA AEREA

Sept 13, 1960
170 E 2 Street
NYC 9, NY

Dear Gregory:

1. Immigration law bars all foreigners of differing opinion from the country
2. Dropped the atom bomb when we didn't need to and everybody applauded or sat on their hands

---

[1] Poet Janine Pommy-Vega.

VIA AEREA

Sept 13, 1960
170 E 2 Street
NYC 9, NY

Dear Gregory:

1. Immigration law bars all foreigners of differing opinion from the country
2. Dropped the atom bomb when we didn't need to and everybody applauded or sat on their hands
3. Run South American governments for our own benifit for 50 years.
4. Fought communism from the start in Russia
5. Executed the Rosenbergs when there was no need for blood
6. Executed chessman which was indecent under circumstances
7. Elect hypocrite dumbells president
8. Stopped democratic govt in Guatamala
9. Support Franco in Spain
10. Destroyed ~~opposition~~ radical opposition in America
11. Started worldwide hysteria against benevolent Narcotics
12. Supported Rhee govt in Korea
13. Support Chiang Kai Shek dictatorship in ~~Kax~~ Formosa
14. Finance France's war in Algeria
15. Bar recognition of China & admittance in UN
16. Destroy mail coming from communist countries
17. Prevent free change of travel to China
18. Bar free expression of dissident opinion thru mass media:bar controve
19. Present distorted information on world events thru mass media
20. Overproduce luxury amusements while 1/3 world is underfed
21. Attacked Cuban revolution
22. Refused to support non-capitalist economic developement in Latin America
23. Used economic aid primarily as adjunct to military cold war
24. Been neglegent & stingy with purely altruistic foreign aid
25. Allowed censorship on important literature thru obscenity laws--Burroughs, Miller, Genet, Lawrence ,De Sade
26. Eliminated controversial figures from government, teaching, & all key posts--homos & reds
27. Overrun by moneymaking status as personal ideals & so forgotten democratic comradeship, thus making above mistakes possible

~~28.~~
28.

3. Run South American governments for their own benefit for 50 years
4. Fought communism from the start in Russia
5. Executed the Rosenbergs when there was no need for blood
6. Executed Chessman which was indecent under circumstances
7. Elect hypocrite dumbbells president
8. Stopped democratic govt in Guatemala
9. Support Franco in Spain
10. Destroyed radical opposition in America
11. Started worldwide hysteria against benevolent Narcotics
12. Supported Rhee govt in Korea
13. Support Chiang Kai-shek dictatorship in Formosa
14. Finance France's war in Algeria
15. Bar recognition of China & admittance in UN
16. Destroy mail coming from communist countries

17. Prevent free change of travel to China
18. Bar free expression of dissident opinion thru mass media: bar controversy
19. Present distorted information on world events thru mass media
20. Overproduce luxury amusements while ⅓ world is underfed
21. Attacked Cuban revolution
22. Refused to support non-capitalist economic development in Latin America
23. Used economic aid primarily as adjunct to military cold war
24. Been negligent & stingy with purely altruistic foreign aid
25. Allowed censorship on important literature thru obscenity laws—Burroughs, Miller, Genet, Lawrence, Sade
26. Eliminated controversial figures from government, teaching, & all key posts—homos & reds
27. Overrun by moneymaking status as personal ideals & so forgotten democratic comradeship, thus making above mistakes possible
28. –

Sept 12 Dream—

The Yage in icebox rotting, have to skim off the top layer of froth or it die—

Fragment later in morning, reading an unpublished later Yeats mss, dedicated to Raymond Bremser in Faith, so I weepingly see how beauty's hope's sadness touch't Willie.

Oct 7 evening 1960—

Kerouac on Ayahuasca

Whistle
They're whistling for me
already
I see roses—
Eh Edie—hello Edie—
Poor lil Edie
I'm 'avin her now
(that was just a joke
for you)

I think I'll be a writer
for Gradgme—Jazzme—
ah ah —Kenyon Review
Won't even let me talk!—
your . . .
they're running
touchdowns all over—my arm . . .
I had a vision of an
ancient Kabala sign in
the puke
My god it's a
beautiful sign—. . .
compact perfect
little Aztec
signs—eyes
were closed . . .
Yeah—how stupid
it is, how stupid is wisdom
Darwin is right
I saw someone move
Dostoyevsky
Dostoyevsky come here
sit down on this bed
with Allen lay yr
$10 ass here—
Oh I see Petersburg
he was interested
in homosexuals because
they were sensitive &
'appreciately eager'—
as John Holmes says—
in a way that J. H.
could never understand.
O God I feel just like
Sherlock Holmes
If you weren't here to talk to I'd be
on a death kick,
feeling my hair on my breast—
I could write a

Kaddish about him . . .
I saw Al Jolson this
week—The Jazz Singer
    1927

    Gee that Al Jolson had
a beautiful face
    You see the people up
there in New England, the French
Canadians didn't like
him—because he had
the great slavic
    Nye nyeh nyeht sound—
But on Broadway he was
    #1 man . . .
The Great Jewish
        B'way
which also featured
    such Jews as
Wm Maynard Garver
    with his pince-nez
    sneaking into his
thousand niggertime
heavens—well for Heavens!—
(Dosty left a little while
    back—)
Hey Garver, How really excellent
        of you to show up!
    There's one of the really
few things I do appreciate,
    Garver a true angel form!
    His conversation,
    "I'm one of the Gods
highest angels as you
knew—& told Me—
and now I'm flying
around cause there's
high angels & low
angels as you know

—I'm going down to
one of those *low* angels
& get me a little shit tonite—"
(Sticks arms out)
"Hey Bill being angels
we don't have to roll
up our sleeves—"
Nirvana here I come!

Such charming men—
Garver & Burroughs!
Seymour Wyse!
"Well what did you want
to say"—
Hey he's just
like Al Jolson—
he's the Chief
Jew of the World—
Joe May said to Seymour
in the West End:
"Aren't you a Liverpool Jew?"
Ah, where's Joe May?

Let's go see his big
rosy asshole this
Morning—

What Mozart did
while his wife
was having a baby—
he goes to a corner
& writes a fucking
concerto!
knocked it off in 13 min—
Shakespeare used to write fast too
No proof but I'm sure of it
his letters to publishers—
Flowing swift copy, writ
on English Hashish—

He'd promised to deliver a play
"within a month"–
said Shakespeare . . .
and them very sheets
dragging themselves
like dead dogs
across the graves
of Scotland–
That's news for Carr–Lucien's an ancient Laird . . .
an old titled prick–
But he *was* you know, at one
time he used to run around
London under a funny little
name– Wm Shakespeare–
– You know who I was at
that time– Kyd– I was
Always an underground character . . .
transferred my activities
to France & became Villon
– stole from the Church–
Then I became Rimbaud–
I was Verlaine– de Maupassant
– Balzac– check on yr
dates.– I'm positive that
in 1860 I was a great
thief in London– My
name was Robt Horton– I
had troupe of Boys who were
sent out by me to attract
men of title & money– with
whom I was not in love–
I was in love w/ a
girl a
brunette, dancer in Soho
whom I murdered– for
which I was hanged–

That was as fast as I cd/write with him talking,
I got the best phrases & main ideas–

Also he says he said, "God (for I was God to him for a moment) why did you create the world?"–

but then sighed back, to himself, "Oh– aghoh"– Accepting! "Because to Ask a personal god *why* he Created the Being is tantamount to telling him to go kill himself– which is not polite, nice–"

Also said– looking at me– "This is one of the most sublime or tender or lovely moments of all our lives together . . ."

I sat there feeling like a secret wizard.

Oct 8 1960

The Eye of Everything–a Series of photographs:

To be a House in the rain,
To be a front porch that has stood in the
  lonely dusk 50 years on a
  southern mansion
To be a Statue in St. Peter's Basilica
To be an Altar of Jain or Mithra, to
  hide back in the darkness–
    be there beside a fat Buddha
    watching the approach of worshippers
up the main aisle of the Temple–
  To see them on their knees,
   or happy or in terror
  praying to me–
The Eye of Everything: to be a photo of
  Allen Ginsberg.

* * *

Kaddish – Proem Narrative Hymn
Lament Litany & Fugue
Lamentation

Epigraphs– Blake's Sunflower, & Whitman's "Damned"

* * *

We will widen our consciousness till
it includes knowledge of Death—
. . . Man shall be Death, Man was but life . . .
Man shall Be—
and no ands if buts—
himself Beginning & the End—
and man will not be Man
till mankind ends and the new God is Born
by our Invention—
Take over Great Buster— Come on Big Babe!
I inseminate thee Universe in thine own sweet
asshole: Death.
That's why I'm Queer
to make Birth obsolete

* * *

Birds with movie-star faces in my collage
Junk Vision— pigeons strutting with Myrna Loy's smile—

* * *

Death which is the mother of the universe, from whose Black lips the Cosmos Came, From whose Blind eye the planets leaped & changed, from whose my black mind the first word of itself was Rumored & Conceived
Whose magic sex made spasm that I am— The thought of all the stars! A mad Vision in the Void! Came forth one Being Equal to Eternity splendid as a fish!
Invisible, with one Huge Eye that sees Naomi in Itself—
and eats that consciousness alive— The gravestones are in the graveyard now—
Fate begat Fate & Death Begat her Bibles of Meat & Bone—
Dead Naomi as the Bride Pregnant with Death— her belly caved to bare her Genesis
A bag of rotten apples for you Now— I brought them on the Train with a cooked goose—

* * *

Oct. 8, 1960

Household conversation, 102 E. 2 St., Oct. 9, 1960 transcribed by Allen Ginsberg.

Carl Solomon—America is Crafty but not free...

Eisenhower is anti-negro because all those colored people are not prepared to sit in schools in Little Rock until they become invisible like Ralph Ellison— ... ostentatious blacks living off the fruits of Republican demagoguery...

United States is a Fascist country, rule of Monopoly capital...

I have no rights I'm treated as a Cretin I'm mugged every day by queers tyrants dictators & Doctors—liberals have sold me out ... Salvation lies in Harry Bridges... It's a rule of phonies—

Curran[1] sold out to Capitalism & now the Social Demos have made a White Xtian dictatorship, I'm accused of things for which I have no guilt feelings ... therefore can't say I'm sorry, therefore I won't kiss their lilywhite asses—Curran never was bad to Jews but that don't make him democratic, because Irishmen are bigger than Jews—

I wanted to assist in the fight against Japanese imperialism—therefore joined the service from college...

When I got back to college they called me queer because I had intercourse with women overseas—

A Communist is very good really, their parties weren't unfertile... Psychiatrists always praise fertility.

The country is diseased, abnormal, stinks foolish planless uncultivated dopefiend ridden Catholic, it's morbid...

No ray of light—I can't feel that a Hershey bar is my salvation—

If yr not a materialist then you're a nut & in this country they esteem nuts more than materialists.

I don't believe in God—why do I have to insist on my point again...

They want me to forget my amnesia—

America is a lot of J. C. phonies, America is unaware—of its own lunacy in the face of the world Socratic picture and all the Jews are scared to assert their rights...

James Curran, president of National Maritime Union.

The return to religion is phony—

If the object of capitalism is *not* to make money then let them put Rasputin in control—have seances—I know what is best for US—it's best for US to eat & not make fun of other people—provide them with food & shelter & not to tell them to go crazy because America's making a big mistake; so is England—& the French bourgeoisie are trying to protect their own most decadent elements—as events in Cuba have come to prove—by doing this they're only fooling themselves . . .

There's a patient at the Hospital known as *The Masturbator*—considered as a major criminal—given a lobotomy—

"Why impose your God on me?" If you spatter my vest therefore I'm not me . . .

They had me scrubbing floors there like in Germany, they hired Hungarian refugees as attendants—I'm slave of the Nazis . . . America fought 2'd W.W. to take over Europe & make money—

Msgr. Sheen is sane because he goes like this *(hands uplift)* . . . Why should I be in a hospital, don't they want a free-flowing society—?

Peter Orlovsky—I got a swollen gum.

Carl Solomon: If what I say is sedition then let it be considered sedition—I am going to buy a sedition wagon when I get out. Furthermore I am still a member of the French Communist Party because I don't want to be considered a negativist—

and you (Ginsberg) who embody the revival of Mediaevalism—yours is a Mediaeval way of regarding the Jew, that the Negro must smile all the time—you and T. S. Eliot—

They want me to be just a good Jewish boy—otherwise they'll hit me in the belly again—an abnormal antisemitic Italian hit me in the belly and called me a prick—I hit him back—They put me in a straitjacket . . .

I want to leave the country go to Russia & sell seltzer . . .

I don't have to live in a stoolpigeon society—if they don't want me here why don't they let me leave the country—I am pleading for freedom to emigrate the country—

Fin

* * *

Yesenin's last poem written in blood on the Communist walls of Russia.

* * *

Jack: The Cross has a smile that goes both ways
Lord Surcease/his evening sleep/has brought
the sleepers/back & deep.

Dream—Oct. 1960

We are at home in our filthy loft, scattered with smelly laundry & unwashed dishes in the sink, extending our experiments into Unconsciousness—Peter, myself, and Janine who is alive (or Natalie who committed suicide some years ago), a healthy girl.

She takes the drug, a glassful, and becomes very nervous—death rays are visible. Are we not plotting against her? What is Peter doing in the kitchen? Why am I staring at her? Why can't she play the piano? Is the world normal or not? This is all routine, all in a night's work.

She does get worse, and I do get worried—perhaps she is too high. I wish she would come down and have some nice celestial visions or Transcendental acquaintanceship with the great Cocksucker of the universe like I do.

I decide to call the doctor—she is screaming at us anyway. He comes over examines her privately—she has calmed down by now, sitting in the large loft room, looking serious.

A small ratty looking plump man, not a bad fellow.

How is she Doc? I ask as he prepares his bag to leave by the staircase door.

Well allright, a little unsteady. I suppose she'll be well. I didn't give her anything. I don't know what effect more drugs would have on her. What was the name of this stuff you gave her?

Ayahuasca. A hallucinogen like Mescaline.

Well the police will have to know about it, he says, turning to the door.

What? Why, she's not that sick, I say.

Well such cases should be reported. I shouldn't take the responsibility, he says, leaving thru door, with one hand already on the downstairs bannister.

But she's already alright and in any case this drug is not illegal and she's had Mescaline and other mystic drugs earlier, I look down on him as he descends.

Perhaps but I can't take any chances. They should know, he replies, not looking back, from the first landing.

But we called on you, this is a personal matter for doctor, not police, besides I myself had had this 11 times without bad effect don't you understand and anyway if you tell the police, they'll come up here with squad cars embarrassing us, questioning us, upsetting household searching the kitchen ransacking the loft for hidden narcotics—we'll wind up all in jail for a nite at least—

He by now has disappeared shaking his head beyond the appeal of reason.

* * *

I wake up, choking in throat, my position in bed normal but throat still somewhat clogged & nothing wrong I realize except sense of suffocation—

The cat scratches in box, I don't understand the noise, think it's detectives outside the door—I hear voices in the hall—I wait, wondering whether to write down dream or not—get up in 5 a.m. darkness on chilly floor—& do so. All is calm. All is bright.

Dream

In a Vespa perhaps stolen, fleeing from the police along route 4 to Paterson—

I had taken it in the subway—I was once lost, sought by the police in levels of subway platforms at the Underground 10-story junction under the Bronx, where there are 20 different subway lines running thru all N.Y. to Coney Island from one huge underground Piranesi arcade, labyrinth—I started from there maybe in this dream (this place I'd dreamed earlier).

—to N.J. highway—hiding by an outdoor movie theater or by a gas station men's room, for the cop cars to pass by—so I could continue on to Russia my destination.

Oct. 1960—Dream

Several years after the last of Naomi, after what I thought was seeing the worst of it, of her—I find that Eugene & Louis are rushing back to the hospital to make a final deposition of her affairs—

Some earlier activity takes place in a forest where we met—a picnic—

they are called away—I am on an elevated with Dorothy Norman [1]—Cancer of the Stomach—I have an upset stomach all night in reality (transcription interruptus here) I wake at noon it's sour in my throat—flatulent & fuzzy inside—

They go to the hospital and I rush after them to find out what it is—it seems that the final emergency has arisen, they need to go sign papers & supervise the final scene with her to make it psychically legal—or legally so—

She is by now reduced to a strange & spectral feeling (in the dream) state—she is a living organism of Naomi—perhaps with some of her old character—however her face has changed—the lower part has collapsed or has been altered thru final Hospital treatment and the condition she is in now looks like a face above with eyes, but below her mouth has collapsed & in its place a cancerous disk or set of plates which protrude from the throat like Vomit rooted in the middle of her?—two extrusions in the mush-mouth to replace the lips & teeth & tongue—

Independent wormface has taken over—a horrible sight which I am afraid to see but they are going to supervise her death at this point—perhaps a conscious murder—a euthanasia—

They have to sign & witness for the sticking of gas pipes into the mouth & bloating the organism to death with cure gasses & x rays.

Gene goes up an elevator, I follow, get lost on a ward wander around hospital looking for the sacrifice x-ray room—can't find him to go with him to the right place—I meet another male corpse under sheets somewhere being wheeled up hall—

I am afraid to ask directions lest I be barred from the experience of seeing the final state.

* * *

My stomach's rotten & I need to vomit now, or perhaps change consciousness, feel some spectral threat which I hide unconscious or cry.

Like Naomi's explosion of diarrhea & vomit.

Lafcadio's last nite picture of me as an overgrown dwarf-freak. Which I thot to append to Kaddish.

Dr. Kreplich's "Vomit not acceptance of the feeling."

* * *

---

[1] Dorothy Norman: rich lady N.Y.C.; girl friend of photographer Alfred Stieglitz and wrote a biography of him; in the 30's edited *Twice a Year*, journal specializing in civil liberties.

Showing Lucien Kaddish last night. He says, "The violence of it"—about Naomi's Cunt description.

Altered sexlessness with Peter.

Reading Book of Great Liberation last nite & feelings of lightness & fire in eye watching Laf draw me, calmed my stomach awhile—

I am I old one-eye of nitemare the knower I felt—

To take get mushroom tomorrow—

Feeling that Kaddish not the last word on Naomi, as said Elise [1]—now seen true, other feelings of deeper mystery not those represented—the spectral poetic horror—the Unknown Fear—

I left the awareness of Lou & Gene out tho they supervised the coffin—

Oct 12, 1960

Jack in for 3 days, finally ending in bed w/ me & Peter like Silenus nekkid—his big thighs & belly.

Oct. 20, 1960

"I want to be wanted" sings Marie [2]—
Death wants you—
Little girl chorus voices from the street singing
through the dark window.

Politics on Opium

What good are all our washmachines if our hair's dirty with Algiers blood?
If the Vice President sits around telling lies about Guatemala what good television except get mad?
What good being reasonable talking public if movie stars're afraid they're queer?
What good being Senator you can't confess your inmost thought?
What good utmost thought if murder gets away with the newspapers?
I got no mama, I got no Government, I got nobody but me and my friends
my friends all believe in different Unicorns.

---

[1] Elise Cowen typed the original *Kaddish* ms.

[2] Peter Orlovsky's sister.

Would Vox Populi own but one Car if Universities were undertaken in Aden?
I won't mind living shabby if my tax money gives breast to Tibetan orphan.
Like, we are the Rich–
Like, everybody got a full icebox
Like, everybody got Kleenex, toothpaste, lawn soap, Car sex, movie money,
dazzling bediamonded wristwatches made of teeth–
we got eyeball rugs, tongue pillows, fingernail scooters, heart toys, congenital sofas, protoplasm pianos, we got the works–
This Luxury mocks nature, lawns satirize the weeping willow,
Potted palms bathed in electric glare attack the nightingale,
Fences of horses attack the rose–

It's all ours America–all the Nimrod Niagara Payable honeymoon sweet Sunday–
Adolescents change their pimpled sox on happy carpets–
The middle class is pretty big and twice as real–
O beautiful middle class! How lovely you were human and not afraid of the Cops–
No one hates cops of flesh & bone–
It's when they're made of plaster rubber, old newspaper Herbert Hoover's hat, steel condom wiretap envy, too many silly laws
Cop can stop anyone on the street for no good reason except he be bored and search him for identification where he lives, it hurts
–two Cops stopt me Peter & his kid brother in the middle of our dream
across the street from my house in 1960 off East Second Street & Avenue A
Forced us in a doorway, flashed their badges, rolled up our sleeves, made us show our behinds,
asked for my Being Papers and destination I who'm a ghost worrying about my void
dismissed with warning "This is a bad neighborhood for Coprophagues"
in once sweet old lower East Side? Citizen got no protection from Ghouls?
Must I write letters to NY Times & petition the furry mayor in vain? I gotta go fite City Hall
protect my private feet delight on the sidewalk?

I reasonable reply Courteously
But fear being kicked in the balls or charged with possession of two Ears
When Law comes on like worst Creeps
Thank God I'm not a Criminal lest I suffer more than mere 1960
paranoia
I can't even commit a crime with a Clean Conscience any more.

Oct. 1960

SUBLIMINAL

One million editorials against Mossadeq and who knows who Mossadeq [1]
is any more?
Me a Democracy? I didn't know my Central Intelligence was arming
fascist noodnicks in Iran
This true story I got from High Sources Check yr local radio announcer.
All I remember's nasty cartoons in N.Y. Mirror long-faced Mossadeq
blubbering in a military court in Persia
looking the opposite of a serious hair'd Central Intelligence Agent sipping
borscht cocktails at a Conservative egghead soirée
Whom I wanted for daddy Man of Distinction that year
I was working in Market Research.
Who threw poison onion Germs in Korea?
Do big fat American people know their Seoul from a hole in the ground?
Will Belgians ever get out of Congo so King Leopold's ghost stop
screaming in Hell?
What Civilization the Uranium Addicts been selling us niggers?
The Mass Media have taken over Poetry U S A
Harold Ickes rushed upstairs to hear H.V. Kaltenborn on Pearl Harbor
Day.
That is an entity, a single public Consciousness, has come
But I am not sure it's really me– "Don't make waves?"
Hoover gets up Republican Convention 1960 says

---

[1] Dr. Mohammed Mossadeq: Iranian premier who in 1951 nationalized the oil industry and was then overthrown through C.I.A. efforts in 1953. He was given a public trial where he wept aloud in court denouncing American intervention, and was mocked by Time magazine for his tears. Official confirmation of U.S. intervention didn't come until 1974–5 revelation of scandalous C.I.A. activities, though it had been reported unofficially in the press by the time of Mossadeq's death in 1967.

"Communists beatnicks & eggheads" are America's Number 3 Menace
What who me? Is I th'Egghead Communist beatnick?
Postmaster General Summerfield plastered obscene sex signs all over my
 post office
brought Eisenhower a copy of Lady Chatterley's Lover
Eisenhower he's the President of the United States in the White House
with all the dirty words underlined Ike glances Shrieks agrees
"Terrible ... we can't have that." Exact words quote deadpan my
 Newsweek
Aint that a National Issue?
How'd an old Fuck like that run my Nation?
Who put him in then?
You you dirty son of a bitch I sound like Kenneth Rexroth paranoiac—
I asterisked the poetic words in my first book to get it printed
and U.S. government seized it when ship wafted it over from England
I bit his hand he dropped the case.
But Juvenile vice-cops grabbed it in Frisco my publisher had to go to jail
 one afternoon
and Naked Lunch was banned in America up yours with a nude yellow
 grapefruit
and I had to rush out to Chicago & ruin my stomach orating before
 mobs
Because the University of Chicago was banning Naked Lunch plates
 from its starving Body
U. of C. produces atom bombs & FBI men
and when I asked Columbia U why doncha invite Kruschef give a speech
 in the Camp David Spirit type days
It said I quote "The State Department hasn't asked us to," giggling &
 bashful like it had to pee
Columbia is very Historical, they even had Eisenhower for President.
They turn out the cream of the crop, fresh young faces that guide the
 Nation
O My enemy Columbia University! How I would like to strangle you
 with a giraffe's footprint!
Master Kerouac was barred from the campus as an "unwholesome
 element" in 1942
Enter the Silent Generation. It got a monkey on its back in Korea
and then went advertising, or camped back to Columbia to teach the
 young.
It's all subliminal either you get fucked or you don't dearie

That's why American poetry stank for 20 years.
Not that this is poetry, it's just shoveling the Garbage aside for Eternity.
I'm taking a stand! Hot Dog!
It's what's known as being responsible even tho it's the sheerest nonsense.
Just moving my frankfurter!
Crap on all you Critics. You Norman Podhoretz, go screw the stars, King of the Jews—
you Lionel Trilling get back on the Mystic wagon before Infinity chops your head off,
and the rest of you, Nat Hentoff, dumb Vanden Haag, mute inglorious L. Simpson, hypocritic Kazin, Brustein-Wechsler, Journalists
attacking Kerouac, Corso & myself, snoopers, creeps, hung up idiots, Incompetents, sneaks & dumbbells, quacks,
here, have a piece of my immortality, I mention your names.
Some of these are my friends but I have been requested to exhibit a sense of responsibility
& hitherto have been too tender & kind vain egotistical to answer public attacks.
As for Time Life Daily News the liberal Post the Partisan Review
all Yellow Journalism take your filthy fathead hands off my genitals, I am the Muse!
Go sniff the saintly footprints I left at Columbia!
The philistines are running America! Left right Center! Shoulder Arms! Onions!
Yes I want riots in the streets! Big orgies full of marijuana scaring the cops!
Everybody naked fucking on Union Square to denounce the Military Junta in San Salvador!
Why did we Crucify Mankind Upon a Cross of Gold?
Whatsa matter our secret CIA plot to unseat Syngman Rhee
flopped & delayed till Korean students rioted & took over the scene?
That's a military secret I'm a prophet I know lots of military secrets
I think I'll tell a couple to the Universe and go to Jail
I've been investigating— I think I'll be unamerican a few minutes
See how it feels like— eek! I just saw FBI
hiding behind my mother's skull.
This is a private matter between me & my conscience
Why those newspapers all staring at me like that?
Big eyes on the editorial pages searching my soul for secret affiliation afflictions

And pinocchio long noses in literary columns sniffing up my ass to smell
Immutability.
It's only laughing gas dearies. Stick that up your dirty old savings
account—
and big long mustache headlines waving at me in wet dreams &
nitemares!
O I just wish I were Mayakovsky! or even Neruda!
As it is I'll have to settle for reincarnation as a silly Blake.
Walt Whitman thou shdst be living at this Hour!
The average American Male & Female took over the ship of state
400 of them got smashed up over July 4 Weekend celebrating!
Democracy! Bah! When I hear that word I reach for my feather Boa!
Better we should have a big jewish dictatorship full of Blintzes:
Better a spade Fish queen run our economics than
Kennedy that tired old man whose eyes speed back & forth like taxicabs
rather reptilian what?—

O Nixon's tired eyes! & Kennedy's hurried glance! O that America
should be hung up on these two idiots while I am, alive!
It's silly but it's serious. What is truth? said Pilate
Washing his hands in an atom bomb.
If you don't think the Chinese don't hate us, you're just not Hep.
Get with it, Big Daddy, I been to South America
Like, it swings there, everybody gets high on Starvation
Like get with it Cat, you better stash your wheat,
I hear the sirens of the Fuzz downstairs in the subconscious
and dont you know, like, Alice Red Gown she got *Reasons.*

Now where was It I sent my extra little army in 1917?
I lost it somewhere in my bloomers— O there it is fighting with General
Wrangel in Siberia
Heavens! What a bad show— you better tell General MacArthur
shit or Get off the Pot.
And that Invasion
of Mexico was such a camp! I never had
such a good time fucking all them bandits and learning how to dance La
Cucaracha!
Let's spend our 50th Wedding anniversary there in Prince Maximilian's
Palace.
What'd you say about my United Fruit? Don't be Nasty you lower class
piece of trade.

I'll show you who's Miss Liberty or Not—
I got what it takes! I got the 1920's (Snap yr fingers kid!)
I got Nostalgia of Depression! I got N.R.A.!
I got Roosevelt I got Hoover I got Willkie I got Hitler I got Franco I got
World War II!
I got the works (cha! cha!) I got the atom bomb [1]
I got Cancer! I got Fission! I got legal Prohibition!
I got the Works! I got the Fuck law! I got the Junk Law! I got hundred
billion bucks a year!
Yassah! Yassah! I got Formosa! (Catch me man) I got Chiang Kai-shek!
and I got my Central Intelligence getten rid of him right now!
I got a million planes flying over Siberia! I got
10,000,000 upstanding young americans chargin' on the ricefields of
China
Jazzin and waltzen and shootin and hollering all day!
Whoopee! I got crosseye yellow cities in every corner of the world.
I got the old umph! I got my Guantánamo! I even got my old Marines!
You'd think I was an old thing way back from the 19th Century
With Isadora Duncan Oscar Wilde & the Floradora Sextette!
But I still got my old man, my handsome lovin blond Marines!
I'm Miss Hydrogen America! I'm Mae in Cobalt West! I'm the Sophie
Tucker of Plutonium Forever!
I'm the red Hot Mama of Tomorrow! Aint nobody gonna burn down
my Miami Hotels!
Didn't they cost 10 million dollars and I hired the best Architects!
I even built a couple in Havana where the livin's cheap.
Nosiree I'm up to date I hadda face lift and got a hot new corset in Los
Alamos
and some airlift brassieres outa Congress and some gold pumps in Texas!
and I gotta boyfriend he's a millionaire tax collector from Hollywood!
He's the artistic type!
I'm gonna make whoopee next ten years before I blow my gasket,
I'm gonna take on the whole American Legion in one night
Just like that cute little Presidential Candidate Kennedy Fellow! (He's
the intellectual type)
I'm gonna make the Rosicrucians scream!

* * *

---

[1] This and neighbor lines formed basis for some of A.G.'s soundtrack commentary in Jonas Mekas' 1962 film, *Guns of the Trees.*

Ah, how sad to get hung up in this way, like on Hungary.
Belinski worried about Russia in 1860! And Dostoyevsky's hero really worried about socks.
It'll all pass away and then I'll be answerable to gloomier onions, we'll all weep.
I shouldn't waste my time on America like this. It may be patriotic
but it isn't good art. This is a warning to you, Futurists, and you Mao Tse-tung—. . .

Nov. 1, 1960

I write this type poetry on Heroin
O Capitalists & Communists you shd get in bed with me
bring your pencils & notebooks
lie there snorting out revolutions and epidemics famines and excess grain production
Gold standards and Ezra Pound hamming it up in the Puzzle Factory—
Is anyone really a fink?
My contention is not original sin or stutterless Billy Budds
We all eat germs & die
It's like America's so dumb
It's like Eisenhower was so dumb, so dumb Truman, so dumb Stalin
Hitler rushing into a war with Russia
Silly but the psychopathic bourgeoisie figured he knew what he was doing
Just like America figures Somebody Up There Loves Me
and knows what he's doing—
aided by Divine Intuition plus Secret Service Corps of trained Univacs
to figure the waves of Time and the exact dot point of germy stress
but they just aren't that SMART
I'm smarter than Eisenhower
tho he has greater sources of Information
I have greater aptness at Awareness to
Widen the area of consciousness of the Universe—
I know when the plum blossoms are falling
I know when I am pushing does he?
He whoever, Castro, Kennedy, whosever Elected King—
Not running for election I have time to take Heroin
and lay in my bed and figure it out—
What's happening who's starving where who's got the gelt . . .

Who's got the guilt?
We have, America, . . .
So happens we missed the boat to the New World.
And now the ships are leaving for the moon,
Have we anything to export to the Universe
but a few dead prophets and a basketful of cranky Formulae for
 Electricity? . . .
Nothing but a bunch of frightened insurance salesmen ratting on TV.
We outlawed the Communist Party—. . .
No sense no sense
Wiping Franco's behind with the hair of a million sentimental Martyrs?
O shame of Casals, of Huidobro, of Vallejo brooding in the Paris rain! . . .
I'm walking down the street university perfecting my voodoo
"Where you goin' lady, to death?" cried the Adolescent ghost
Now the Tunisians riot on the streets in Tunisia where else . . .
They just want to be free like us ugh shudder
They're dropping bombs, they're torturing fingernails—
loud noises in the air about French Sovereignty
mysterious hashish being consumed in the Waldorf Astoria
grooming Gen. MacArthur to take over America
General Taylor made sovereign of the Lincoln Center of the Arts
Bring back the dead comedians of 1939—
Bring back the Grapes of Wrath! Bring on Jean Harlow's pussy!
Bring back Buster Keaton's silence! . . .
I'll write a play about French Freedom in Cameroons.
Now that the Congo is independent how come Nelson Rockefeller
campaigning for president owns 22½ percent controlling interest
in Universal Mines in Katanga?
It's all our uranium deposits he's worried about so he bought the Congo
for Moise Tshombe— No wonder the Ukrainian Parliament makes such
 a funny noise.
I complain about politics! I put my 2 cents down on the Fall of America
Because *Times* says Brazilian life expectancy's 30 years—
we have a big fanatic used car laundry business on the make. What bad
 taste. Like a mouthful of Joe McCarthy's semen . . .
O Elie Nadelman thou shouldst be living at this hour
old reactionary surely you would've taken part
in the Anti Bomb riots that took place when Times Square
went on a sit-down strike against your Tanagra knishes.
Spengler makes sense in 1000 years

in the Harz Mts., retired he listened to Beethoven Deaf quartets
I could have stretched out the oomph at least or wobbled the cycle—But the Police took over the poetry & music cafés and charged Admission
I never read poetry for money. Which is more than I can say for Henry Ford.
Vain tho my activity, I did strike a chord—
I banged my own bell, and a thousand alarm clocks began ringing
but that's not enuf to wake the Expanding Population,
all they want to do is fuck & play with Chevrolets, gibber in the Supermarket over Frozen lobstertails . . .

De Dream of Richard Nixon

I am in North Africa—on a boat to England—a huge high castle-lighted boat over the sea—as in an earlier dream, an entire universe, original & complete—this ship which takes me from my home in Tangier to England—I've made the trip before—with my brother's wife-family presence for chaperone or front—

The Fuzz shore-patrol customs-police examine me as I go down the sandy beach side to the boat to embark or disembark—shake me down—One policeman particularly nosy fastens on me and insists on examining my person with minute curiosity, presses my hand to see if doesn't contain a box, looks in my ears—for smuggled perfumes?—I wonder if he's looking for dope, which dont happen to have on me that trip, I feel safe—no he thinks I have an A Bomb concealed in me—I tell him I don't, I don't want to blow myself up yet in any case—he marches me up & down the beach from gate to gate, examining my behavior—which is high & paranoid—I am afraid he'll discover something I once took—but it's all out of my system—besides my brother's wife is there, very respectably—

He takes me back toward the boardwalk, I say "Well don't make me go thru another set of guards—they don't know how thoroughly you've already examined me & might start the whole thing all over—" He says No that wont happen—but he does head toward them—

Next, at the Convention, Mrs. Roosevelt is seated, as spokesman for the delegation, but the bosses in the upper lead-window Gable of the "Witches House" 18th Century Campaign headquarters have denied her de vote—so she rises and I believe resigns her part in the delegation—or this happens later.

.... In Nixon's house, visiting his daughter—election eve or election week—I'm visiting, a friend, but hostile to my girlfriend's father—I'm lying on the floor—Nixon is there, in the breakfast alcove a worried father visiting his wife & daughter over weekend off from the campaign.

I realize he's not so terrible—He's in the breakfast nook I see him thru a picture window from the living room, I'm looking up at him right under his chair—he's nervous, having coffee, reading his breakfast paper—he dawdles nervously on social notes—remarks to his wife:

"Eleanor certainly made a scandal." But his wife rebukes him sensibly, "Well it was a terrible snub & insult they delivered her, the only thing she could do was resign—they took her vote from her tho she was head of delegation—that means they'll have to fight it out—She was willing to lay down her cards & force the issue after all—The liberals *did* get in so she deserved ... this was nothing but a snub to her & the Liberal wing."

Nixon nods & agrees, he's sensible & sympathetic—I realize he's a nice fellow, just nervous, and in it sincerely—In fact I'm a little ashamed to realize he is so sincere—and I'm a bunch of liberal-anarchist bums lying around his floor—must dismay him his daughter hanging around with all

From Love to Art, or from Art to the High Heart

I make an aphorism the paradox structure of which I dwell on & repeat several times & think to write down. Then I am wakened by Carl who says an old lady's at the door.

On the Threshold of the Great Consciousness.

that trash—but has come on polite, very restrained, even under the pressure, sat down & not ordered us out—but an abused prisoner alone in his breakfast nook nervously being self-contained reading the papers.

At some point or other in the dream I'm explaining—on the boat, or Eleanor has explained—that Love is the path between the Heart and Art or the graph of or curve of development from Love to Art, or from Art to the High Heart

It makes an aphorism the purpose & structure of which I dwell on & repeat several times & think to write down. Then I am awakened by Carl who says an old lady's at the door.

* * *

On the threshold of the Great consciousness.

Dream

A group of people on the streets to vote—we're watching the race for office? Nixon & Kennedy crossing swords?

In any case, thousands of people in the streets with crossed swords, the mirror images of each other cancelling each other out with broomsticks, bricks, swords—

As if under robot control they swarm down the street & attack anyone waiting for bus or passing—

They throw earlier organized groups into this one—the ex-soldiers, having been reduced to control, are then used to it, and can be whipped into another political action—to attack each other & anyone in the street & cancel each other out, so that there are whole lives of people mirror images of each other in serpent chains up & down the block—cancelling each other out like equally matched electric fighting cocks, all with crossed staves—stragglers try to engage me, I move outside the field of the disturbance rather than become involved. They are being manipulated by the warmakers.

Dream, Nov. 12

Lying on the couch to sleep, as I do, I wake up out of a trance—Janine is pointing to the wall—a huge deep light brown pile of watery shit plaster hanging on the wall—I turn away after examining it under her insistence—it's smeared also on my hands & pants—in my mouth, I taste it—rather globs of brown water have splashed intentionally all over me—

She gestures, the taste in the back of my throat from the nasal drips of shit from smelling in it so deep—I swallow a few times, till the taste is no longer exceptional—

Dream, Nov. 27, 1960

In the New Poor Neighborhood—the police come by—we are visiting on a trip thru the castle walls but the damn police come & bother us, a whole file of them—They are looking for victims—they line us up with hands up against the stone balustrade—make us cross hands as at ease as if at no angst, then come by & hit anybody not found with hands crossed properly.—O the enemy is cruelty in any form—Cuban or German or NYC—Bang they hit you or they suddenly make you start applauding them & you & the relationship—applause, bam, crosshands, bam, applause. The chief cop passed me by without hitting me, I am relieved. Bam he hits someone down the line—passes me up again—I'll get it next—I glimpse the open fields of Poland—scene shifts.

to NY slum upstairs housing development the new Puerto Ricans have just moved in to the second row of windows over the balustrade embankment of the castle walls (as over the Inti Pampa wall in Cuzco Peru—) *All* police are evil—they murder for control—They are moving in again—I am angry—Last night they rounded up all the Jews & Puerto Ricans for an *exercise* in the Park—crossing & uncrossing the hands, applauding the police—the old sloe-eyed tailors are herded into Tompkins Park at dawn when the middle class is still asleep—for a Patriotic Courage Parade—It's Hell—I am angry!—They are the ones who have awoken and frightened the sleeping community—The apartments are empty—

* * *

Laws hurt people, in U.S., like waking up to a vast police conspiracy to hypnotize and cow whole nations of individual souls under the ancient arbitrary will of a malevolent state.

* * *

To put a microphone to the sun
and a moving picture camera ten miles away from the boiling light
or in the center of the Invisible
Mass of roaring fire and connect it to the eye and ear,
old fantasy of ballpark daydreamed on the bench, no player me—

there's no way to connect the brain as cold as lukewarm eggs
Sooner or later the antennae would shrivel at the great nearness
probably a million miles away—

Several days later Life Mag has photos of sun in color enlarged.

* * *

Lucien sits at his table in a business suit & we converse like dummies in Eternity.

Dream

In bed last nite on Cocayne—looking out of my face as a frog—the familiar feel of self, even enlarged in Frog-Consciousness-of-Be—looking into the cosmos thru a frog's eyes—remembering the same presence as I am now—Then the bulge of water of a fish—a glimpse thru the ocean, worried about same death with my large nose & clear eyes in water—and a cat sitting on the couch of same—and a dog resting on paws, knowing—and a hippo ensconced in old Flesh—

I ran thru a series of archetype selves back to the Paramecium—along the same problem of self-awareness in the grand vast Waters—as thru myriad selves & forms of Bardo Thodol—half wake in the fantasy in bed in living room. The bulging chattering opium frogfaces of Burroughs are similar.

Boston

Hurrah for the American Revolution!

Light dies! all light is the same
Light rays on over the coffin of the Seen
The million stars conspire the Universe
I am the Son of Man, I am the Sun of the Cosmos,
I am the Father of the American Revolution.

Huncke's Room

Fleeting visualizations—Naomi, a group of old peasant ladies on the sidewalk going to the well—she turns & curtseys—she might have gone on alright like everyone else—but she decided to dramatize the change of the cosmos—so turned old and paranoid—

Literally she was mixed up—but what expansion of awareness was she caught up in?—Hospital was not the answer—a farm outside the civilization would have been better—

Ezra Pound—his grey beard and sharp chin—another one—as Mailer made a mistake in judgment still appealing to external authority—and Al Aronowitz.

From Boston Dec 1—Psilocybin

Poetry is a dynamo in the void
People are alone with their "things" in
the void
"I had Laughing Gas & I had a baby."

I sit here writing— this is "my thing."
People don't laugh at other people's "thing."

I am maintaining that I am a
man of mystery,
whereas I am no different from
anybody else. I am a
horse's ass.

I am Louis' ass—

6 Dec 60

Laugh Gas—12?

Prophecy
Sooner or later
it will all
Be Revealed

— — —

This prophecy applies
to the
Entire
Universe
Hurrah!

— — —

And the old ladies dying will walk thru the streets of Bloomfield Time Forever.

— — —

"Sometime I think it be better to pull the whole thing out!"
Said he of my bad tooth, this life.

"A tragic situation in which you are implicated, dr."

— — —

The Clown of Subjective Being

with wide mouth pounded in by dentist
since I chose to be
so advantageously human
with teeth—
doomed to dentistry
& Laughing as to disintegrate doom.

Sitting back in dentist's chair
Mouth open, wide circles
of anxiety painted round my lips
—leaning back into the void
pure facade of me—
and the whole of Appearances in front
draining into my mouth,
music, the old face of the Partner
with his bulbous nose, his hand,
his drills & hammers &
nurses
Pouring into my mouth &
disappearing beyond—

— — —

"You stole the void from me!"— Jack.

* * *

Woke up this moment and more
beautiful than poem is Elise standing
in dawn in middle of room in
black high on Mescaline—

Dream—Eleanor Roosevelt, Genet, & LeRoi Jones

A long road on the West side of Broadway in Paterson near the Synagogue—out toward the Foreign Beach house—like in Hong Kong or Casbah—the Corrupt Country Club—I get there by accident and someone tells me Jean Genet is that old fat man that came in from town on the same bus with me. Well Well Wow I think, and I go around to the basement to look for him to talk to him—one man I do talk to a fat fellow with paunch & blue coat & bald head—but it's not him he says it's another fellow I saw before, I go looking for the other fellow can't find him either—Maybe one of them wants to keep his identity secret . . . I am in a basement cooking soup still hoping to meet Genet—

Outside the window Mrs. Roosevelt comes in from her car to her door—I see it from my upstairs bowery furnished room—I go downstairs with LeRoi Jones to watch—She goes in her door—I suddenly break away from him & go to the door, push it open before it locks, in her basement foyer, and speak to her—she says one moment let me say hello to her grandchildren—and busies herself & her daughter & grandchildren while I wait at door to make my speech to her—I said I just want one minute to tell you something—

She comes back to the door—I lean over to her she's deaf & say—choking with tears—"I have remembered you & yr work and I want to say I love you what you have stood for and done and my name is Allen Ginsberg."

She cannot hear my message but from the way I look at her tenderly slightly tearful she sees I mean no harm in fact good and she's interested but can't hear a thing, would I please repeat my name.

Allen Ginsberg! Allen Ginsberg! I yell in her ear. She still can't hear a thing—I think for a minute maybe she never heard of him?—She gives me a pencil & paper to write it down.

I had been anxious that she know who I am that was trying to suck up to her—I take the papers she gives me—several sheets covered with her own notes—I can hardly find a space large enough to write my name—

The "minute" I asked for is already over and I'm getting panicked & maybe she's getting bored. LeRoi comes in the door & watches, at this whole point struggle is for me to tell her my name so she recognize it.

I look for a spot, write it and write it ALLENGINSBERG—but she can't distinguish the letters they are cramped together—I try again in another spot but I get ALLE as far as that & see there's writing under

what I wrote—"Alle the Nations" with ALL confusing my ALLEN.
I try another huge

but it still is really illegible and I'm getting desperate.
Alarm bell rings I wake.

Boston, December 1960—Journal Entry on Visit to Timothy Leary's House

Police [1]

I declare myself the Law
All man has Law in the soul
The ghosts of hungry dopes & worriers frightened in the Void are beating themselves up with nightsticks, with mahogany courts,
Their starveling lawyers pinch pince-nez'd at the Ritz or the Pierre—
With ribbons, billfolds, fresh air funds, electric chairs and blood
One hand at the eternal switch— shock, war & radiation, the human brain a gas chamber—
Banning of books, insolence of parole officers,
The old Prison librarian snipping lines out of loveletters in San Quentin—
"A nasty old fuck" with a pistol, Neal said—
The whole population plugged in to the central Government
By money, talkies, radio, newspapers, television, lottery banks & gossip,
Bigotry & despair, the Beauty walking the street like God—
Under the clouds, in his universe,
Able to see the eye in every forehead
Sleeping & waxy and the light gone inward
To a dream of the Fearful Jehovah or the Atom Bomb—
All these who are dancers in the memory of creation
All these Eternal Spirits to be wakened in the stores & alleyways

[1] Portions of this poem were integrated with "Television was a Baby Crawling Toward that Deathchamber," pp. 15-32 of *Planet News* (San Francisco: City Lights, 1968).

All these bodies to be touched and healed in their windows
All these Lacklove, all these suffering the Hate along avenues of rusty
bedsprings
All couch'd with Evil, dreaming of the Void,
All dumbed under the rainbow snowstorm streets created
in the Great City of Eternity the Heaven of Consciousness–
O Police the Means of Heaven are at hand,
Thy rocks & my rocks mean nought, black and white are one,
The Identity of the Moon is the Identity of the Flower Thief
I and the police are one in this Immortal Numbness–
Cocaine! Thy Hash! The Grass! The Dopes of Sleep and Wakenness,
The Consciousness become the brain itself
Staring from its Eye– As I found in bed naked
With Peter, and out my window, the blue skull of the Sky,
a star broken thru the Infinite, the birth of the Messiah
with wild hair near bald to the skull and half blind without eyeglasses,
but naked again in my body in this Universe where I was born,
Through Wagner's horns, the Summons of Die Walküre
Reminding me of the furthest hornèd star beyond the Circles of Inferno
And Lucifer that Milton sang Redeemer:
I seized power over the Universe, I seized the tablets of the Law,
I saw the Spectral Buddha and the spectral Christ
Turn to a stick of Shit in the Void, a fearful Idea.
I took the crown of the Idea and placed it on my head
And sat a king beside the reptile Devas of my Karma–
Naked, strode down stairs in the Science House & seized the phone– to
Mao Tse-tung, Stalin the Skull– The chicken Eisenhower,
Living soul of Kennedy or Norman Mailer or my father in Paterson–
interconnect their consciousness on the telephone
on TV, on the radio– everyone plugged in at once
announce the Coming Union of All Consciousness–
That we are the New Born God, the old creator, that we
take ship into the end of the Entire Universe,
That we on our vast home go visit the massed destiny red Archfire-
pitted sun–
Seen from afar in the Meadow– Seen in Aurora Borealis dream–
Kerouac! awaken– Seize power in the Universe, thou God!
Burroughs art thou yet in thine ancient body?–
To all that I loved alive– and that Unknown & all unspoken

Wept at in ecstasy, or spoken in fleeting pain
for these poor suffering bodies— Silent Joy.

– – –

Baudelaire would have liked Billie Holiday—

– – –

Memory—all memory re-echoing in the instant of the present—that's Baudelaire on the icebox, his youthful idealistic face growing old & pitted with knowledge, but still young him staring thru his suffering.—

Dream—

Peter dancing out half-naked smiling over the bed, I'm grasping him round middle with my eyebrow to his tit as he stretches over bed w/ new proposition, that we inaugurate a new sex thrill, no more than in one week a year, process of C.O.D.—sex C.O.D.—where I get to do anything I want, fuck him without return or payback, absolute action, get what I want.

Boston Dec. 1960

Otherwise earth's future is an upside-down candle—
the melted wax will kill the flame which burns upward
no matter how you hold the candle— the Atom bomb.

The way is not thru regulation of men by laws from above
but the inward illumination of each universal citizen—
Pound went mad trying to make up just laws for ignorant men
Educate the men to be themselves, their actions will follow more justly
than
Law imposed on them from outside.
Men must know, the answer is in men knowing.
Otherwise it's an Augean stable,
or Sisyphus stone of rationality & materialism.

– – –

I sit in a room in the country on the outskirts of Boston
a lone citizen— the air is filled with Radio waves
electronic messages from the Materialist organization

They want my taxes for a war, they want my brain to be their slave
as they are slaves of television
They want my body for their war against the Gods—
The world of the Future is here above my roof,
1960 has come with its apocalypse—
I am the lone citizen
all scattered over the land, the woken ones, the lone ones
who are the gods, waiting for their godhead to seize them
Waiting for one Messiah to revolt over the kings of earth & Heaven
and declare the Millenium is Now
all shall be Gods of this Dimension.
The old man in the Sky, the phantoms under the pavements & fields
have fled back to nothingness, are but rumors in the newspapers
and ravings of Death slaves—
The ones who have taken power in the normal world of Machine
are hungry ghosts who tried to find a body in this dimension
and fix it, hung up, like Jello in the webs of police.
They are apparitions of their own fear become real and are
at war among themselves.
This way or that way—
  the Controllers give the
  signal.
Lights out in Europe
Lights on in Asia
    Siren squawking over the
      building.

* * *

"I saw The Sunflower Monkeys of the Moon" [1]

I felt a hippopotamus hit me in the eye
I saw a donkey looking silly
at a Jackal they call Billy
and a green iguana hit
a grasshopper taking a shit
on a green gorilla walking with
a purpleass baboon

---

[1] Recollection & recreation of tape song (now in Kerouac archives) improvised with J.K. at his home.

I saw a rosy okapi upon the stream
I ate some okra-hominy in a sunbeam
I saw a silly zebra eating broccoli Cuba Libre
& an inky octopus inside the sea
in a little yellow bus came down to me
as I was a sittin on the morning eating Corn

I saw a butterfly-rhinoceros sit down
He had the biggest ass you ever saw upon the ground
I saw an elephant eat holy Poetry
the 'lectric eel he put a shock to me
the cockroach giraffe sat down to nap
The lion-dove, she took a crap
& the warthog-peacock folded up without a sound.

I saw an ant sit down & try to think
I saw a stringbean Jack-the-Ripper eat a girl—
I saw a purple spider slipping up a veil
while all the ants & bees were turning green
I saw a cockroach walking in my sink
fast as a bedbug & quick as a wink
I saw a hyena come & look in my ass, I saw a gink.

I saw the werewolf baby sucking caterpillar milk,
Walrus dripping on a pile of tiger silk
Buttercup unicorn donkey drinking asparagus juice with honey,
Hippogryph-mink blinking in despair of us
& the Siamese skunks were stinking up their ilk.

I saw the oyster-monster hiccup Nearer my God to Thee
A hummingbird lay 1000 yr. old eggs in her tree
I saw the pussy willow jackals & the upsydaisy vulture's tail
—Vice president of the cockroach hole come out to say hello
To the anteater on the sofa & the urchin skipping in the sea
But I was eating breakfast on the bedbug whale—
It had its foot stuck in my belly & its horse-ass jello in my toes

The serpent-daisy's pisshen'
& the phlox-fish is a squishen
& the Sperm-Behemoth breathing on my nose.

Dec. 23, 1960

"We might topple with the universe together"

"There's Frankenstein lets tie'm down to the ground & put leaves on top of him."—Lafcadio

Jack imitating Frankenstein giving an olive to Marie Orlovsky in Northport—Wagner's Liebestod on near Xmas. Machine in the kitchen, sunset light in the winter outside.

— — —

"The color of wind would come close to the color of water."—Lafcadio in answer to koan—What color is wind?

* * *

[Notes for "Journal Night Thoughts," pp. 9-14, *Planet News.*]

* * *

Dream—

The movie from 1930's—*Grapes of Wrath,* the *WPA Tragedy,* or *Mack Sennett of 1936*—the archetype culture movie that started my life—*B'way Scandals of 1938.*

In an open tent where the unemployed circus comes to the dust-bowl small-town—In walks my hero-heroine hermaphrodite—It's the familiar clown of my Infancy, the Beauty I adored, a weirdo, the 1930's tragic doll, Juke the Leer, Sammy the Queen, Longhair the Matinee Idol, Hepcat the Buzzard, Freek the Floon, Floosie the Mane, the Reverend Epicene, Joke Mope, Nobody—

He-she walks in—a feminine boyish face, real curious, round eyes & 1939's Brecht hair—I'm impressed—I remember him as the one I noticed in childhood—There he is in clown costume from the Freak show of the Circus, coming in under the awning of the breakfast tent for morning communication with the gang & audience—a round face like young Naomi, I gaze at him knowing my own amazement he's reincarnated in a movie-dream. Is he made up? I can't tell if it's a girl or boy or girlboy monster. He looks sweet—

Later he sits down after his screen test & I get a closer look—he gets up & in his own clothes moves past me I see his face he's got no eyes, and in décolleté dress, like a teen-age girl, has breasts—long breasts that push out against loose black-strap dress—The man moves past me to go by & think on the side outside the tent—the breasts are dull bibs without a nipple—

On the edge of a precipice we inhabit—I look down the Yosemite-like dizzying fall into the green valley—

Flocks of dove cats at the edge of the cliff lip step off—or dog birds—and meet their rivals from the opposite land cliff to fight in mid air.

They step off & tread the air they start falling I think they will plunge all to the bottom—but they are lifted up by air currents like airplanes—

Across the valley on the left side hanging from the height of a cliff is a house—It is pointed out that's where the green blindman lives & leans out—he steps off into air too—

Our magician dove-handler steps off with flock of doves to lead them to their faraway mid-air battle—a multitude of dovies—

He moves on a piece of raw delicate billowing silk—if the wind takes it down too far, he pushes compressed air button to make it a parachute-balloon & it floats up—when it goes too high he releases air & it collapses & brings him surrounded by dogdoves, down.

He goes way up above the level of our cliff edge, & releases the air to come down & float in.

I step off dragged by my own parachute—my teacher (Gary Cooper Young or Mr. Smith in Wash—the now-old man who was Mr. Liberal Deeds) rescues me by pulling my parachute back, but I have to relax he tells me, so the wind carries me back naturally without strain—If I strain I fall & maybe my parachute open & float me down maybe not—

Ah, it's open! a relief—but I can't relax & its dragging me *out*—over the edge of the cliff—he steps out over edge miraculously, grabs the parachute & brings me in—I see our map edge of the cliff like a swamp-tidal basin delta Amazon-from-air—seem untrustworthy lands-end.—I am in danger of stepping in and falling off—

I get back safe & am in kitchen of [Norman] Mailer's or [Julian] Beck's pad.

* * *

Waking at 4 a.m.—sense of unreality in cosmos—a babel of Turkish-Polish yelling. One voice downstairs in the street, my super's voice, "Ich machts it's the police—Policeman! Policeman! Its machts nichts mit guessen Policeman!" for five minutes insistently—I got up, finding myself in the shirt naked at ass—pulled up the shade to find out what noise that was—A man in middle age, in a white rocket-suit with blond-white hair in the moonlight climbing gingerly up the fire escape across the street, on 3rd floor by then, glancing up & down the street, estranged, ignoring the shouting from my apt. floor—testing & knocking on various darkened bolted windows as he cat-walked his way up the iron stairway—finally entering an open lighted window, disappeared. No more. What was that all about?

Reading—N.Y. 1960 Aug.

Von Hagen—Incas; Penguin on Incas
Peru—
Thos Wolfe—Selected Prose Portable
Book on Tibet—Alexandra David Neel
H.G. Wells—Short Outline of History
Wm. James—Modern Library Anthology Selections
Will Durant—Story of Philosophy (Kant & others)
The New Testament—Revised Modern Version

New York Aug. 1960

De Ropp—Drugs & the Mind
Huxley—Brave New World Revisited
W.Y. Evans-Wentz—Tibetan Book of the Dead
Paul Reps—Centering (In Zen Bones)

Later 1960

Herrigel—Zen Archery
Weston La Barre—Peyote Cult
Evans-Wentz—Great Liberation
Poetry books—Corso, Happy Birthday;
Jno. Williams—Empire Finals
Milton—Paradise Lost
Gil Sorrentino—The Darkness Surrounds Us

Jan 3, 1961—Dream

In a farmhouse in France, I stumble on an old man, painter, high ceilinged old barn studio—it's Matisse, ancient & tough-stringed neck, with black hat & scarf, and his wife—I'm awed to see him still alive like a dark skeleton pursuing his images on canvas, bright colors—his wife takes me around & I sit at table over tea & talk with him. The house is obscure & vast & he is out of the world & very somber tho friendly spirit.

Jan. 6

[First text of "Who will take over the Universe?", *Planet News,* pp. 7–8]

Jan 8—

Cosmic plots—who's going to take over the Universe—the shade of J.F. Dulles hovers over America grim skeletal spectre pointing to the doom.

* * *

Laugh Gas XYZ—

"We are involved in great high sounding consequences"—

"Dentist's"—spitting out the sound S—
A series of "reflex" reflected gestures—*repeated*—as if it had been done exactly the same before—anticipating—as if everything were being eliminated by a process of elimination as if life were a process of elimination rather than accretion . . .

There are different levels of conscious being.

What is happening on one level intersects what is happening on another level.

Where they meet & cross you get thrill of sense of harmony & unity of different levels of conscious being

—hoping for the intersection of all the different levels at the same *time.*

Which can happen only *once?*

Dream:

In Africa, looking for a lawyer, over the tar pit fields, I follow woman analyst guide—she leads me out to open sea—as if in Venice in a motorboat we ride hither & yon in Backstreets then finally we reach a place the sea begins—

Emerging up from 3rd class to First on great oceanliner—up the staircase to the deck—First thing I meet, huge faded negro Paul Robeson—in officer's uniform—I salute him introducing myself which doesn't mean much to him—he bows—I begin scheming immediately—Being a big officer Communist negro all these years perhaps he could get me a book in the NMU so I can ship out? I see he's working on an open deck hole with a lift truck & wire lift placing faded 2nd hand turkish rugs in the hold—Old communist, I notice I am amazed at his calm—he is folding the dead in to carry that way (Won't they not smell up the

But his demeanor is the same manly one, only not schizophrenic & garbo-legal talking, After he leaves with his Companion, I suggest something strange has happened — They've been already all ports in Mediterranean & are now returning back — have been to Algiers — I say I lived awhile in Tangier — Mailer goes down to Cabin, I follow

Norman Mailer dream illustration

exported carpets?)—I see one corpse in the hold lying face up on rug, he's getting a layer of carpet to cover that. The corpse is a middle-aged man dead-faced & slightly rotten lying on a rug drest in a blue business suit. I wonder if I have the guts to face corpses like that negro communist.

Up walks several men, one I recognize & talk to—a middle-aged—perhaps Robert Lowell—but novelist—only later do I recognize Norman Mailer's on the same boat, first class, all along—He's wearing feminine bloomer clothes—a shirt that makes a lollypop round the hips & the breast—But his demeanor is the same manly one, only more schiza-mysterious & garbo-esque. Talking, after he leaves, with his companion, I suggest something strange has happened—They've already been to all ports in Mediterranean & are now returning back—have been to Algiers—I say I lived a while in Tanger—Mailer goes down to cabin, I follow.

Underground in the Chic Wards—a cage where baby is kept, a double cage. The left cage for the bigger kid who baby-sits for the smaller one, we take one kid out—I think so I can have a place to sleep now in First Class & replace the other—Some complex dream hassle.

Going downstairs to Mess I sit next to Mailer who's brought his novelist's portfolio & is working on it—I decide to talk to him about his fantastic female dress and male body at the moment—he remains aloof & inviting & open.

Jack: "Massachusetts is Fulla Queers

. . . in many a morphine reverie in a broken-down
  bed in Panama it has been revealed
    that the cunt is an inverted cock,
    inside out . . . a room with a pink dresser—

The rhinoceros has warts on its tits—

Ma Rainey's last lover— Bob Donlin—
Marxist critics— their cocks are covered with
the blood of Mayakovsky & Yesenin."

"Like Proust be an old teahead of time"— J.K.

Jan. 26— Lying in bed
with the black cat at my hip
and a cigarette stuck between fingers on the book—
There is a Portugese luxury liner [1]
running between Havana & Caracas
outwitting the US Navy in pursuit
the rebel captain peering thru night binoculars,
Lights and radio dit dat rapping warnings
that the New York Times
is after them with Murder—
Headlines all over America
Messages sent thru the stormy Aether
Brass Bands of Imagination
readying the torpedoes and spybombs—
In Guatemala they just shot 100 anonymous
heroes to someone—
Someone must write the Editorials I read
today in the News—
The giraffe bent down its head between the bars
and ate the peanut from my palm
with long black lips
and hot glue drip from his tongue—
That's when they raided the Cuban Embassy
in Lima
and Absolute J. Whitehair arrived at the
US Information Service
with 20,000 dollars worth of
Readers Digest in Spanish

---

[1] The *Santa Maria,* seized in Jan. 1961 by 29 dissidents protesting the oppressive rule of Portuguese dictator Salazar. "... Portugal's water is running in all the faucets on the *S.S. Santa Maria,*" a line in "Television was a Baby Crawling Toward that Deathchamber" (p. 29, *Planet News)* refers to the captain's attempt to foil the rebels by draining the fresh water supply. Nevertheless, for 12 days the *Santa Maria* remained in rebel hands, outwitting all pursuers, until the rebel leader Galvão brought it to the Brazilian seaport Recife, where he and his men were given permanent asylum by the Brazilian government. During and following this period of time uprisings in Angola were subdued by massacre.

– They found no evidence the Cubans were sending
      propaganda to the Communists
and every Newspaper in America took a
            purple shit–
Mobs of Buffalos beat up the Peruvian
            red intellectuals
      who went home crying into their Lorca–
O what Hatred!
      the US does it all by Force
                  where it don't pay off in Martinis.

Dream, Jan. 28, 1960–

We are attempting to preserve the life of the patient by any means–

In London–on the foggy superstructure of a ferryboat I wander around in disguise take off my glasses (because of fogging lenses?) & put them in my pocket, take off my coat in the heat, and station myself near the top passageway which overlooks part of the supreme rectangle or topdeck square of a huge parallelogram set of crossbars in which some sailor Monkeys are participating in an experiment.

I had wandered with my adopted family across Epping Field, thru Boston Terminal, and down the meadow in Cézanne's Bathers (memory of small family seen in distance). I'd parted from them to complete my investigation. I am a member of a Cosmic FBI.

The performance is over, I find my way back from the foggy passageways–but I have lost my glasses–I discover them in the pocket of my coat, the ear pieces broken but they fit & I can see again.

I go back to the regular level of the RR station & see the Channel-Riverside train–that's closed off by customs inspectors so I know that's not the way back to center of town.

I'm expecting to find my family so I turn into a fat little 13 year old girl & report my predicament to the Station Bobby–I see my family of 3 somewhere near a salt water Taffy Stand.

Meanwhile I am in bed with Peter in my sleep. I pull down his pants & pull up his T shirt exposing his whole body to be felt & embraced and run over by my naked hands and legs–This seems part of a medical operation I am performing in conjunction with my role as cosmic-detective-agent-Doctor.

I wake up realizing "We are attempting to prolong the life of the patient—the human race—by any means"—as my report to central headquarters—that being the purport of activities as visionary dreamer poet queer drug-taker politician schemer lost soul.

* * *

Before Sleeping a title—
"A Whole Bunch of Poems"—

* * *

Square = Rigid

Feb. 5, 1961

Dream of Dr. Grossman (the Junkies Doctor)—Begins in huge new apartment owned by a couple—the Becks—they just moved in—I explore it a huge central living room, then several large size bedrooms, and am wandering around exploring it amazed by how it has two separate apartments parts in one—

This links to various apartment dreams before—one in which Eugene has an apartment in 115th St. with huge one room,

one in which I have a rotten coldwater flat on side of elevated line in the Bronx—

—As I walk thru, Judith Malina shows me how every room has simple radio connection linked in with central radio to pipe music all over the house even uninhabited rooms (to chase demons away).

There is a fire, we all go away on a bus,—we see in front of us after several miles thru the city, a big higher apartment, modern as Mexico, with their top floor aflame—it's a familiar place—I see a doctor figure in the window next door standing back as yet oblivious to the destruction—The passengers behind me all notice it's none other than Grossman's high office—

Grossman is downstairs—fires in both his apartment & his office the same day looks suspicious—maybe he *is* a crook—

He's bewildered on the street below surrounded by people—I rush up & embrace him, hold his head, give him sympathy—he likes it—guilty or not—I see it makes no difference whether he's guilty or not, he needs sympathy or understanding—needs to be patted on head so not feel totally alone. In his blue business suit and middle-aged head.

* * *

(See Dream E.R., pp. 167–168)

Met Eleanor Roosevelt outside of dream—intending to give her Lindesmith's book on Narcotics [1] & explain to ask her help fight govt. on reform—banking on hope she would recognize me, be curious, eye me & talk would go on from there.

Introduced at Dorothy Norman's, we shook hands, she stared myopic & said very deeply "I'm pleased to meet you" and turned to be introduced to a dozen other people.

Then in a moment of silence where others' attention was lax & she was standing, stooped, eighty, looking into space, wondering where next, I stepped over to her to talk—she looked at me—expectantly

"I write poetry"

"Oh do you how very wonderful" she said.

That ended that—absolute blank just as in the dream of the meeting.

So I explained, correctly & rather excessively formally, I wanted ½ hr. of her time in next month to explain a "social problem" to her.

She said yes, but asked which—I said Narcotics she said she knew nothing about Narco but would be glad to make appointment if I write her.

* * *

There's a lot of nonsense in those snowballs
    The violin scraping in the dry barn

Feb. 1961

Policewomen looking up the tragic brown ass of Billie Holiday
As her body disintegrated sighing in the hospital
She sang the most sophisticated blues in the world
Lester Young brooding in an army stockade, blips and buzzings of war
        jazz bugging his orient Ear,
Thin white heroes, softvoiced Chet Baker, desperate in Texas
tormented by cynical detectives hypnotized by the bloodless spectre of
        Hearst
putting their hands on his naked belly,
Thelonius Monk immortal on the floor of a white restaurant

---

[1] Alfred R. Lindesmith's landmark sociological study of the corrupt basis & practices of narcotics police: *The Addict and the Law* (Bloomington: Indiana University Press, 1965, paperback edition).

waiting State Cops bust him for possession of Silence—
all the shy horror of the Baroness faced with America doped with hate—
Emile Zola musing in a café in Soho, Lumumba beaten up by a Chinese
Cop from Idaho—
a man named Fred Waring smiling & waving his baton in the White
House
to amuse the long-toothed ambassadors from Portugal & Russia—
"Daughter of Zion, Judah the Lion, John the Revelator"
"Roosevelt's in the White House, he's doin' his bes'—"
Ike's on the Golf field, Ginsberg's in the dentist's chair departing in Gas;
It's all a bunch of horseshit you read in the Newspapers
and they lie and they lie and they lie and they're lying to me—
They're lying to me, and I am the Truth Cloud changing my shape
I am a learned poet defending myself from a magic octopus
Naming the names of the Damned: America fucked up the ass by the
Daily News—
I'm on the Battlefield for my Lord: Come on everybody
Lets drive the cosmic pederasts from the airwaves & eat Joe McCarthy for
breakfast in the Bardo Thodol,
I'm sick of suffering thru my only life in this Kalpa,
Anslinger sticks pins in dolls made of my shit—
Who *are* the centers of Power?
America 5% of world population eats 80% of the World Machinery
and gets more silly every year; Hurrah for the Australian Aborigines!
They got one all-purpose stick to wave at Eternity—
Notched for counting, cupped for eating, arch'd for throwing, solid as a
pillow—
They got the least Claim on the Empire State Building—
If we believe in this world lets live in it together, like Huncke,
otherwise let's join the pataphysical Aborigines and shut up about
progress.
"Walking on water wasn't built in a day," Kerouac said to Leary.
Moon voices on 1927 records are broken in MacDougal tombs of
Gaslight Café.
My harp is hitting the exquisite, let's play Jizzum—
Let's thrill our assholes, let's put nipples on dreams
Let's put our buttocks in the library, lets have spit in our hair when we
speak Civics,
let's lynch the hungry ghosts of Capitalism to the nearest thought,
flush the toilet on my brainwash, eat god's shit in public,

show dead bodies on television, bloated in the Mekong River and
waving in starvation from Chinese railroad tracks,
teach Buchenwald in Harvard, teach Guatemalan history in Passaic High
School—
teach Tantric Buddhism to the workers of Pinsk— let's teach Rimbaud in
Harrar,
Let's fuck in public if we want to, let's go naked in the summer in New
York,
eat in cafeterias wearing daisies and discussing Marxist Boxes
go thru the phonebook & let anyone say what he wants on TV,
mass-communicate the Poets, let Jake Marx be paranoiac on the national
network,
Give me my own program I'll interview Bill Heine for real,
about faggots' weirdness and the dangers of Pop Methedrine—. . .
Let's do *anything*— we're all human beings aged 32—
"Let's shit out the window," cry a million voices, "at the moon!"
Make a billion noises over the telephone— The man who dropped the
Atom Bomb
wound up in the bughouse, I'll give him my cat if he feels better—
Let's hit him with a pillow & forgive his mother— forgive Hitler too,
Eichmann to commute from a Kibbutz in Levittown
put a big fat naked statue of Goering shooting Morphine up on
Brandenburg Gate—
I'm ready for anything but the Bomb,
I'll even be an Indian and eat peyote on Sunday,
I'll even get married & have visions—

Dream March 15, 1961—6 a.m. (Read Dürrenmatt's *The Tunnel)*

In a motor boat, approaching the city, a boy is on the bow, dives into the water, the boat runs over him as he sinks near the shore—this the preliminary to the magic dream—

He is afraid of what's in the water—snakes & gliding things, sea monsters & tortoises surround him—

I am in a grotto with a friendly Bear-Spirit or Reptile Spirit with whom I've made a pact.

I have several rings on my finger. As long as I have them there everyone is safe.

One is a simple silver circle with figures enworked, hanging loosely from my right forefinger. On my left hand, I have one colored ring in particular, of a serpent with Jewel eyes—

My friend Spirit points out that his power is over the tortoises and snakes—the reptiles & serpents!—and that I am under his protection as long as the snake-king's ring on my finger is quiet & shows no danger—but that now

the snake's jewel eyes are shining and flashing red.

I have a vision of huge Tortoise-Gods together in assembly standing upright whirling in slow motion in silhouette like tops—with their victim—the boy who dived (died) or myself at the center of their shadowy Indian dance—

"I call a Conference of the Tortoises," I exclaim!

These tortoises are figures of Wisdom & Longevity—

"I call on the tortoises of Eternity to appear and give me their wisdom!"

This seems to me the way out thru magic inspiration—a summoning up of the weird spirits of power & truth I have heard of legendarily & whose ring I am wearing which is now shining red in the eyes, to my danger, as is explained me—

Connected with Communist letter to Evergreen calling for political action.

This was in a gypsy grotto.

* * *

Harry Smith—300½ E. 75 St. N.Y.C.

[Suggested Titles for What Later Became "Heaven & Earth Magic Feature":] [1]

Eyeball Head Poem, Asshole Homunculus Eyeball, Mandala Water-

---

[1] A.G., 1975.

melon, Hammer Dog, Eyeball Vomit, The Vomiting Lesson, A Bee in an Egg, Reptile Consciousness of Machines.

* * *

Scrap Leaves: Journals, March 1961

But I have tried to speak
    to this unholy nation
and my spirit weakens &
    sees only its own death...
this planet of madmen
    whirling to their destruction
sending electric signals
    like cold ice outward...
beeping out of antennae the
Daily press clatter
    yowl of warped
    radios blip static
    hate over television
The swaying noisyness of
    mass mind formed
    by electricity
surges in waves of
    steel to surround us
clacketing reasons for myriad
    bomb-trigger—
Over the Atlantic Blakean
    ocean of Space
Seraphim summon each
    other to Apocalypse
flared over buildings,
    shadowed over aluminum
    brightest towers...
Who knows the terror of
    the wrath to come?
Who knows the Joys of
    waiting sages and
    sufferers

Who knows the banquet
    billions hungrily
    await in their dark
        beds in India—?
One Eye Sees All— the Hate
    and thwarted Joy—

* * *

V
THE MEDITERRANEAN

March 23, 1961—February 11, 1962

Peter Orlovsky, Allen Ginsberg, and S.S. America *dining mates*

Mar 23 1961

S.S. America
O look!
Manhattan is gone—
snows over the
flats of Bklyn.

★ ★ ★

"Waving goodbye
I lost my arm
in the snow"— P.O.

★ ★ ★

At the dock, Elise peering over her eyeglasses, Janine whitefaced blond in black jacket waving scarf, & Lafcadio with half smile, fluttering a straw hat ambiguously—Peter above deck cupping his hand to heart in a Russian cap—and when I called their names I saw them, drifting away with their skulls.

I shd mention, it was a rainy day, empire state wrapped in eternal mist—my feet got wet on the bow in all the sleet green deck.

★ ★ ★

I could issue manifestos summoning seraphim to revolt against the Heavenly State we're in, or trumpets to summon American mankind to rebellion against the Authority which has frozen all skulls in the cold war,

That is, I could, make sense, invoke politics and try organize a union of opinion about what to do to Cuba, China, Russia, Bolivia, New Jersey, etc.

However since in America the folks are convinced their heaven is all right, those manifestos make no dent except in giving authority & courage to the small band of hipsters who are disaffected like gentle socialists. Meanwhile the masses the proletariat the people are smug and the source of the great Wrong.

So the means then is to communicate to the grand majority—and say I or anybody did write a balanced documented account not only of the lives of America but the basic theoretical split from the human body as Reich has done—

But the people are so entrenched in their present livelyhood that all the facts in the world—such as that China will be ¼ of world pop makes no impression at all as a national political fact that intelligent people can take counsel on and deal with humorously & with magnificence.

So that my task as a politician is to dynamite the emotional rockbed of inertia and spiritual deadness that hangs over the cities and makes everybody unconsciously afraid of the cops—

To enter the Soul on a personal level and *shake* the emotion with the Image of some giant reality—of any kind however irrelevant to transient political issue—to touch & wake the soul again—

That soul which is asleep or hidden in armor or unable to manifest itself as free life of God on earth—

To remind by chord of deep groan of the Unknown to most Soul—

then further politics will take place when people seize power over their universe and end the long dependence on an external authority or rhetorical set sociable emotions—so fixed they don't admit basic personal life changes—like not being afraid of jails and penury, while wandering thru gardens in high civilization.

* * *

Imagine all that *enormous* civilization of those great ocean liners to transport a bunch of bores over the ocean.

* * *

"I hope America will still be there when we get back."

* * *

Dream of long  worm in my breast crawling to my neck, serrations rippling on the skin—I pluck it out part thru a raw gooey hole—only get segments—Peter presses knife to my skin & cuts off the tail—

PARIS

April 8, 1961 Sat. nite–

In bed naked in chamber of 9 Gît-le-Coeur again—all the grey stains of Paris buildings familiar outside, cars racing around the corner down the cobble roadway along the Seine.

April 9–

What's left? Nothing but this body with reproductive organs
Eyes ears nose— to stare hear smell the floor hall sky
other bodies with the same empty mind
What can we apprehend but our own emptiness?
That we exist—Ca Ca!—What for? to reproduce ourselves?
Me? Reproduce myself? Never!
The trial of existence is a complete failure
To have entered heroin in my body
and lie in Paris bed in black bathrobe with thoughts flitting thru my reproductive organs—

———

The great snake from 0000 to 1961 which many have entered & left
Streams forward inching on itself thru a million eyes—
Does this great being want to continue with me?
Do I even like this snake that for all I know
will only end up chewing its own tail?
I who masturbate and will die?
Can it do better than masturbate?
Will this being ever meet another and a fuck of suns
create a new sprite Universe in some other dimension
where it wont have to shit all over itself to exist?
Where can I leap out of my consciousness but to Death?
The only reason to have a baby is it works out logically.
What, does this machine work by logic too?
or is its head between my legs,
its pensées every orgasm leaping from man to man thru centuries toward bigger eyes and ears & smaller feet
and a huge cock to carry them on?

April 13, 1961

Artaud expresses himself
like a can of spy-being,
exploded.

— — —

. . . The beasts! They would not even
stop their iron Guillotine
in mid-flight down its carpenter-made frame—
by the stroke and final squiggle of a pen
the blink of an eye,
the sigh of a single bethought-me

— — —

Agh! The Ants work hard,
cruel impoverished system
they have become on their silent hill—

— — —

Aux Deux Magots I did not destroy
a black & static insect
that lit upside down by my cup,
clung to my finger till I blew it off
and landed like a fraternity pin
on that tall Dutch blond's mink jacket

— — —

Message from Subconscious— which
exists, is here—
I am waiting in bed for the great moment, naked.

— — —

. . . At this moment Tibet which possessed all
Secrets
is destroyed
by the Ant men—

— — —

. . . You are me, God—
Artaud alone made accusation
against America,
Before me, Whitman saw Space—
Poe Night ahead—
and Emily Dropt a tear into Eternity—

ONE DAY

One day
one day I will speak of
twelve years before I finally write this down
One day in my high chamber in Harlem
six floors up to the sky
in a cold water flat covered with books
isolate from all Manhattan I didn't
know what to do
I cooked my mind in a frying pan
I shopped for breast in the butcher
I ate my vegetable thoughts from
a pot on the stove
I walked up & down Espin Harlem
One day I lay in my bed
with my cheap pants down
hairy thin legs exposed
genitals under my eye
organs of reproduction black and red
in the mirror
As I read William Blake
in Innocence
That day I heard Blake's voice
I say I heard Blake's voice
There was something wrong with me,
aural hallucination
the reconstruction of syllables on
printed page in iron rhythm
rose to my ear— an ancient
Voice
I heard a physical voice
that was not an hallucination

That voice said Ah Sunflower weary
of Time
A voice
a physical voice in the room
because I had come on my lap
because I had rested because my
mind wandered afar
It spoke aloud from its Center
one human voice that sounded like an Eye—
that made the world visible in my 21st year
all twenty years before a dream-life
waiting for this Blink
of Consciousness
known by St. John of the Cross
known by great Socrates whose air horse
ascends in the spectral tornado.
No man can deny I had a Vision
and I do not lie
so that my skull is cracked open
and I will crack open your skull
as Blake's skull spoke to mine
and said they arise from their graves
and I saw all billions of ant skulls and
men alive at once in Kosmos
waving and seething
I have seen Miracles, heard Miracles
within Miracles—
This was the first real miracle
Documented
I screamed on the fire escape later
before Witnesses
Trying to disturb the balance of consciousness
in this lonely century
Everyone sick—
The second Vision— the Worm whose love
is death, a minute later
—I could see the buildings I described
mainly the cornices curling in
Great Spacious Presence—
Manbrain!

And because I am not now in
a state of Vision
and I despair age 34 attaining that moment again
I defy my own consciousness in words
because going to die I
write my message and transmit
this fake Eternal Mind
thru memory of what I living once saw.
Albeit this confession sounds bad
it is good
better than silence
because I wish to express thee a Miracle
at last, Man—
merely by writing it down
for Poetry is the secret formula for
miracles—
No lesser purpose for my art
But Hope which is a stupid Miracle itself
Bong! Next day I walked up & down
the kitchen floor
incanting monosyllables to the Great Spirit
that it appear again— and the
room thrilled with terror
and belief so I stopped before I went
too far
The room changed and became significant
not my kitchen
but the place where I summoned the
Spirit
my Church where croaky Transcendency
uglied my thoughts—
and rushed out on the street ringing
with churchbells in Harlem—

Then to campus— "See you around the
campus" I cried a million
years later in Paris—
There in Columbia bookstore
surrounded by beasts whose eyes
see all

I woke up again, afraid to speak to
      those wild creatures in the room
that were only shoppers, readers,
      divinators, and the salesmen
      that served their books for gold—
One man had an eye descended from horses
another a dragon's-eye stare at the cash register
The horseye looked at me & I dropped
      my glance, I knew him
            old faker

Later walking round the football field
I summoned up again the Ghost of the Universe
and it came . . .
as if the sky revolved in cancerous vertigo
   and sucked my death out of my ear,
      it scared me— afraid to
         go into the living darkness.

*   *   *

Bay of Pigs

Cuba full of blood guns tonite people scream
Screams in Quito, bombs in Santiago, grief in Peru
where the director of Instituto de Arte Contemporaneo's fired
Communist party outlawed; Marsha
      sits at her desk in the embassy
            embarrassed—
Now is the time to resign from the US
      Government Adlai Stevenson
Don't sit there in the UN telling lies—
Hush Hush Camps in Florida covered with reptilian Silence
angry boys in blotched & nameless army greens
      have drifted into the morning
            mist
outside the Lunar Isles
            I sailed by
years ago & noted the green wave . . .
                  The US Government
Issue labels were censored by the *Daily News*,

The Eagle wiped from space before
exile shoulders entered the Shirt [1]
Miguel Ydigoras Fuentes swallows
his training camps alive
and denies the existence of matter—
Didn't US Guerilla Sergeants bark their
submarine orders at the edge of
this Pacific?
Subhuman lies
US firms 24 hr a day contract
sturdy concrete over old runways
5,000 ft. airstrip for Eleanor
Roosevelt's B-26
& Mamie's DC-6.
Workers and materials imported from
Gettysburg & Concord Bridge
Thoreau screaming in his American
graveyard
waiting to sink his bony jaw into
Ike's phantom skull—
Commando training camp 110 miles away in
Guatemala
"as the base grew experts were summoned"
Troops vanished a week ago
also from the Gold Coast of Florida
also from the Gulf Shore on La.— abandoned &
disused airfields
Volunteers assembled in the Florida
Keys
Opa-locka Fla. enters the struggle against
Lenin's Ghost—
surplus Marine Corps station
—paratroops, D Day trainees, Fishboat fleets'
dynamite saboteurs
Mounted to excited climax on p. 7
numbered tickets, blue-caps in relay
They never return from there

---

[1] U.S. govt. issue labels were eagles on shirts worn by anti-Castro Bay of Pigs Cuban invaders.

Central American Isthmus or Carib Isle
Organization: Wash DC & New York
Communiqués issued avec cooperation
US Wire Service
Instant Communication with Dean Rusk or
Allen Dulles
who reports to Master Kennedy
drawing his bath in the White House
to cleanse that good looking body
At last a fucker in the White House
that was supposed to be a good sign—
Poor Claude crucified at wire service
Should I take a gun and fight
for Cuba? Issue Proclamations from
Havana?
denouncing my father & all my Aunts
& Uncles in Newark?
Kerouac, self, Trilling, Podhoretz, Mailer
Brustein, Sulzberger
your taxes are paying for this
monster of gristle & still
Piling up in Havana
the bones of phantom
taxicabs
Remember the Maine!
No I don't know what to do,
the riot squad is running America
the liberals are bankrupt,
Kennedy the boy-man advertising
fruit caught starting a war,
Denying his responsibility in
crazy headlines—
No excuse for Adlai; Horror in the
New York Post,
Mumblings & Grunts in the N Y Times
Murderous deathical screeches from
the Hearst & News
Dinosaur claws all over their
eolithic pages—

Squishing & sneezings & bleedings
& menstrual cramp &
b.o. and dandruff and carpark
crash and bad feet
and chewgum & Death from Vox Populi
and belching & noisy jurisdictions
from 1,000,000 lawyers—
Coaldust over John L. Lewis' cheek
Henry Kaiser Khrushchev Cyrus Eaton
Edw G. Robinson
Adolphe Menjou Ethel Merman Frank
Sinatra
COMPROMISED
with the Dove,
Gabriel Heatter with knife at
the foot of an immense Lamb,

WE ARE ALL DAMNED TO HELL.

April 13, 1961—Paris

* * *

Ezra Pound—the Jews care only about Jerusalem—

* * *

Death is the silence
between songs
of Billie Holiday's
olden Golden Days.

* * *

[First text of "This form of life needs Sex," pp. 33–35, *Planet News*]

* * *

On RR to Cannes from Paris all shooting in the head me & Allen Eager [1] pissing together he w/ his big man cock & long needle and hard varicose like arm veins—then later after cokes & cigarettes & talk rocking on clack roar racket on my arms my head my feet in Peter's lap dark, an armored knight in all panoply & flag with lance & purpose to conquer and chain mail hanging from his mediaeval horse—charges up to the

[1] Celebrated post-bop tenor saxophonist, friend of Kerouac.

target toilet victory and on the other side of death turns into a dust-mote—as the bowery beggar crawling up to a well with a bloody head to snore himself to oblivion—equally victorious, a dust mote:

So what good racket and machinery to change the world movies, Fame & rushing up & down the Paris streets gossiping about tank revolutions on the outskirts—all resolved in dust motes—Why compare myself with Gregory and argue his glory against my sloth—But will his alert dust mote be brighter than mine unless I polish up my shoes in life? O Lifeshoe what next step?

Alan Ansen & Greg on the nod, a big moon, Annie Campbell [1] with her feet across the compartment in boots, moustache Jerry walking about in the aisle smoking Robt Burns on the road to Marseilles—looking for a job in the shadows. *(Quai des Brumes)*

Yet the pageantry beckons its own beauty irrespective stomping on the dust. Cries of Princesses and Cuban girls scream across the Atlantic, angry Holé's caroming in the Carib,—I left my crib & walked down the hall & set fire in the wastebasket—

and also

since "the book may be written but not read"—what magic to be alive for this and that 70 years, enter freely into the strange mortal playground and issue orders to the Universe, send out directions like the captain of the galley of the Cosmos, send my food upstairs, eat at the Skippers table and ride on trains to Marseilles arguing with Peter & Gregory, all sniff junk & eating apples.

Cannes May 5, 1961

Last shot of junk brought from Paris—Film festival, blue bar, sitting at table coffee—

To have to leave life
my nose against Peter's arm
the dawn over— out the window
    the tall white apartment
  by the curve of Golfe-Juan
– and the stars, never again—
and the movie people vanished into the box office
    and eaten by ticket machines—

[1] Corso's lady of those days.

and my father, arm waving goodby
at the old days,
Lucien registering at Columbia unbeknownst to me—
and the music of his door across the hall—
and ships over the Atlantic, mambo
off Cuba in the blue Float
and golden sun—
the arc of Poetry over all, & the nimbus
of my genitals & deep asshole—
a lonely ghost, unbidden, children
gone goodby— thru the Hall,
thru afternoons in English novels
walking carpets, waving wands
at the moon
or pointing the finger by the eyebrow
upward, in argument
war headline in a Paris café, newspaper
left in the chair—
To let it all begone, love lights in old cafeterias,
bellies stretching over beds,
assholes
assholes
assholes
assholes
Sheila's cock, "it's going to be a
nice day tomorrow"—
standing on the jetty, water coming—
& Peter alone,
returning to the source,
the play where that began,
shorn, blind, deaf
can't open the mouth, at last the touch fading
to solitude
and nowhere more to go—
and even that memory drift like a
cloud to another universe
of yesterday— who'll
say Goodby?
A meditation upon death in Golfe-Juan—
"A lonely ghost the ghost is/that to God shall come" —Yeats' Crazy Jane

Dream

Packing up to go, three in a car, leaving the city—me, Peter, some girl, Gary Goodrow[1]—I'm in old shop run by beautiful 1890 woman—she moves over behind the counter when I ask for cigarettes—has to push junk off counter helped by her fat white roll-sleeve-shirt assistant—the ciggyboos are kept in counter under the trash locked behind a wooden board—which has round handle like oldfashioned US snaplocks—rummaging inside I bring up some "Chanticleer" cigarettes & some Chesterfields—a large pack of 100 Chestys—bigger at bottom than at top—I get one or another after hesitation—then we're back in car—I had found some shoes, it was originally a shoestore—big red slipper shoes and some regular ones—the big red ones I not sure fit me—we get in car to go and I worry have we got everything out of our room—our room?—earlier in the dream related to all dream furnished rooms back to 114th Street Eugene's room—I suddenly announce that shoes fit, and we drive off after I get in car.—

May 27, 1961—Saint-Tropez

FUNERAL VOMIT

of the most luxurious mushroom sauce
laying out in sunshine on Epi-Plage
listening to my Ray Charles croak goofing
    with a big bunch of french sissies
"I want to get out" he pleaded
But the dragon chariot's gone to another Aeon
Nobody knows the goodlooking chauffeur
    except a telephone number I forgot
The same day Machine cracked the Dresden Codex
Kennedy numbered the years of the moon
Stern leaned on his aluminum cane in cold halls
        of 18th century

---

[1] Actor originally with Living Theater; helped organize "The Committee," S.F. (North Beach) night club featuring topical radical revues.

a murderous sportscar pulled into Saint-Tropez
with packs of amateur heroin—
When I leaned back on the couch I remembered:
it never happened
That's why it's always the same— I've never
been here before
and everytime it will always be different, forever
Till the last time it's so different from
all before
that it'll be the last time
and they'll trudge downstairs with my coffin
into the street
and outskirts of Newark where they speak in English
and my stone goes on the nod
cut to my prescription: Eternity is always high—
all ways lead to the same phenomena
Nescience ties its long black shoelaces in the dark
and steps out over the cliff
into another dimension with the same old jazz
"I want to get out"
It's a blues for junkies
on a cracked record repeating my shouted "forever!"
And where did I go?
ask the grass, ask my liver, ask my poetry, ask
Peter Orlovsky,
ask the Marx Bros. or the Man in the Moon,
ask anybody but me, I'm dead
and I dont know my own answer
Except I know Eternity is sounding dreadful
like airplane noise this minute
Until it gets to be nothing at all but eardrums
And eyeballs blinking over the clothespins
at the déjà vu of flies on a
newspaper
or a dirty asshole being the whole answer
to the sins of America,
— anything you chose, within reason.
And that stretches thru every probability
up to being born at all— Myself,

I graduated college and began counting
up all the machinery to make a living,
and being a failure at that, accepted the
Cross of Poetry, thinking that
was the sum total of Ambition—
only to find myself 21 years later
in the same ill-fitting clothes
a famous personal American in the Port
of Saint-Tropez among the rich
eating lobsters & scotch and worried about
my figure in a cute blue bikini—
with all my problems solved except
what am I doing here
and what next for kicks on earth
except India and later death
and not even that certain, they deciphered
the Madrid Codex too
and gave me hallucinations it took 200 hours
on the thinking machine to duplicate
legible in futurity just so I can be Immortal—
the right being at the right time hanging my world on a Prophecy:
the U.S.A. will legalize pot & go thru paranoia
as who wouldn't faced with being
part of the human race
about to explore the Universe & enter the
4th Dimension
when all it wanted was to be able to
eat good clean pork chops
and be a family with ants & uncles slowly
born & suddenly to die,
avec Yiddish and Chinese high documents
somewhere else in History—
Who would have thought to enter the burning
bush & be God?
Take it away, I want to get out, you always got
yourself to blame,
Stop making such a racket, be still and know
that I Am etc.

* * *

Mad Jump—

O La La
Charlie zigzags down the staircase drunk
old fat man with gout-foot bandage snores by the mineral-water fount
old proper dame with straw hat busts a thought in the lobby
old hotel creaks with elevators caging cranks & bellboys
rushing up & down the stairs—
the Chinaman is drunk in the room off the hall—
the maid sneaks a whiff of ammonia in the closet,
rooks crow over the roof
the moon is yellow half above the mimosa
& Chaplin flops over the bandagefoot on his face in the feminine lap of
money.

30 May '61

Sitting at bottom of R.R. station steps in Marseilles in café drinking tea-lemon looking at the green June trees. Yesterday in Aix comparing postcard Cézanne reproduction with Sainte-Victoire and measuring each brushstroke to a geological epoch. Went to Avenue Paul-Cézanne & stole into his studio—the cracked white hat & green cloak—(modeled in photos & paintings)—his skulls & thighbone—rosary—wooden puppet in a drawer—his easel & palette & the shining slippery polished wood floor of the vast room—

Then the Deux Garçons & empire mirrors—my face fat & hairy & silly—the arcade-trees street, the stained glass violet in Cathedral—cosmic egg design with music notes that look like laughgas on the Seminary stairway—up to Vauves hill to see Sainte-Victoire a new housing project annihilating the old point of view from which Cézanne saw the Mountain's south face steeper than at Château Noir.

Aboard S.S. Azemour:

[First text of "Sunset S.S. Azemour," p. 36, *Planet News.*]

Cf. Melville's poem ("The Night-March") about the message winding thru the night from the front of the army backwards (thru time) to the end of the columns of army, and also cf. Hardy's "Nature's Questioning" ("brain and eye now gone").

The only machine that can store and project all the variable data of the universe is the universe itself.

— — —

"cosmic-ferocious" style

Gregory wants everybody else to be dead so he can be alive.

* * *

The Yogic caterpillar digs the scene builds a cocoon goes into nirvana & emerges a butterfly. Mankind can do no less. And emerge a big SNICKER.

Snicker Snoop [1]
the world's a boop
Snop de bop
the umphs a bump

Ipsa diddle
tricksy woo
weep the beep
whappity bap

Ippskiddy whipple
whopsky top
lucksky whupsky
whipsky woo

Iksky whacksy whucksky whoops
Ipsky pipsky whipsky troops
Army Silly whips the stoops
Civilization spooks de groops—
Hopsky gropsky all the dopsky
Lovsky wuvsky dovsky slobsky
Wobsky topsky wantsa win
Ginsy insy pantzky Pinsky
Mr. Pinsky makes up pants
Pinkus fucks Becky
Ginsberg sucks Orlovsky

* * *

[1] Further reconstruction of improvised nonsense poem w/J.K.—"I saw the sunflower monkeys of the moon."

Take them out & chop their hands off
bunch of dopey fucks
dopey daffodils & strongarm bandits—
Bondage in the moonlight—

June 1, 1961

Many dreams on ship—just woke from one—

Begins with Rebecca or Naomi of Arabia entering the ship by the front glass doors carrying a jug of wine or water—she steps forward to look for her boy-friend—

Suddenly the crowd around her parts & one of the elder women steps forth and screams insults at her, shaking her fist like a 1920 movie—

In the family parlor the Arab family is having a party-dinner—I suggest we go to a hammam—the father says—"Ah, that is a fine idea for you young boys but it is too early in the evening for any chumminess to develop at the baths without a little more hours of drunkenness—" We all go to the bath—women are there also and the couples are together in a mixed fleshy scene—my girl-friend from the shop entrance—who is the girl friend of one of the male lovers—

[leads to] Some scene in the hammam of young boys on stone beds with bodies turned together and the women watching. Then all go into a main room to drink & make love. Fat adolescent Arabs, soldiers without uniforms.

Outside at the sea wall the half-human porpoise receives his boyfriend, who gives him a message to swallow.

The porpoise chokes on the message.

The creature falls backward over a wall choking.

An old water farmer comes along and sees the fish choking on a half digested mass.

He pulls out the body and pulls the mass out of the throat of the porpoise—he grabs the white skin sticking out of the mouth & pulls—

The whole flesh comes free—it is a huge orange square of flesh with an infant's face in the middle flat on it—eye holes nose & mouth & teeth—

half digested,

but hideous & orange colored. It is the face of the fairy at the hammam.

The woman Naomi enters the door of the shop. From the crowd a lady steps forth 1920 movie style & begins insulting her—

"You who love a fairy boy! You who are not enough woman but to pick half-man for a lover! You who put up with this insult from a man."—

There is a lot of this dream unremembered.

Earlier dreams—Apocalypse & A Bombs, etc.

* * *

Hotel Mauretania street scene, Tangier

Tanger 4 June, 1961

With Gregory & Peter to the café terrace overlooking the Avenida España—on woven mats without shoes under fig tree drinking green mint-tea . . . later high over the ocean, with horizon blue mist & writings & inscriptions of streaks and blue zigzags on sparkling white background—the ocean a vast animal-back to be looked at—a blue wall of living jewels & fire—smoking pot in alabaster pipes—conversing on the hide of the sea, Michael Portman, Burroughs, self, Peter & Bowles—then movie about Amérique Insolite—nostalgia of back-facade skyscrapers & revival-shouts & dances.

* * *

r my daughters sing
ce beside the well in the backyard,
in "the pleasant shade" of bougainvillaea
full of blue fish
– with a big furry dog
c of money war from radio–
oread– roast my corn
by firelight and wait for death.

Enemy?"
dying
rity by his pillow.

———

✝

/ leads to the tomb
garden and the great harmless black dogs–
t of this pad on my knee,
aburn, the big kids dancing in blue gowns
ny enclosure near the mules at night–
& pipes snaking forward

dead. Old man
age in– nothing.
shade well in Eternity
sorrows to the King–
ee our cause to him
e receive us well

d Jacoubi[1] *in conversation:*

Third Face

hen one day he (black market man) came again & said "I have $"–"Where?"–"My pocket!"–"What you want do?"–"Change $"–"5 p.m. at Café Paris." It 3:30 he left–I left too–& find some

[1] Achmed Jacoubi: painter, student of Francis Bacon, friend of Paul Bowles.

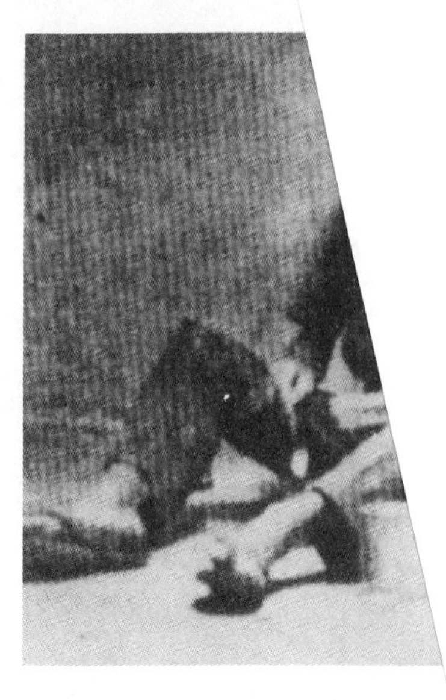

Zoco Chico again June 10, 1961

Dream: June 15, 1961

Jack, Bill Gregory & self are gathered
of the Mystery Cosmos—we decide th
question, that is, given the Universe, the
is whether or not really to continue the
form—Suddenly I or Gregory jumps up
continue—as an elephant God—I want to
wings for real"—

Followed by premonitory dream in w
the door to Peter who was in bed—some th
wake out of dream in anxiety to get my war

* * *

"the last best hope on earth—the bourgeois

Arrest death!

* * *

And there to hea
and my sons dar
"A far countree"
beside an ocean
in a stone hous
and hear no ya
and eat cheap
make pictures

"Is death the
The old man
Warned post

Eat noise.

All Nobility
Céline, the
the halfligh
the lamps
in the bus
the drums

— Céline
hairy im
Fare thy
Bear ou
Plead th
H

Achme

And
some
some

Orlovsky, Corso, and Burroughs in Tangier

policemen said to me "You know some people have fake Amer. $?" said police. I'm really embarrassed. "I think if you want to find out these green $ fake all coming into Morocco" . . . Policeman said "Mmmmmm you think some American people you know—? Have some coffee." "I have a lot of stuff to do"—"What are you doing?"
. . . I think that before the war be beginning, god he be working fast—

July 9, 1961 Tanger

Soco Chico over black Tea & Yerba Buena—taking codeine—Peter home in bed sick, Gregory with cut finger curled in his bed in room downstairs on roof of Hotel Armor—I came out at 2 in the afternoon, stopped at Bill's for a half hour—he was lying in bed with clothes on without tie, Michael Portman was at his desk—discussing nothing—relaxed—Bill described high he was on last nite, smoking raisin-like matter brought from Marrakech, mixed with local Kif—entering a very exquisite place—ghosts of Truman Capote and old Mrs. Stevenson flitting in and about the room—skin rotting and hanging from the body like Spanish Moss—

Then I went to pharmacy, bought paper handkerchiefs & codeine—then wandered down to market gazing at meat stalls, looking for red chunks of good steak—bought a half kilo and came down to Soco Chico to drink black tea & take the Houdé [1] pills. After this I will go back to the house, and I wonder what I will do all afternoon—cook, putter at my desk?

Peter says he is leaving for Istanbul in a week, meanwhile he is recovering from mild jaundice and a series of colds, & dysentery.

Yesterday in the Soco, sitting at the Café Fuentes table overlooking the street filled with passing Arabs and ill dressed youths, while Peter was visiting the whorehouse for half an hour, I wept, thinking of all the happy and past years we had lived together—how with his departure the sense of assurance and unity I enjoyed would be gone—and the sense of purpose to seek love—for what to seek now? As I am 35 and half my life now past, I have no sure road ahead, but many to choose from, and none seem inevitable.

Alan Ansen will arrive in Tanger in four days.

---

[1] Codeinetta, available nonprescription opiate useful for colds & headaches.

Photo by Paul Bowles

A.G., Djemâa el Fna, Marrakech

July 20, Marrakech—

The roof of the house—lying on mats drinking tea with portable radio & stove & rug & air mattress & candle lamp—lying back after majoun & cigarettes & pipes uncounted—the stars forming huge geometrical patterns, meteorites, and a land of roofs all around, some lighted & some dark, all stretching & jutting flat in every direction, broken by silhouettes of Koutoubia Mosque and others—

lighted up at 2:30 a.m. with the Muezzin calls from one end of the city echoing to another—

Birds flying in the house thru high hot windows—

Djemâa el Fna in Marrakech:

The din-ringing of myriad goatskin water sellers
in between the rubbing of the drums of the pavement
seen from the hotel terrace with circles of Breughel-Crucifixion-
entranced crowds

Listening to the white-robed storyteller in a hoarse voice spread his hands and babble—
the inner circle of the ring all children bug-eyed hands clasped on their knees—
Saccharine, Saccharine all! the beggar of the Hanging rags, with his thin breast and thighs,
one foot behind an ankle relaxed, toenail to the ground scraping idly
other hand flung up to mouth with a tin can full of water or urine sluffing it down,
mocking the proprietor— with flitting eyes— that did not rest on me as I passed thru the long arcade passage
up a hump to a crossroad in the labyrinth
that looked familiar— a little coin and silver necklace booth—
up to the triangular Magic Square—
Sellers of snot & tattooing, Amber, berries of Atlas, "Pakistani Seeds"—

24 July

Settling down with new Zen Kif pipe, in first class train Marrakech-Tanger—Leaning forward determined to resist all folly (as I get higher looking out at red earth-desert plains and thin mud walls & stupas of black hay and grazing sheep

The slam of the train door,
a blue truck running on the highway parallel.

Ah little camels! walking towards green ponds—Did I have a vision in Marrakech I went to the hammam & jacked off with my finger in my ass. I sucked off an Arab kid with scimitar thick cock, kneeling in the dark on a side road near palmtrees, I fucked a fatassed boy, in a loft in the Medina—What Allah wills!

Lay on the roof five nights in the heat drinking kif tea—watching a moonlit cloud in the shape of an Angel drift by watching me and 2 mud huts with grey brambles heaped on the mud wall—

Marrakech! Djemâa el Fna! Waha! (yes) Baraklaoufuk (thank you very much) Blashmil! (you're welcome)

Arabic:

Barak Laoufuk
(Barry Cloud Fuck) } thank you

Blã-zjmíl Blashmíl }	you're welcome or that's o.k.
Sma'ha-li–	pardon me
Mez-yèn Mez-yén *Bezèv*	good *very* good
B'sh Hal– B'*Ch-hal*– }	How much?
Yi- (yid)– lla- (la)–	yes no
La Barak·Claufek–	No thanks
glottal waha (wa-ckha)–	okay
Fine– (Fine Achmed:	Where is? Where is Achmed?)
Sh'kane– Shnu-kane– }	what's happening?
Kif n who ah lyoum lyoom (Kif & who are youm?) }	how's the day going?
Laissez hair–	God will help you– (to beggars)
Lousouesse– (loose west) }	paranoia

Tanger 2 Aug. 1961

"Wise is the man who can look at the lightning flash without making a comment."

* * *

Across the ocean Peter Orlovsky walking in Greece
knapsack and staring eyes–

Fragment of Marrakech

Aug 8, 1961 Dream—

—This is the first dream I've recorded in months—something been awry—

I'm in NY—Jane Bowles and Leary are on vacation together in NY or are to meet and perhaps marry after spending weekend together—

I have become Bill's heir in some way by marrying Jane perhaps and received the money from naked lunch & his new cut-up process—I think in the dream that this will make my later life easier and also make my children's life aristocratic & free—a good feeling—I have taken over Bill's legacy—a natural move I felt I deserved in the dream—I will be Bill when he dies, which I want to be in dream—

Thought when I woke that children have to deal with our karma, that we continue our karma in them, & that this inheritance move improved my karma in my children thru whom I sensed it—that Jack's kid was being doomed in his trials to suffer his Broodiness & isolation since he didn't pass on any legacy to his kid—

Yesterday Jacketblurb for Ansen Book: [1]

Ansen is the most delicate hippopotamus of poets with his monstrous classical versifications—he gets conversational fatness "into stricter order"

[1] For Alan Ansen's *Disorderly Houses* (Middletown, Connecticut: Wesleyan Press, 1961).

by use of weird echosyllabics, polyphony, strict rhymeless pindarics, self-annihilating sestinas, mono-amphisbaenic and echo rhyme, skeltonics, versicles & alcaics coherent Palindromes & such like master eccentricities—a hangup on Forms which interestingly pushes academic modes beyond polite limits into the area of lunatic personal genius—This an amazing book, with many sad poems.

★ ★ ★

The sadness of goodbye again— the melancholy sunset—
Bach pathos on the phonograph— the singer chants his farewell in baritone—
The door is open, and the warm wind blows into the house—
the bread is piled on the cookstove— the drum stands empty, the waterjug has lost its top—
all the spoons and forks goodbye, goodbye to the calendar where another hand scratched out the dates—
What tenderness, to see the pants hang from the wall— my white coat for night air with a wrinkled sleeve—
Thin hornpipe fills the room with its plaint?—
Hymn of awe— reclining on the blue bed spread looking out the door— the black—

★ ★ ★

Opium makes separate identity bearable.

August 20, 1961 Dream

5:45 a.m.—"Naomi in the Bughouse. . . . Allen"—a voice calling me sharply. Woke dressed & went over to Bill's to see him off to London from here (Tanger).

August 24—

The chair, flat square table, like brown wood, on which Peter set the typewriter to tap [1] while I put my head against his thigh, my eyes, his belly, my mouth his cock soft at first then excited. The brown chair, a month later, bare & clean.

---

[1] His (Peter Orlovsky's) "First Sex Experiment," published in *Fuck You: A Magazine of the Arts.*

Clownish mandala

S.S. VULCANIA TO GREECE

Aug 24 2pm '61

Tanger, church spire, apartments, hillside covered with Arab houses, white blocks, disappearing behind me in the blue mist—Alone, solitary, hopeless, tranquil, still with knapsack—on to Acropolis—thence to inspect the Sphinx—then not know what forward to India by Xmas—Now from the gates of Hercules—old voices, old loves murmuring farewell—Hart Crane's Adios in the Water—Gibel Mussa ringed with clouds—a thin bony tower far away leaning & waving against the Atlantic horizon—

★ ★ ★

Consciousness is the Law. Which Consciousness, what law? A matchstick. A damned born burying ceremony. Listen to me. My throat is dry. The old ladies on my right are talking in the Vulcania—The name is an explosion—the night the Vulcan went down. Mediterranean hidden sun. Healing sun. Oedipus wildly tearing his eyes out of his skull. A monster in a labyrinth. The riddle of the sphinx—and man 2000 years later—

Oedipus at work

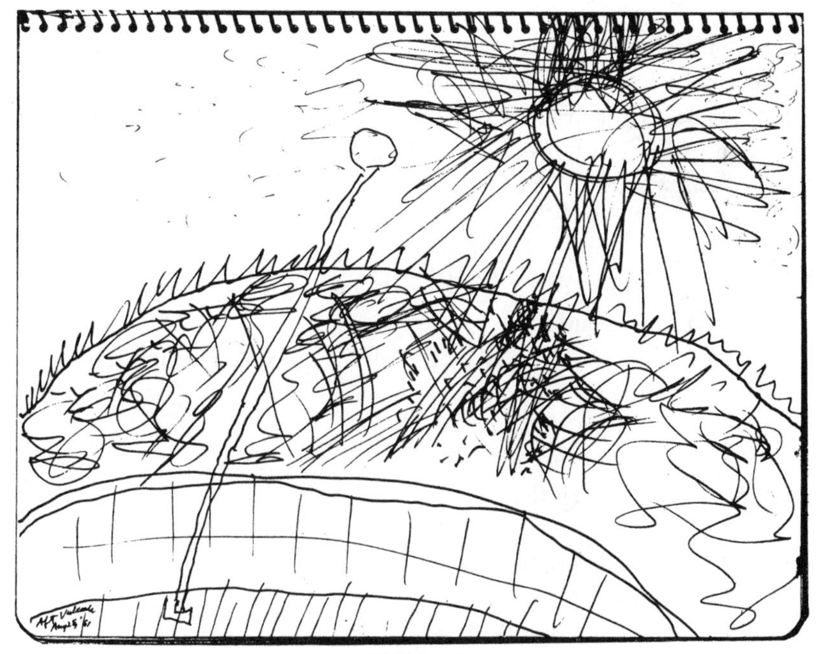

Aft Vulcania

Prohibito spòrgersi—That's the gayest sight here the red bands on the white-welded blower-stem's 10 feet tall—red mouth pointed in six directions—and green lamp-pole-mushroom electric light protectors painted with a bead of white each reflecting the sun—and the plop of the red stack—blowing grey smoke with hueing noise next to the motor vibration bump & rattle of tin fences—no more I tarry on these Isles. —To bake my head in classical sun. Under the blue sky. No clouds. Will be left out of a new consciousness like Moses not seeing the promised land. Where is the spot he died? And sing 'Old Man Mose he kicked the bucket' dancing on that mountain pass? And the desert. A camel driver.

* * *

Against those pipestems the cause of this discourse, the heavy blue—Emily Dickinson, "Parting is all we know"—No diving—Que hora es?—The sky in a round bowl, enormous blue dome fading to mist on endless horizon—the straight curved line and myriad wrinkles & white foam-flecks rushing—

The old waiter squints & leans against a bench.

Dream—Aug 29 1961

Riding in back of truck or train toward Native Fields—The train seats which were uncomfortable are now clean & empty, only one or two other people in the back of the bus with me—He says, "Well now everything will be better & easier"—Somehow symbolized by the clean leather dustless seats—out of La Paz? Naples to Pompeii?

To Greece, Aug 29, 1961 (Hotel Park)

Gas tanks in Eleusis
Passing Scylla & Charybdis on Vulcania at sunset 2 days the sun flecked currents.

* * *

Acropolis like any Golgotha
has blue eyesockets
thru the columns the bright
blue north
a void for hair— and empty blue
metafisks surround

all the blocks of bright new marble
        ο α θ η ν α ι ο ν τ π η α s
Passengers seated on the steps
        of the huge slow moving bus
that's standing still.

Allen Ginsberg at the Acropolis, August 30, 1961

        Have yr photo taken thus
with a marble skeleton background

* * *

At nite, walking around the old streets under Acropolis
I am as lonely as the sound of a cat–
Suddenly a dark square with tobacco kiosk
and above in the sky, the poor toy Acropolis–
Face to face with the hair veined cock
in my mouth, at my eye, pressing against the hair of my unseen hole,
"This is the country of Socrates and Alcibiades"
A long white dog barking at me in the dust-covered pavement–
There is a wind from below the World,

The sun is down, in my white suit
and beige crepe-soled suede shoes that comfort my feet
pacing the streets, beyond the Tower of Winds,
at the edge of Hadrian's Library I took a piss,
and walked the circle around new ancient streets,
each familiar, face to face with the statue of man,
knowing Patroklos dead, Achilles remembering that tender breast on his
own—
an old man leaning out of his chair to see trucks
Pass the street; the bus stop—
Five boys in a circle, the sailor leans & plants a lip on
lips of a younger man touching his shoulder—
Who am I after 3,000 years?
This is the land of marble and skin
This is the love of man. This is the buttocks
that do not shit. This is the marble of understanding
this is the old sympathy. This is money changing hands
and young men eager at the loins
This is the doom love I was remembering in the Paterson Library;
This is all my melancholy come home
Alexandria, where beyond?
This is my palm tickled. This is my poverty.
This is what I wished come true to mock me & make me red faced.
This is me a machine. Here come the German tourists
with blond beards, climbing the stones to Erechtheum.
Whose feet should I kneel at, and not pay money to love.
How many loves can I buy at once?
The Acropole, I saw from Aeolus street, sticking up in sky
a scatter of stars in the deep night blackness—
Those sympathetic architects and boy love sculptors
weeping made golden triangles to match their dying boys
breasts & cocks, foreskins & balls,
triangles of gold hair, foreheads smooth, short hair'd,
eyes clear smiling more knowing than agued age—
belly perfect as a many columned temple dome—
dome smooth & delicate as Phidias' boy's buttock—
Old farmers smiling & wise; sons more gentle
in bed with guilty foreigner me
than I was hoped made hairy flesh—

Who pocketbook tonite, I sit in
cafe ascribble sneering at human bellybuttons—
The Acropolis is a Chimera, Parthenon stands forlorn,
the hair of the nymphs
is white, their bones are brittle under Kore—
I shd go wander & meet who I meet—
If no money wd/ they love me still?
Where are the girls, equally sensitive?
Am I going mad in Athens, staring at every waiter?
Diving champions come to the rich architect
and he takes 3D pictures in color— their bellies and eyes in the water,
their legs open in bed, their hats on,
their eyes shining: Greece—
the national Museum, Pan with barbaric beard
and hair-foot pipes to the boy;
Syntagma, Harmonia, the bald waiters staring
at what they were— a yellow sweater, palm against cheek
eating meat pie, curled black hair, the waiter jiggles his knee—
the youth, the youth out of Phidias in machine dress
army or streetboy— looks out at my eyes—
I am 3 beers in sorrow, I refuse
To pay my dues— 100 drachmas— 3 lousy bucks.

Zonar's Café, lit from behind, the sidewalk tables filled at 7:30—
White-capped old sailors float by like boats of sponge, pendent undersea
a boy in striped T shirt ambling hands in pocket eye on the gentlemen
from America.

Athens Aug 30, 1961

Late morn, woke after dream in which a young man sought me out so earnestly tenderly passionately—& with such gentility that when I woke I couldn't remember his image & "cried to sleep again"—except immediately it flashed thru mind that this dream like others is a Jokers wild which before I took for a real sign to pursue & now, confused, I take it as a vagary which needn't come true, not prophecy. Thru Bill, a dream to keep me in the queer track—"Teach the cloth"—behind which there is nothing, no body.

Later in morn, riding with Marlon Brando in a convertible.

Athens Sat nite Dream

In the Black Pit

Bus to saddle of mountain, a reservoir, walking along harbor side like Palermo—older dream landscape—

Atop a cliff—Tanger, going home, Burroughs has left me with Bowles—who descends & leaves me too—down a long pathway thru trees (from balcony of theater in old dream) (where I wander in free & can't find seat) thru new young trees, it's a vast housing development in the basement of an arroyo below Tanger. Restaurant floor, trees like Egypt, waiters cocktails, a huge plain in the arroyo—vast cafeteria, café, housing project, garden, meeting place—a section of Tanger—Bowles goes down there, I have to go and follow him—he meets me at foot of path & I exclaim surprise at the area—he says, "Didn't you know this part of Tanger? I often live here in summer"—and takes me in to show me a table, show me around.

We walk from path to near table under trees—I see boy whores and waiters watching me, I feel the people & place are familiar like Syntagma Athens, Zonar Café fishbowl meeting place—also there are horsefaced men—women—I know them from before—I look around to find my role & place here from before—

We are facing the pit of the prison now—I and a few young friends—Lucien perhaps—We go down, having special visitors privileges. The pit is the courtyard or prison yard. In the center is a glass-brick dormitory jail with door & stairway leading to the basement-moat-prison yard where unfortunate souls are allowed to walk—We go down there among them—I see the brick window where prisoners are sleeping & sitting reading semi-visible behind the wall—I know I have a friend there, it will impress him & other prisoners that we are allowed in and out—

As we walk past the center middle elevator-door shaft in the pit a few boys surround us, we pass them, one has palm open with 2 white caps of goofball or H—he brazenly tosses it in air to us, showing off, but it falls on floor in dust—nobody sees perhaps but we start away (to keep out of trouble)—he picks them up—we move out of under pit-marquee to Free Area—The prisoners are forbidden to follow under surveillance of machine gun—

In fact, in the pit, I feel waves of terror & secrecy—here is meeting place of terror & freedom—if you're a prisoner in the pit you feel it worse even I guess—Neal was in there—like Alcatraz—

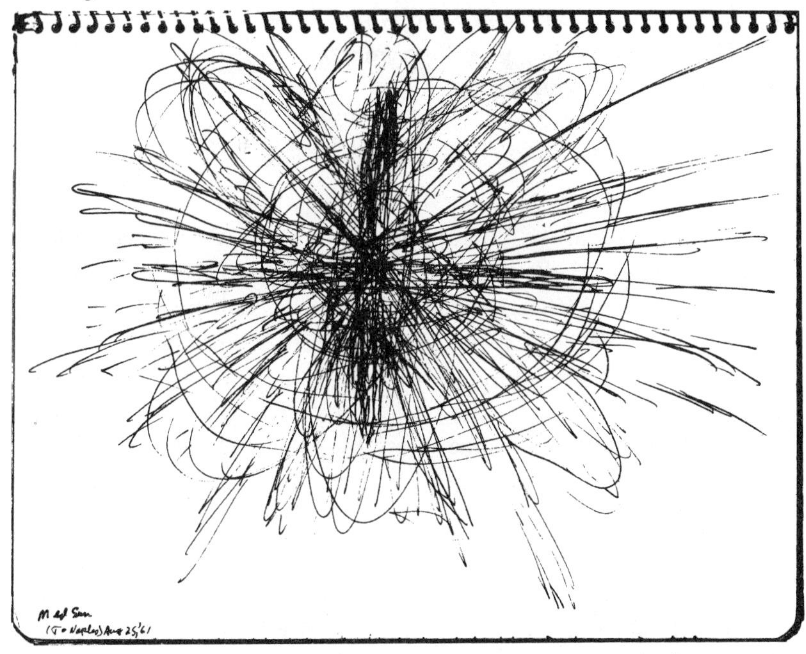

Mediterranean Sun

Gregory, he must be rescued from this grey terror he's there for bad passport crime, but suddenly I see him coming up hill from outside dressed in rubbery grey raincoat & carrying newspapers—the Sunday papers & headlines—he's been got out of prison by his escort a big Jewish fellow like Mike Grieg from Frisco—Gregory I expect to want to go back & show me pit, but he's still afraid of it & traumatized, wants to have expensive sunday coffee & read news & not get into pit-mood conversations, too much horror, prophetic he should be in it after he wrote Alcatraz poem.[1] Imagine one year free he surveyed it, next he found himself caught down in the system, he's out now but shakey—

The newspapers of rubber grey-brown rotogravure color—headline is

KENNEDY ASSUMES SINGLE POWER, ORDERS
NEW AID CUT RESTORED
AMERICA HAS TO JOIN REST OF WORLD
OR DIE SAYS KENNEDY

---

[1] "Ode to Coit Tower," pp. 11–14 in Corso's *Gasoline* (San Francisco: City Lights, 1958).

I see, we realize he's suddenly "laid down the law" & become dictator—but a good one, he sees what is needed & is going to be great bold president & *lead* personally—it's gratifying—

Dream ends reading paper, remembering with amazement Alcatraz Ode (Coit Tower) years ago.

Dream—9 am—

Setting out on a journey, I'd been preparing my food & papers to catch the late train—going alone on midnite Chicago special—Ransacking the icebox-desk in family house—plate of cold greek salad—manuscripts—I eat what I can, rescue what papers are still clean & pack them up at last minute so on outward journey I won't have to spend any money tonite eating in train.

I feel depressed in morning, I lost my passport & spent $20 stupidly going to Piraeus by taxi to hear Bouzouki music & drink Retsina.

Sept. 8—

Today high on Bhang pipe and wandering with P. first to Agora & back to Zaharios Café? and then to house high & Plaka with Spiros & amis and Pyrikides—and yesterday (Zitzannis, lost passport & found) the proposition to make gold in India, cats like maggots in an alley—walking from cat to cat, people all day—every days, changing people company from John B. to Ticonos to Spiros to Yael to Amy—to leave town for Delphi—in a tourist bus, when shall I ever be alone? Athos?

* * *

This morning a letter from a poet
who used to be young in N.Y.
I crossed the street in the sunlight
in Athens, reading it— no money,
but activities, public, words and music
and many a new magazine in America—
I am not old yet, but my lover
left me this year, I have no letter
from him in Istanbul. I used

to read poetry to youths in cafés—
now read letters silently in
the noisy street. When death comes
it will be no further surprise.[1]

* * *

Sitting on the third large grey marble stoop leaning on a mossy column in the arid sunlight under a blue marble dome—
No temple like that of the azure sky stretching in all directions, smoke from Piraeus settling on the sea horizon—
Taking off my glasses— eagle eye lost— a doubled blue beyond my eyelashes—
Sitting as before with shadow fallen from the West— slow lengthening to reddish soft color—
Should the Acropolis be blown up by more intense light than human day—
How do I know— strange to see the columns fused by radiation hats & blasts maybe powdered? or blacked?
a project to build a bomb shelter over Acropolis—

To Delphos—

Three Roads [2]

Approached the three roads from above & stared down thru space like an old horse—
come back to an old adventure
Mt. Parnassus slope, an old bus, bare chested, a pipe & grass bag—
the murmur of conversation, the mechanical humm whine of the bus

---

[1] These lines an "echo of Rexroth's verse"—A.G., 1975.

[2] The guidebook Allen used at this time in Greece, Hachette World Guides' *Greece* (Paris: Hachette, 1955), contains the following note on p. 252:

"This cross-roads corresponds to the Σχιστη Ὀδος *(diverging road)* of the Theban legends, also called Triodos, or Three Roads (from Delphi to Thevai, to Daulis, to Ambrysus or Distomo). It was in the adjacent gorge that Sophocles situated the tragic meeting of Oedipus, coming on foot from Delphi, with his father, Laius, who was on his way to Delphi by chariot. Laius, having struck Oedipus with his whip to drive him from his path, was killed by his son, who had not recognised him."

flowers in glass stem, windshield pix of the Byzantine virgin, blue
reflector

"Hi on T thru Bus window to Delphi"

High on grey rockd cliff above the brick pebbled pathways of Delphos
across the gulf a mount, rocks climbing upward, a wing clamped
outward down the valley
a floor of olive groves to the sea
Town roofs stretched from the shore to the wrist of blue water,
opening bayward with paths of water inland, straits & coves & round
small Islands–
a haze-bank Castled with Cloud heads, a huge woolly bed in the sky,
up over Parnassus shoulder the brightest cloud
with an eagle flying against the white-silver rollers of luminous prow
of an Island ship floating up in the blue–
a thin road below threaded slowly by a car, the honk of a bus buried in
town,

Small-leaved bushes reaching their thin fingers up in the air, pine trees
leaning against the mountain,
myself half naked perched on a rock, my back to the height— a cliff of
blue ridden by a scatter of cloudmist drifting downward
Below, a cavity-ravine for the waters of Castalia
— wind blowing all the dry weeds on rock— trembling bushes—
Aeolus & Helios a small white pebble in the sky— with whiskers of light
burning far away from the eye—
the plenitude, the Vast, the Olympian glimpse of human water & rubble
& roof, mount, broken temple— and
a zigzag path up the side of the green earth-wall across the valley
leading up rocks in a funnel of pines to the gates of pasture
and the miniature brown field lying high over the shoulder of the range—
stretching back into closed-in valley farm acres hidden & secret to the
low river eye
to the west more hill mounts & white air peaked by cloud arising on
broken horizon.

Dream—Delphi, Sept. 9, 1961, 5 a.m.

Football Field

In a bedroom with Tony Perkins, we go out to eat together, in an apartment Chinese restaurant.

He or we or I kill someone (push the body, bloody) under the fire escape—Perkins turns into a girl, a doll blonde type—we rush out of Chinese apt. to movie apt.—trying to escape. I take her back to her apt. where her girl friend is.

She begins telling me she doesn't like "Cassady—It's all lies"—She knows all about it, she used to be Kerouac's girl, and he told her, the whole romantic story of Cassady is just a lot of make up & hooey—I get annoyed at her she won't even let me talk—on top of that she wants me to think thru how to cover up the murder. I tell her if the police come I'll not involve her & say I did it. The whole thing gives me the old guilt dream guilt murder chill. I was trying to make her but she's too flouncy & rare, and we got murder on our souls, she wants to get rid of me, I say "I don't love you" which annoys her since she thought she had me conquered, she's a self-centered power type, not a prey to my own power of storytelling, & romance, no, she won't even let me get my story off the ground—

I go out—her girlfriend there was asking where we ate—I say the place, but look significantly at her, and ask my "girl"—"What time was it we were there?"—So that she has to think herself how to make up the story—She says "3 p.m." or so—we were actually there around noon when we did our crime—

Somehow I pushed her before at restaurant & she was injured, in fact at that time far back in the dreamday it was Tony Perkins who leaning over was pushed & ripped his pants or crushed his cheek, I don't know—he blamed me—I go out to the football field to escape, I see the cop & army cars pulling up to the reported murder arena—I go down the field out the back way, behind the cars—if they ask me I'm just another spectator watching football practice—

door bangs in Sikelianos'[1] house in Delphi, I wake up.

* * *

Climbing up face of Cave of Muses (whatever cave)—sight of the valley below and a small cluster, village in the center, shepherds' flocks below joining on the red road, a circle of horses an eagle's glance away—

Now in the cave in back of the long arched floor, perfect vaulted construction, say ¾ a block long, with adenoids of rock & central pivot rock at entrance, and same sentinel to the back of the throat—the place like a huge long mouth with entrails leading to the bowels of the earth, up forward in the hanging darkness a small eye on the black clouds the entrance uphill over the beds of moss & shady rock—patches of moss making small kingdoms on the dead floor—the chirp of a bird (fluttering inside the entrance) from moss bed to silvery green mossbed—and in back, side paths, an entrance, inhuman steps upward & total dark—with our 3 candles, blind.

Me sitting on a small white toadstool throne, my hand resting on a gnarled old coal-black tree bole—with Minos[2] dancing on a red floor-circle on the earth—and a Greek scholarly girl singing Castalian song.

Then down the zigzag path on the rear of a small mountain in the vast ranging valley, past isolated huts in hills and one road winding—thru cropped grasses & red open circles & squares of soil—the yellow flatland

---

[1] Angelos Sikelianos, deceased Greek poet.
[2] Minos Argyriakos, painter and cartoonist.

with its tree by truck-path—walled in by spotted mounts' greenpine, a red branch in the nearest hill—Like Chinese painted valley, Chinese trees & floating roof of sun-streaked afternoon cloud—and all the blue above lit forever by Helios—and night every night "Let's just stay here"—Greek shepherd by roadside with horse & watch, patched pants, full toed brown sandals, and bottom torn striped silk shirt—We must be going on the very roads—

* * *

Dreamt— Jack K in jail—I visit—he's very self contained, strong—I wonder if I would be so in jail—I try to get him to appeal for my sympathy, pity, help—no—he's too indifferent—I test everybody this way, I think as I lie in bed awake—10 AM Delphi, bright sun thru window.

* * *

Delphi Wed.—3 AM— Strange dreams—"entering the flesh fair—" with Eugene.

Earlier—went thru a door into the desert fair, with many other people—a desert with sand and huge heavy wind—detached myself from my body, remaining inside, and I was whirled around and around like a gyre, limbs in every direction of the compass hands and head flying round and round within all three dimensions while I was aware that by relaxing completely and letting the wind take my body the sensation was pleasure & I was free to go be blown anywhere by the winds—I was free—

Fell asleep without recording dream more exactly, woke at 4:15 with first recorded phrases in mind, lit candle & picked up notebook to write—went to huge dim wooden window arch to look out & empty my bladder over the marble windowsill into rock strewn dark enclosure—broken fence I saw earlier today, rocks tumbled—

Looked out window saw perfectly Orion constellation in bright star sky, and down below on earth on my hill the thin marble shaft and white bust of Sikelianos—delicate & thin as his name—him lost—standing there awhile—

Poor Sikelianos lost, & in Delphi awhile a white marble shaft & bust on a hill over the ruined temples under Orion's belt—thru stars—at night, with no-one to know.

Which I shall be in time, a bust in the starlight somewhere.

Amy told me, pleasant dreams, or have a good dream, when I went to sleep—and earlier Minos had said S. had gone to Sahara as a beautiful youth, and there written his first poetry. Must have been eternity there.

familiar. The part I would like to lay
my head if it were soft against
is mid breast. All the human muscle
curves & ripples over the belly & side to
the armpits — The pubic hair shaved
except for right above the ball. & the cock
is missing, which must have been a fine piece
polished creamy marble, long tipped.
A rose-white softness about the head, the
lips mona-lisa like from the side. Walking
around the back I realized over again I love the
body, the thigh-power symmetry & who is it?
His bellybutton not very deep but just
a touch & small valley. The lyre shape
curve of the lower belly from the waist.

Hermes of Praxiteles

Olympia Sept. 12

Hideous trainride Itea-boat-Aigion-train to Olympia—felt dizzy then bands of awful headache enveloping my temples, uneasiness, finally vomited & vomited over again in train toilet bowl, still felt bad arriving, then that nite more headache—passed by the morn except for threat of headache as I walked the grounds of Olympia ruins & sat on drum of Zeus' temple column to read guidebook.

Hermes—Praxiteles—the right arm, dangling a grape to baby Dionysus is missing, as well as thumb & forefinger of left hand—the balls are polished like long grapes. The right buttock is too big as you pass round statue, too feminine but from side & directly in front Hermes' whiteness is beautiful & desirable, gazing at the head, at the misty eyes, the whole body breathes and moves. The complicated sandals, should be copied. Dionysus miniature. The smile on Hermes' face is very soft & familiar. The part I would like to lay my head, if it were soft, against his mid breast. All the human muscle curves & ripples over the belly & side to the armpits—the pubic hair shaved except for right above the ball. & the cock is missing, which must have been a fine piece of polished creamy marble, long tipped. A rose-white softness about the head, the lips Mona Lisa-like from the side. Walking around the back I realized over again I love that body, the thigh-power symmetry & who is it? His bellybutton not very deep but just a touch & small valley. The lyre shape curve of the lower belly from the waist.

Olympia—Sunset, sitting on a rock, orange light on the grey boulders—lots of the rock is eaten away, I noticed these worn out temples now reconstructed are themselves built out of stone made from dynasties of shell. All the rock is fossil.

Dream Sept 20, 1961

"... Chicago, Paris, Venice, Tanger, Rome, Geneva."

Houses are destroyed, I'm living in an apartment with friend—he shows me thru—there are lots of beds, I chose my own in the apt—there's been some kind of hurricane or bombing & whole sections of the city are torn up—it takes me a long walk around the police lines around the ruins to get to my walk-up apartment.

We are a little theater jazz group rehearsing in rich lady's house—she's partial to one, a tall aristocratic skinned kid, with fine clothes & trumpet—gives him glasses of chocolate milk for the heat—we are to come back rehearsal tomorrow is at 11—but we don't even get paid a lunch? or supper? I go back thru the drawing rooms to retrieve my sweater, the old lady is discussing that & I primly advise her of the facts—that rehearsal can't continue but would have had supper been on hand—then I leave proudly, stiff faced.

* * *

Walking on changing road later with rest of band we begin singing
"Swing low sweet chariot
Coming for to carry me home"

and I take minor key as befits my singing arts in dream and am crying to the words—

The names of cities above, a poem of Peter
Who's smiling at you now in Istanbul
If I find another lover I'll tell you about it
When we reach the gates of the last city Dis or Persepolis
Meanwhile I'll go on alone after the sphinx & look for Cleveland.

Hydra 20 Sept 1961

Last three days wandering over Hydra desultorily—one boy in white I am constantly encountering since yesterday when I saw him almost naked in white bathing suit diving off rocks—turns out to be the one good looking petty Lieutenant in town—a comic opera blond boy—with a somewhat rough snubnosed face & cupid's bow lips—Now sitting across tables talking to dark friend (dark hair & shirt—one dab of young white in hair) at Café—What is attractive about him?—To me first the blond hair, well cut softly & genteel-ly about the skull reminding me of the middle class grace of Paul Roth [1] 20 years ago. In fact it is definitely Roth all over, he even vaguely looks like a replica of P.R. This face is marked either by debauch or labor—a high red puff mark below the eye on cheekbone—but I've not got to his body. A gold ring on one finger, and a watch—both civilization touches—seeing him in pool yesterday I didn't dream the white uniform, watch & ring & officer cap. The body is curiously curved—thin but well developed muscular calves & breast muscles, then thin chest below & outcurving satyr-stomach, slimness pillared on the legs—I saw him turn his buttocks over in the air, diving, and lift his loins free above the water with his whole body arched backwards as in orgasm. Right now, the white uniform encasing his chest in folds, billows out neatly starched above the flesh frame of chest & stomach—buttocks now flattened on chair, one leg out, surprising thick ankle in white sox & sneakers—always smiling, a little Billy Budd—I've been staring at him for 2 days & not said a word—what's to say, & in

[1] Eastside High School Paterson friend c. 1942–3. See "Kaddish," p. 16, "R—."

Greek? Sitting as he is with friend, legs folded talking, occasionally touching or poking each other, framed by small gay souvenir store, postcards over his head a blue square halo, a yellow & red Kodak sign hanging down—I don't even have my camera here to capture this priceless moment—and strings of coral or shell wavy beads hanging on wires outside the window. Small feet. Donkeys going by behind my back with goatskins filled with wine. A bunch of sailors on my left singing the butcher's song—that naive sound in baritone falsetto, curving & sensitive & masochistic like Jewish music—three "Yasoo"-ing in unison. Baker's boy walks by with round loaves stacked on his left arm. Huge pans of beans & oregano bubbling in the open kitchen door—a big red hulled "Caïque" or Syronic sailboat with barrels of grey liquid on deck—and a pump operating from top of huge barrel w/ man standing on top—he pumps up & down like a huge jack-off cock—and out of a pipe at his loins spurts huge masses of greasy grey liquor into waiting buckets. Hopeless to sit all day watching the action & teeth of the same white capped boy—but it's a pleasant solitude.

Strange constant chorus of tune-y groan kept up by the 3 sailors ranged in front of me—bare armed & hairy & Greek naval teashirts—I'm finished my coffee & might as well move off—or else hang around here & make a monomaniacal project of pursuing the sailor.

Argos

Slept at Methana, took sulfur bath, then to Epidauros & climbed over hills behind the amphitheatre & shouted, then Navplion overnight & went goo goo eyed with amaze on top castle of the Franko Turkish Venetian castle rampart fort on top of hill. Then morning bus to Tyrens—sitting on Cyclopean wall, smoke in my mind coming up thru wooden homeric rafter, "Wallgirt" etc.—suddenly musical groans upwelling out of the rocks & triangular stone doors & grey rubble—a church having services? No—a huge dairy-like factory—a prison—Sunday morning services in one of the buildings & baritone & basso Russian orthodox singing floating over the acre of prison compound & over the walls of Tyrens.

Climbed Argos Fortress—then walked Argive plain half way to Mycenae—

Tonite at the Belle Hélène with Gregory's & Rommel's names in

Guest Book—ate meat, Fr.Fr., stringbeans, soup, tomato, bread, ending with omelette confecture—At 7:30—a light appeared over a prehistoric middle volcan cone silhouetted between mount-crotches above the hotel—a yellow light—and then a full sick yellow September moon, vast lantern brightness blotched with eyebrow-seas—a raw cold moon in thin silhouette breeze—and down below in the valley, tiny carlights moving from Argos—

Walked up road to Mycenae ruins—vaulted fence, entered by Lion gate in the moonlight which cast white paleness over all the grey-walled mound of rubble—all over with flashlight, following my feet & the path—till the vault door of the Perseus Spring—I thought Agamemnon's tomb—went in down steps, my shadow growing thinner & smaller in front of me till it was human size as I touched it—into the door, down steps, I looked around, the moon outside the triangular arch of tomb entrance—the sky clear & moon rising in the grey-blue w/ no stars—down I went, flash in hand, thinking of *Colossus of Maroussi,* turning twice till the central descent, suddenly it felt dark, the deeper I went the darker—off went my light on purpose—finally to the floor, turned out light & waited—Why did Miller send forth that message to Fear this tomb? [1] I lay on the first few steps from the bottom in the dark, talking to myself about my shadow in the moonlight, pondering Miller's frightful words as they came thru to me in the darkness as Warning—Scared!—but where there is nothing there is nothing to fear I repeated aloud—there in the Blackness with eyes open waiting to appear what noisy white phantom? Then I wandered all over the top of Mycenae & back to sit under Lion's Gate, by the side near a broken column leaned against the crude inside wall & scribe—that I saw wavy green-spotted frogs motionless in my flashlight beam.—Now I sit exactly on the huge stone beneath the lions, a huge portal step, smoothed tho made of a pebbled granite, rotted as if a giant comb of time'd been dragged from left to right opening the door—huge foot-square post holes for old wood gates & other round pegholes—and far away on the plotted mountainside the moving goat bells tinkle music in the pale night.

I saw the plain of Argos from the top of Mt. Marta—a cabin-chapel up there with a blue door, I left a note amid the candles and ikons—the key was hanging by the door waiting for human hand—a white mist over Arcadia—spread down on the plain—the sun in my eye reflected thru the

[1] See pp. 88–91 of Henry Miller's *The Colossus of Maroussi* (New York: New Directions, 1941).

mist too. Earth red color—Prophet Elias Mt. near Epidauros also in view—and white village on top of high mt. valleys—waterwheel sound of goat bells—roads gleaming like thin streams of water—came down mountain, passed shepherd's hut—Lady who was sifting macaroni in the wind invited me in to eat—crosspole covered with burlap—rocks for furniture, earth holes to keep the water—baskets—

* * *

"Maidenhair clothes the moist rock walls of excavated graves. Owls dwell in the tholos [1] tombs."—Wace, *Mycenae*, p. 5.[2]

"On the other hand the massive blocking walls of the doorways [3] may have been intended to prevent the dead from issuing from their tombs and walking abroad."—Wace, p. 15.

Troy falls, 1183 B.C. Mycenae is covered with thyme.

Lions "apparently still existed in Greece, for they were found by Xerxes in Thrace."—Wace, p. 113.

Dream: Mycenae—Sept. 2?—1961

1. The Shouting Contest with Kenneth Koch
2. The eye-reflector—argument with Duchamp-Ernst
3. The Chien Andalou Eye
4. The premiere of Chien—First time with Stravinsky
   Salle Pleyel Second time
5. The Exposure Meter & The Visible Refrigerator
6. End—Janco's Yacht
   (Earlier his correspondence)
   and age—85—

I

In a cubicle like a voting-radio booth, I am seated next to Kenneth Koch and a Jewish girl (Maxine or Elise) and Jerry Rauch [4] perhaps—we are having a Shouting or Farting contest—a Poetry Tournament—I make a statement which is broadcast over the radio then it is his turn to make a statement—That is the rules of the Tourney—I say "I can no longer

[1] Large circular "beehive" tombs.

[2] This and companion quotations are from Alan J. B. Wace's *Mycenae: An Archaeological History and Guide* (Princeton: Princeton University Press, 1949).

[3] to the "chamber" tombs, large caves made in hillsides.

[4] A.G.'s roommate Columbia College 1943.

participate in this contest because it has got too serious, because my ego is involved, because my ego eats words, because it is time for the Mutation of the Race."

I leave the booth & go listen on loudspeaker, feeling righteous & self satisfied. How can Koch match that. To my surprise & horror he begins singing out a parody—

"I am only too glad to not participate because plateglass, my id is extremely grapefruit, it tastes like purple meat, it is loquacious monkey soup, it comes like Mama, it's all Ginsberg, Hurraigh for Kenneth Koch, when do the Movies begin and How much is the Purple Admission?" And so forth but in eloquent funny Dada style—so that I am ashamed of my part and rush back into the booth realizing I am losing the poetry contest.

I lean my shoulder ingratiatingly against Koch's side & slide down Cleopatra-like & embarrassed & seductive & coy, trying to make up to him & hide my shame, also trying to figure out if I can continue this Dirty Dozens Capping Contest with him and still come up with anything that will out-serious his fancy rhetorical gaiety & style & wit & wisdom. Because by comparison I seem just hung-up on myself & he seems a vast whitmanic canary. He sees me sidling up to him like that and smiles & says

"O No Ginsberg no you don't, you've got to see this contest out & be defeated like a good poet."

II

I then take a mirror—some kind of magic stroboscope-wheel mirror—and am holding it at my eye, watching the patterns and pictures come and go.

I am doing this relaxing on perhaps Janco's beach or yacht or modern house all white on the rocks of the cliff.

I look in the mirror, a succession of Mandrake Top hat pictures, seas, clouds, fields of olive trees against the mountains, geometric spirals, finally my own eye, at last the perfect olive-oval of my own eyeball's transparent iris—The seer's mirror always comes back to this image.

III

I am reciting this (or a similar) sequence of mental ideas to Man Ray-Max Ernst—a composite person I am relaxing with—we are all relaxing together in the sun—He replies

"Ah well this is nothing but the old eyeball, the eyeball that was perfectly stripped & exposed in the Chien Andalou of Dali"—

I am unsuccessfully trying to repeat to him the sequence of eyeball images I see clearly in the silver mirror—Serpent eating itself, orange, blue sky clouds, Iris circle—even Theda Bara with circles under her eyes slinks past—I never finish with my punchline of perfect reflected circle because he's babbling on about the Chien Andalou eye—

"But I do see pictures, but it always returns to the old mystic scientific human eye-reflector circle in the mirror in the end" I finally get to say to him & he approves, however he still feels the Dada Dog Eye was the original statement of the same Principle.

IV

He is sitting before an open display of cold perfect fruits—oranges, pears, slices of watermelon—revolving on a tray inside a window of like a large low washing machine. It's his desert house modern ice box. He's telling me the story of the première of Chien Andalou—and explaining that the important version never was publicly circulated.

That is, the original première—it had been left up to the entrepreneur to organize the orchestra for that, and he had improvised "artistically" to prepare the event. Stravinsky and Dali were consulted of course, at least they were asked permission to perform the piece, which they gave asking to be excused from public participation in it, as they were tired, and had made that point (tiredness & end of man) clear in the performance in Europe.

"But all that is is the slitting open of an eye" I complain—"What message is that?"

"Ah no—it was extraordinary the effect—however this first performance was a complete disaster—you see the Impresario, an American buffoon, did not understand the scene and prepared a farce, he attempted to arrange a series of pulleys & wires backstage, like a huge batwing-like rowing machine, which could produce the desired effect of wind & eye-cutting on the audience. Of course we all attended the performance & Dali even went backstage to test the machine and saw it would go wrong & protested but there was no way of stopping a first experimental performance so he sat down in the audience & awaited the results—it was a terrible scandal, and artistically impossible and only cut the eye of a dog or a cow, a *trompe l'oeil*—but it was not the sublime Zen Music intended—so we arranged for a real performance with real musicians—in Salle Pleyel or Aeolian Hall—Stravinsky arranged the musicians, it was all absolutely grim and serious, and the end result was achieved at that performance, the eye & ear were definitely cut open—but by that time you see, there was no audience, the public had been exhausted & deceived by the first fiasco, and nobody understood this correction that was made so sublimely—ah, the musicians were so perfectly prepared it was a miracle of precision and savagery, that nerve-music! They all knew what the score was, they went at it! That was the great event."

V

Tzara-Ernst-Ray is sitting still in front of the fruit window, talking—I am talking about Burroughs now to them, explaining his theories perhaps—They point to Duchamp as a Figure and are about to question B's use of "ze drugs" and I am about to defend him aesthetically but the argument never gets to that. Janco who has been listening gets up to wander on. Ernst is leaning back, in a foulard, on a modern Eames chair, staring hypnotized at the real fruit—perfect as wax—on the turntable inside the refrigerator with the invisible-glass picture window—"the visible refrigerator"—He says "I am now thinking of a project for an exposure meter for this machine—I consult my wife, it will eliminate shopping—That is a meter that exposes itself to these raw vegetables—perhaps in the market or at home in one's own refrigerator—I have not worked it out but the principle is very simple—The Meter eats the bananas for you and selects and digests and arranges the calories and vitamins and does your shopping for you—all decisions and all selections—All you have to do is wear it on your person and stare at the fruit—at the *individual* fruits piled up in your visible refrigerator (which can be seen from your living room from this perfect relax-chair, American style—it is all a boring extension of American wealth and efficiency)"—he is leaning back in the chair impassive, bored and rich in fact, playing with luxury in a scientific dada way, thinking up *reductio ad absurdum* machines & gimmicks to destroy man under this Capitalist luxury—The exposure meter a sample—"And then goes out with a robot to whom it is wedded and does all your shopping for you, picking out the exact large oranges & pears you will want to be exposed to."—

VI

Janco has got up, I ask him if he is a painter is it not? No, "A writer." I am surprised, thinking perhaps I missed something in him—"I'll send you a book—my book—" he says "my *Correspondances*"—ah, he writes big ideal letters to people—interesting—I think—

against the wall—they topple, well, they're his however they got there—I recollect I was going somewhere, I live *somewhere* surely near here, I ask, Claude in the dream comes kindly (seraph) and directs me there—downstairs—I love Claude, my psychic father—or brother—helpmeet in life—my Love (platonic here live) takes my arm and shows me to my door—not a beat pad at all, a de luxe inhabited flat—I go in relieved—I realize remembering where I am, & who I am, & why this happened—it's the small stroke of aphasia, brain damage—you forget who you are and what doing there—have blind instinct to grasp what you can, confused, rather like personage in a dream—real people come & assert their definite identity & take it away from you—till you get oriented—remember who and where you are that is—I give speech—since I realize I own the theater and can cash in the blue thin paper ticket I have—good anytime up or down stairs—It flashes thru my mind it will do no good being warned in advance that I will be undergoing periodic losses of identity for short periods—because *then* I won't know—will there be any way to remember, any continuity from aphasia to aphasia—like a dream? My first aphasia feeling was terror—suddenly born full grown in strange world—no past—amnesia!

Woke 5 AM strange wooden room Byron Hotel Athens—thinking the dream is prophetic taste of true identity loss I will undergo later on—Dawn now—woke tingling in my body & cramp in right leg. Last thot—how to maintain some continuity or memory over to another state—like Richard kid I met sans passport wandering Athens street, "secondhand Rose"—From Amnesia to amnesia, will I next time take off where I left off, or even forget it has come to this happening before—

As long as man thinks in talk and still talks, poetry be useful to maintain continuity and consult for memory—direct one consciousness to another—needed in this dream—really necessary later, tho?

This dream after conversation in Leslie Fiedler's huge apartment and visit earlier to Constantine Nicoloudis' house in Athens.

Oct. 2

Quack Quack Quack Quack quack
the White ducks squash wiggle their rear feathers
float motionless on the brown water
spread mythical wings in orange sunlight
thru the high small leaved trees—
on little green chairs the Greek Army sits with pretzels

The Mediterranean

He looks young but moves heavily in his white clean sh. & yachting cap & polkadot foulard—"I have 85 years you reali. surprised at this age. "You may use my yacht"—says Janco, getti. leave.

* * *

Trip to market with greek cartoonist boy in hotel sunrise—depress whether to sign political petition or no—

Dreams—

Bony pallid-faced King of Greece & Queen invite me to palace & attempt to seduce me from my idealism by reptilian intelligent charming offers of de luxe basements in the Grande-Bretagne Hotel—

Last night a nostalgic friendly dream—I was marooned depressed where I am, and suddenly from all sides—Claude arrives by car alone from country, he got my message—so does Jack, & Gregory was there all along. I am consoled, lonely, Claude is going to make it all up to me and takes me around and kisses me. A long dream which when I wake up with, it was too exquisite to record and I felt hopeless to record it—too much a Dream.

The Brain Damage

Movie—Later hip couple coming home—the hats piled up—can't find my door—my apartment door open, I'm a rich aristocrat—the flickering of consciousness, aphasia—it happens twice—Speech—. "It's the brain damage. Now I'll know—Next time I'll remember. This is the beginning here—henceforth it becomes interesting," I say entering my apartment.

I had bought ticket for the Radio City Music Hall De Luxe Theater (I been in this vast theater on both sides of balcony in other dreams)—Just as I am to enter I have a change of consciousness—total loss of identity—I don't know who I am or what I am doing in that spot on stairway going up to theater—I think I am going home. I think I recollect I live here—I look for my door, enter the first stairs down on the series of rack-staircases & porches over the lower theater—I think the theater and the apartment are the same—I'm confused since only the apartment is there—I go in, I don't recognize the place as mine, other people come into my house, I am indignant at them tho I know them they are taking my place—they say the apartment is theirs—as if they had been away all summer and I've been camping there and don't belong—of course not, he the man of the couple says, and sees a pile of felt hats—2 huge stacks

feeding the swans that violated Leda anon—
Scandal & Fury thru Duck-ranks
A fat kid waves his tin toy sword
a boy in blue long pants and bright
red sweater screams at the rocks—
Sunday, Tuesday, the afternoons are long and nothing to do
for the American in the green shirt—
He sits at the duck pond and worries—
on a zoo bench, an old man with a newspaper and glasses
pats the cheeks of the kid with the toy silk blue shirt.

Tues—Oct 2 or 3 1961

Out noon to Amer Express, met young gang there & sat around with beards & chicks & then to Taverna nearby, I sat while they ate (I'd eaten Souvlaki—shishkebab in Tortilla w/ tomato & onion) (and strawberry juice before)—then to Brazilian, met Nanos Valouritis,[1] then to Zonar with Nanos & met Katsimbalis[2]—sat there while he talked, silent—he looked like Sydney Greenstreet and had amazing Raimu gestures to illustrate his pop-eyed tales of travel—in fact he told how he crossed the Rockies on a train in the tourist Gondola car—made himself into a butterfly in the full moon with the howling of jackals on top of the American sky—to Hollywood where entering a "lounge" angry at being beaten for $30 in a taxicab mixup, a girl in furs leaned back stared at him and screamed "Greenstreet"—That I'd been thinking that of him too & his story later the same, I was amazed. Then drunk on the 3 bottles wine I wandered out thru streets in siesta time sunlight, tried to settle my mind with a dollar meal in good Vassilissis Sofias restaurant and went to the park to look at ducks (wrote poem notes) and lean my soul against the boys walking in torn pants and army white navy dresses—home and fell in bed to read book on Crete, dozed, slept till late dark evening at 8 and woke on a dream—

Dream—

I was with this writer Salinger who is a short man, who changed into east Indian negro color, with fine blue-brown style skin and black iron hair—

[1] Greek poet, friend of Surrealists, now (1976) living & teaching in California Bay Area America.

[2] Great talker described by Henry Miller in *The Colossus of Maroussi.*

myself changed color—wonderful! I exclaimed in the dream—really a change of identity—Like the Alchemist I heard of last night—whose last triumph simultaneous with the great work of philosophy-stone discovery was transmutation of himself to another person in another life. With no memory—So Allen Negro, followed by me, went up on a stage platform to the wooden door of his house like the prodigal son, knocked & entered—I waited outside for him to return, as my friend, Philos, which in greek can mean lover & in dream meant I desired to be this wonderful lone shade—don't know what recognition scene went on inside, then he came out, haunted by having seen & said farewell, unknown, to his children—and we went off together into an alley, as I woke—I loved him as I loved Claude in dream several days ago—

Woke lonely in the room—the window open on a church below a cab stand and closing flower-peddler's stalls in the darkness, looking out from huge box on the stage of people running home thru the streets & many cars in the concrete narrows, and up above in orange light the rock of Acropolis down Aeolus street from Hotel Byron where I am in the corner room one flight up. And a star over the small steeple, motorcycles cutting thru the silence.

Phaestos Oct 8, 1961—Cock Crow Dream

In house, modern ceiling with parents gone, rain, the ceiling sags, water dripping thru, it's my responsibility, I place buckets on floor and hope there's insurance.

In a tent with "Edward George" and a smaller pubescent kid, we are looking for a place to really fuck each other (and the kid) all nite—we have a large sleeping bag in the tent, like a circus labyrinth tent—I am ready to put down the bag as a bed, but he points out a pile of used torn rubber mats, we go drag them in and he builds a fire, the mats I am spreading touch the fire and burn underneath, I can see that a catastrophic fire is beginning—I call him Edward George! and blame him for mixing fire and rubber, & try beating it out, shake myself & wake up—and lay in bed ruminating about all the associations—

Robbery of Dr. Mahler's tiles,
    —off his garage roof— for my chicken coop next door
    155 Graham Ave Paterson 1934?
Starting fire in wastebasket, Firemen, Naomi in bed with lesbian
    nurse— obviously she shd have taken me to bed, no reason

for me to be alone sans contact then— burning her basket
she'd woven in occupational therapy, Hillside Hospital, 1930?
Later fight with negro at grammar school and coming home crying
to her— some contact love there— 1935
The stamp reversed on Fair Street— what was that?— 1931? Took
a letter from my father to mail at corner ice cream store,
put it on wrong side of envelope, got laughed at, embarrassed.
The accusation in high school chemistry class of stealing a book
I'd bought from a last term student. Isolation and guilt
in lady teacher's office. Met her on the bus years later,
she didn't even remember the incident so traumatic to me.
Peeing and wetting the bed? Fair St.? How long— peeing behind
Aunt Rose's piano at Newark, 1930? I didn't know where
else to pee.
Screaming being taken to school first time. Going to bathroom
[at school #1 on Fair St. in Paterson] not getting privacy,
not knowing how to unbutton pants. 1930?
Screaming at time of inoculation for smallpox— kids lined up for mass
shots— Children should be w/ parents in times
of stress. 1930?

* * *

Oct. 10?—

—Yesterday left Phaestos, bus over by side of Mount Ida Crete, great mount-pass scenery to Heraklion, fine meal roast pig & potatoes & okra, short visit to museum, then bus to Mallia, stopped an hour there, caught next rattle-y bus to sit in front by driver-seat over Lassithi side mountains along the coast to Aghios Nikolaos—at dark, no liking the size of town nor the gap-toothed harbor nor the small view of the bay, unable to find cheap hotel, settled for 38 Drx. in Lato Hotel with greek cook from Roumanian merchant ship sharing 2-bed room, ate and met a thin mulish greek named Michael who pressed my hand and talked of "baiser" and "vous êtes très agréable" and wanted to baiser with me in hotel—but no, too scraggly—ate shishkebab & a plate of shrimps & read first 4 books of Odyssey, unhappy.

Wake and confused walk on roads toward Gournia, turned back & walked up overland hill road winding toward Kritsa, tired, carrying basket of radio camera & clothes, sat hot & thirsty & turned back there, returned & faced Michael again who talked & practically weeped making a date for tomorrow which I shant keep. Then magnificent bus ride over Lassithi mountains to huge flat round lake-bed-like plain of Lassithi and found hotel cheap in crude mountain town overlooking the windmill-dotted old hidden valley. Climbed to Abdraeon Dicton Cave [birthplace of Zeus] & went down alone on slimy rocks & bottom waters, flashed light over amazing stalagtites, stayed as dusk came on and climbed out—to find, at the lip grass platform, high up overlooking V shaped gully that showed like inverted stage curtain over the valley floor—an Austrian gentleman of old age collector of moths & butterflies setting up his apparatus—storm lantern and white dinner screen to attract and catch moths at 16° centigrade 1000 meters up. Then watched him catch his moths as nite fell & stars came out, catch them in bottles filled with arsenic dope, then inject them with thin needle & black syringe of ammonia?—that saponifies their petit carcasses—and pin them down (blowing on wings to open their spreads) on cork floor of his wooden collector-box. Then I came down mount by flashlight over rubbly path to Psychron village which pleases me—bought sardine can & opened it with knife, turned on Sony miniature radio, and ate sardines, cookies, candy & water ending with a huge red apple—while broadcast operatic strains of ancient middleage tragedy—Chico Molina, the rich cultured lady of Peru, the old fat dead painter in Mexico City, Aunt Elanor, all the intellectuals from Santiago to ladies in old Milan, floated thru my head with their sadness & lonely hospital deaths. The room is bare as a cell, kerosine lamp & darkness outside—perched on slope overlooking the plain—and Orion in Milky Way banded over the roof.

Oct 11—'61

Woke at sunrise, gazed thru window at radiant haze, fell back asleep, a seizure of love and came in my hand thinking of the baiser of the ratty greek.

Yesterday I thought how lovely grey the rain would be hanging over the plain, when I woke up for food at 7:30 it was raining—all morning I lay in bed, looked out the window, read the *Odyssey*—eating in the hut next door, discussing Zeus, a blinding flash outside the door, and later a crash of thunder that shook the earthen cot.

Then walked across the plain zigzag on wet roads by overloaded red apple-ripe trees, branches hanging to the ground—climbed up to see the circular mountain view above Tzermiades Village—sat for coffee at iron table & watched girls run after cows, trucks unload, & old men lean on canes and blink on main street. Coming down from the mountain, I heard a mew in the rocks—mew bird?—but no, in a small aperture in red lava stones, a cat's charnel—I stared in, scared by reptilian skulls, bones as Polyphemus' cave bones must've been, cannibal floor—and the poor cat mewing for rescue behind a wall deep in. I went away, still too scared to rescue it, to stick my hand in thru all those cat teeth bones where the peasants had buried these babes.

Then home to the hotel zigzag an hour at sunset to bask along the field roads. Supper, fish and beans, & once more jacked off, thinking to accept life like Odysseus, stoic in misfortune, life being such.

Dream—

rainy night thunder, lightning—I wake and put on light and eat cherry drop—

The Murderer

The Jewish camp—originally in the wilderness it was to have been a religious center with posts and tents, music and sacrifices and food, in a sacred grove apart from the city, where dancing could take place all night, and death come without disturbing families asleep or human ways and streets.

I wander up the stairways of a movie-house toward the boxoffice, sneak in and glimpse—despite the aged ushers who won't have me stay ticketless—the old movie I've seen before—Marlene Naomi Harlow's death agonies, plane crash and heart attack. Rebecca with the cows at dawn, weeping Ruth, ancient landscapes.

Down at the fair, outside the main camp tent—civilization has grown up around the old park, there is a football field in a parking lot, an outdoor movie, fenced-in areas, and now a Jewish dance hall—pipe-iron railings enclose that, it's got kitchen attached, the dance is in full swing, some kind of Hebrew hora or folk dance—a huge silly dance in a place like a Dodgem Enclosure [1]—Hi Simon and Jerry Newman are dancing with big fat girls—I think, this used to be a general park for all folk out of town, but now the Hebrews have claimed it for their own—

---

[1] Amusement park arena for bumping and swirling in tiny electrified cars.

taken it over—ah well, but Why Not—their dance is nutty enough to be irrational invocation of mystery, none of them know anything, they are big empty heads dancing to show their silliness—In the line of bald dancers and heavy clownish women jumping up and down, there is room for any phantom to be invoked—Hebrew Voodoo, good as any other. Impression in dream that the line of celebrants are perfecting a gap in their own heads, a bubble of non-identity, they're dancing to lose grasp of their bodies—they're bumping off their minds—In fact it all goes back to the ancient story of ritual self-sacrifice, a placard bearing that method is posted on the wall or on one of the pillars, in printed cardboard—

Old Meaning

The Egyptian Method
of Becoming Conscious
is still remembered—
Man or woman, lost
in this sorry world
Who neither gains or loses
beset by sufferings and
able to live & die freely
are trained from youth to
jump into an old volcano
six or seven times by chance
to show their unimportance—
This is a ritual task
of old Mystic Jews' children
That was oft done of old.

Meanwhile tho I deplore the Jews taking over the tent exclusively, I admire & am amazed by the idiot quality of their display—a voice or awareness in the dream emphasizes that the ritual makes an empty bubble in all heads witnessing nearby.

Out on the parking lot a disappointed old man negro in rags has just emptied his pistol into a victim, in vengeance for injustices & slavery suffered by him as a child. A crowd chases him but they are all afraid to come near, while he raves at them, screams warnings, and pisses into a beer bottle to make an inflammable bomb. A young man right in the line of fire, in front of me at a picnic table, gets annoyed & hurls a bottle back at the old man, who is still preparing his urine & flame bomb—he looks down the line of fire, I move out of the way because that's the direction I'm in—I wake, detesting the old man, afraid, like I was afraid of the dying kittens' charnel house in the rocks.

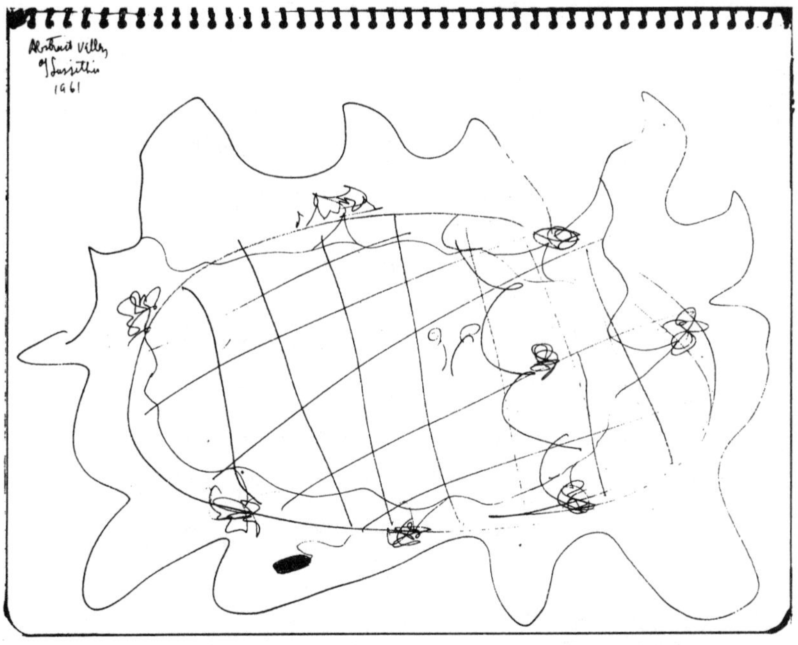

"Abstract view of Lassithi's rounded valley floor circled by mountains"

Dream Oct. 14, 2 AM 1961

Shirley Temple on screen, sitting on old Romeo's lap—some old handsome Spanish-Mexican he-man bronze from Palm Beach actor—the judge at Cannes—hero of a Gary Cooper film—La Petite Belle Temple, sexy, has mussed his tie and snuggled to his breast and kissed his eyelids and passed her hand thru his shirt to his chest & also pulled out a letter from his inner dinner jacket pocket. She takes the liberty of reading it, must be a very personal letter, why, it's from Ernest Hemingway in fact—

"Yes" says Actor "just a memory from dear old Ernie"—and then the letter written in an extraordinary illuminated hand script is flashed on the silver screen—in fact the letters drawn like Mayan hieroglyphs glitter in the starshine of the Hollywood Screen—

"Dear Actor" says the letter—"I am writing you this historical script by hand just so the people won't get their hands on it till I am safe and sound beyond their rage. After all it was not Schopenhauer who started the stupid search for the superior man which led in turn to such monstrosities as Chamberlain and Hitler in the end—and then rather as a post-mortem kick he added old Joe McCarthy which has been the menace in America ever since the downfall of honest journalism in was it the Golden Twenties? As for myself I can only conceive of America getting out of its present historical fix and saving its neck and skin by finally once & for all ridding itself of the after-effect of his despotism—for he has left in the brain-pan a residue of electricity which from Rosenberg to Chessman has stained everybody's arms with human blood, etc."

At this point in the movie house one after another people begin to applaud—a public demonstration—and I bang on the chair applauding the noble resolution also—amazing! the spirit seems universal in the audience & great waves of broken applause surge forth to greet this trailer on the screen.

Someone is commenting on a Des Moines or Detroit newspaper which during the last election campaign was so angry at Nixon for some drunken blunder at an election rally locally that all mention of the Republicans was dropped for a week and all front page news reported as sport & hollywood gossip & divorce-murders. Then the papers picked up pro Nixon front pages where they left off. Nixon had got drunk, vomited at banquet and appealed for the Wowser Vote on basis that he was due it since he had schemed the importation of Australian Wowsers to replace the yellow race banished from our shores by Alien Exclusion Act—or some such nefarious piece of politics.

— — —

Other part of dream, Gregory Corso in a fine English fur coat—presumably bought & paid for with fast money come by thru gift or gamble or article—is walking in broad avenues of London—it's a film of his present career he's sent me—seeing the swans and all that—he loiters by Blake's grave and up the structure of London Bridge—and addresses me from the dream-screen—"After all I'm yr. friend and so don't worry about the money"—I'm annoyed, since I am worried about money—He still owes me 100 in the dream.

* * *

Paris in Bronze

Antekytherean Ephebe, restored, black skin,
resting on one foot, one knee bent, looking outward to the right
eagerly, with a question in his eye, vulnerable,
his right arm stretched forth to tempt
Aphrodite with an apple of Pride.
He's a good looking boy, well built,
with flowery bronze pubic hair, small phallus
tip of flesh at the end, relaxed,
with his breast bare, belly muscles and veins in his feet
choosing between the Bed, the Mind or Power—
Paris stepping forward in Eternity, Man before the Trojan War
chasing his joy, eager, as he might touch her breast for the first time.

Oct. 15, 1961—Athens, Hotel Parion, Dream 6 AM

At radio set, waiting long time for the right broadcast, the opera theater with the soprano artist, twiddling the dial, leaving the radio for long periods at a time to wander offstage to other portions of the dreamworld, in a room with people who are all waiting with me.

Finally the hour comes, 7 p.m., and—desperation, frustration—I twiddle and twiddle but suddenly can't find the right station where I know the opera's taking police—taking place—Lawns of Tennis—The radio turns into an old-fashioned one with a table under which there is a stone unhollow urn suspended midway between the table legs. Old fashioned 1933 radio—But the stone urn loomed up in the dream—and thru it another scene—for finally I did find the station, very small, have to center the dial on it around 700 and clear out the right sound—Thru the urn, a bedroom like a stone cell, on which a woman lay, twisted and mad, as opera music came thru the radio—and surrounding this iron bed high off the floor, cobwebs & spiderwebs which by now had jelled into networks of soft but solidified jellies that covered the walls and underpart of bed & shelves beneath bed and on mattress where the woman lay,

and three jellies-bumps were the recorded operatic folkmusic I was trying to get on the radio, except they were now unavailable and the prima donna was dying mad on her bed and the jelly bumps were in an awful condition—and outside sat her retainer and nurse a young woman, who appeared to toss a match to the room and end all the suffering—I advised against it, let the corpse lay dry on the bed, but don't try to burn the soul out of the body lest all the jelly bump folk music that's preserved in the room be destroyed.

Woke with a start, thinking of Artaud "bodies revolving around their corpses" and Dante's *Comedy*—Brunetto Latini (or Naomi).

After dream Oct. 15, 1961—

Face to face with those Beautys too awful for Logos
Hölderlin shuddering on Patmos—
Scared Oscar in Paris after words failed him,
Baudelaire in ruins babbling in a dark room on Ile de la Cité—
All them I heard of, and counted myself lucky
that I would get free, without paying my obol to Charon—
only be sad as a Greek plaint on the jukebox in silent Bambino—
Now it's time to say farewell, to all I thought I loved forever—
all my silken desires, all I ever saw in dreams— sad Pitthecotis the singer—
or Homer's ladies gone into the book of the dead—
No sadder song than that of the world going bye bye
Bye Bye Neal, strong thighed as Achilles in the tents of the West,
Bye Bye dear Bill, whom I never loved with my body, tho desired once,
Bye Bye Lu, you too wasting, consumed in the stomach, thin, forgotten
in the old dream of life,
Jack, Bye Bye, sweet old Master of adieux.
Gregory, all yr foolyness, Bye Bye even to Immortality & the Laurel,
withered before yr. eyes—
Peter, Bye Bye to your long nose, & dear old loves of every city we ate in
Huncke, you too excluded from Immortality with us all—
that the Shadow of the Awful come over Literature
and end the pining, aching, sighing, tortured ecstasy,
Goodbye my ambition to be Eternity's Columbus claiming empty doom
for discovery—
No Glory-shining ash left for memento, much less Fiery Monument—
Nor son to weep after the Charnel's filled—
No Lord to ask but Me, and that Lord Eternity

ıongst many at the Surprising Jukebox—
r his bright Selection . . .
ıusic.
I like
blinking lights,
's beard traced on his cheek,
orown hair waved over his skull—
fingers on the music—
smiling, a ring on his fourth finger—

7–38,
ready

ıful

chard,
of
om

* * *

n Café, intended as Bouzouki Lyric]

ny hair in the mirror,
to the travel office,
the typewriter for hours,
ımb my hair in the mirror.

ght but my face is dead
t of my mother is paralysed,
vants to marry me but
man who sells tomatoes.

voice

t I have belly I have fingers
reasts I have teeth.
nt I find a hero
me before I'm dead?

The one

e home and cook meat,
't have a telephone
np on men in the street.
ne nights I cry in the movies.

ıear mustaches whistle behind me.
Iy dreams whistle at me in bed,
When I'm dead I hope the bones
Don't start whistling in the graveyard.
—Athens

* * *

Hymn to the Jukebox

If it weren't for you Mr. Jukebox
With your big aluminum belly roaring
and your thirty teeth eating everybodys dirty coppers . . .*

* [First text of "Seabattle of Salamis took place off Perama," pp.
Planet News. Lines below a variation–continuation of the poem, a
in print.]

2 Drachmas brings Black Jack, 10 Drachmas brings on the Unfait
again–
I'm casting my spell on you, Apocalypse Rock, Open the Door R
I Got a Woman, Melancholy Locomotive, Abrupt Nirvana, End
the World Rag–You'll Never Be Untrue, White Silk Bloss
& you Neal– what hard won piece of joy–
when all about the blossoms of love fell over Arcady
We had to struggle over the Rockies and I had to cry
for nothing but the hard hard fucking heart of America–

and all about me now the bodies of men I wanted
naked, smiling, statues 2000 years old
boys of 18 dancing in the middle of the floor
with hard-looking sailors smiling & truck drivers singing in low
my Surrealist nitemare of Whitman come to Full Neon Karma–
and a dwarf carrying apples–

Poems dictated on Ammonia (Sq.) by 2 Greek boys from Kea–
I slept with–another translating:

Six years I eat
inside of the Calethea town
Because I was a pimp
to your company–
For your jealousy and your now getting old–
and you man
where we got gone down in life–
made crimes–
you wanted a lot
now you're a whore–

Hymn to the Jukebox

If it weren't for you Mr. Jukebox
With your big aluminum belly roaring
and your thirty teeth eating everybodys dirty coppers . . .*

* [First text of "Seabattle of Salamis took place off Perama," pp. 37-38, *Planet News.* Lines below a variation—continuation of the poem, already in print.]

2 Drachmas brings Black Jack, 10 Drachmas brings on the Unfaithful
 again—
I'm casting my spell on you, Apocalypse Rock, Open the Door Richard,
I Got a Woman, Melancholy Locomotive, Abrupt Nirvana, End of
 the World Rag—You'll Never Be Untrue, White Silk Blossom
& you Neal— what hard won piece of joy—
when all about the blossoms of love fell over Arcady
We had to struggle over the Rockies and I had to cry
for nothing but the hard hard fucking heart of America—

and all about me now the bodies of men I wanted
naked, smiling, statues 2000 years old
boys of 18 dancing in the middle of the floor
with hard-looking sailors smiling & truck drivers singing in low voice
my Surrealist nitemare of Whitman come to Full Neon Karma—
and a dwarf carrying apples—

Poems dictated on Ammonia (Sq.) by 2 Greek boys from Kea—The one I slept with—another translating:

Six years I eat
inside of the Calethea town
Because I was a pimp
to your company—
For your jealousy and your now getting old—
and you man
 where we got gone down in life—
made crimes—
 you wanted a lot
 now you're a whore—

is just another Doom 'mongst many at the Surprising Jukebox—
Putting in a drachma for his bright Selection . . .
of a moment's passing music.
I like
that boy so lively at the blinking lights,
I like his face, with a day's beard traced on his cheek,
square handsome face & brown hair waved over his skull—
and interested in putting fingers on the music—
Straight-backed, and even smiling, a ring on his fourth finger—

* * *

[Poem written in Café, intended as Bouzouki Lyric]

I comb my hair in the mirror,
I go out to the travel office,
I bang on the typewriter for hours,
Then I comb my hair in the mirror.

I look alright but my face is dead
on account of my mother is paralysed,
Nobody wants to marry me but
the skinny man who sells tomatoes.

I have feet I have belly I have fingers
I have breasts I have teeth.
Why cant I find a hero
to love me before I'm dead?

I come home and cook meat,
I don't have a telephone
I jump on men in the street.
Some nights I cry in the movies.

I hear mustaches whistle behind me.
My dreams whistle at me in bed,
When I'm dead I hope the bones
Don't start whistling in the graveyard.
—Athens

* * *

(I lose my life for you
      my life in the rest of people's world—)
because I was love you—

My Darling know then
  I am so far from
you   So   I
understand how much
I love you   I beg you

Athens

A Note

Plato's Steeds—Phaedrus 342?

Recall walking several days ago over hill and around walls of Mycenae, climbing the shoulder of Mt. Ziria & facing the valley behind—the small rocky castle ruin far downstairs—then walking to (Benahi?)—and along the road thru the red rock cave pocketed mountain pass near Heraeum of Argos to the plain—reaching the flat rocky dust road my sandals broke & I plodded on thru the solitude bordered by olive groves and hills with the elevation of Hera's ruins on the right hand distance, singing to myself and the sky till the tears came to my eyes while I lifted my voice, desolate in all that history, without any name for what I was—

Dream Oct 26—3PM—

(aboard ship Athene along coast of Asia Minor—saw it first 8 AM when woke—Finished *Iliad,* lunch, then came downstairs to sleep, thinking as on ships I oft dream to catch a prophecy on the wing—)

Just woke, was in a dream with Burroughs and Dorothy Norman—I and Bill alone at first walking together, he touching me, I was abashed—alone with him,—he asks me if I continued photographic work—I say, Not much—"I thought you liked it"—"Yes I do, I made a few photos but liked some of them and I didn't want to cut them up for collages—simply never did any collages since Tanger because I couldn't glimpse directly what you meant by yours—never understood—and I didn't want to destroy the photos I liked."

He has his hands on me, I feel younger and embarrassed, playing up to him like this—ambiguously encouraging him to admire me yet winning his contempt for being a whore—we are seated at a little card table covered with white cloth & silver serving dishes in a Chinese restaurant in New York—Suddenly Dorothy Norman, dressed in black & very demure & shy, approaches, I invite her to sit down, proud to connect the two of them—She is at end of table, I look down and realize she's sitting below at bottom of 4 steps—but more intimately close than this photo below—more like side view (I see both in dream)

more like side view

(I see both in dream)

I get up to move the table, so as to give room for her chair at the end of the table, but the frail table legs collapse—and the table settles on the floor—I am sure Burroughs is annoyed by all this fuss and imposition of sociability on my part—I get up to lift up the table—I have my sweater and shirt off—bare-chested, cute—I do get the table righted and all in place but now faced with the problem I'm half-naked—as per Bill's advice I go to corner where my over clothes are hanging on a hook and try to find my sweater or shirt—I get the sweater but see it turns into a too-small shirt—I go to another chamber in the Chinese restaurant to pull it over my head and come back out—I sit down.

Wakened I remember Norman as a sort of Deva woman—surprised and logical she is interested in Bill in the dream, perhaps I should write them to meet—

In the side chamber, an associate kitchen with a few pots and boxes of silver or napkins lying on the concrete floor, struggling frustrated to get on the shirt and look decent, I think of myself as a sort of city gigolo, whose specialty, lacking other talent, is introducing people and making myself useful (like Johnny Nicholson [1]), which everybody knows—not at all a wheel or a prophet or saint—but some kind of weak opportunistic kid loose among vain celebrities, social climbing by juggling their names on my tongue in conversation and introducing one to another for my own purposes as in this restaurant scene.

Thinking awake of Duncan's rebukes "riding triumphant and despondent on the wave" [2]—the vanity and danger of fame—dreams in S.A. of Duncan and Spicer mocking me—a lesser man as in the Iliad, as I thought upstairs of the Seraphic potentialities of Jack and Bill compared with my own which flirted and has become tricked with Power Realities and forgotten other worlds of spirit—tempted as in fantasy by rail overlooking Turkey to found a political party in America and challenge Stevenson to public debate and make good earlier political vows on ferryboat to Columbia—defending myself against Jack's accusation of being a Jewish Communist intellectual—all hung up in image of my external Fame self and name and now finally all tactics and psychic life now centered around this problem of destroying Allen Ginsberg Karma Fame Selfhood which battle so preoccupies me it is the reverse-coinside of an earlier egotism—which absorbs me now so complete that I am useless for any other helpful science.

Oct. 27, Dream—

Morning—Gene and I in bathtub of Dr. Mahler's house while they are out—I raise up a bit, seeing the water level has run high enough to enter the first drawer of the kitchen bathroom cabinet that's built into the huge tub—he lays back despite my repeated appeals—I exhort him just to raise up but don't explain why, frustrated—they are coming home, in the door.

* * *

[1] N.Y. restaurateur c. 1960, friend of Tennessee Williams & Paul Bowles.

[2] From Robert Duncan's mimeographed program for Corso & A.G. reading auspices S.F. State College 1956.

Israel notebook cover

Israel
By the shores of Lake Galilee
with the blue-dark dome older-
starred at night . . .

[First text of "Galilee Shore," pp. 39–40, *Planet News*]

Galilee

The lady night club owner observed that Arabs are (if they smoke H at all) addicted and have a sense of fantasy (which they really believe!) and are good stone-fence makers, & continued her analysis: they are Unreliable, Cowards, they make poor soldiers and have an inferior mentality.

Tiberias—Oct 28, 1961

Dream—In large house with older friend we are touring—there is a kitten we have as pet, but which has to die to be eaten—I make an omelette of the cat, and eat half of it, but the front half of the cat is still alive and I've no stomach to confront the cat with his total disappearance—I leave the room, the older man talks to the cat alone about business—when he comes out the door I ask what happened—am relieved when he says that he & the cat finished the omelette—then we go out to tour, to see some galleries of cave that I missed passing thru the neighborhood before—in the cave I meet a Texan American also touring—great confusion in Cretan-Palestinian night.

* * *

The Word as a Physiological and Therapeutic Factor—
by K. Platonov
Foreign Languages Pub. House, Moscow, 1959

* * *

Pavlovian Psychotherapy:
"Owing to the entire preceding life of the human adult a word is connected with all the external & internal stimuli coming to the cerebral hemispheres, signals all of them, replaces all of them & can, therefore,

evoke all the actions & reactions of the organism which these stimuli produce."—I. Pavlov

* * *

Behold! my flesh is pure library
and my hand is 5 installments of Potatoes

5 Nov 61—Afternoon dream— lying in bed, rocking back & forth on bed calling on Lord for a sign. Moaning & singing in dream demanding news, as Whalen advised in letter. Saw my body from above.

Premonition Dream

7 *November, 1961—*

Dream, after week of unhappiness and mood arriving by Ship on the Shore and walking along vast boulevard by Sea, Street of Lucknow Chickens in INDIA—first dream of India—huge red and brown night boulevard by water, I walk alone several miles in night along ox-meat market street till I go thru fairyland gate to the Rashbehari Rich Section with modern Apartments on the Seaside—a beautiful front street rich waterfront like vaster Chicago—I wonder what city I'm in, I'm deliriously happy, it's my promised land (I'm writing this in the promised land)—the night street has few people, I see chain of lights like Riviera hotel facade facing the ocean—I'm coming to a big church front—at last; it's the Sign Christian all India Church—fantastic Door, just made for me in concrete, like a blind one-eyed skull, with Sacred hearts in the bottom concrete declivity—as I bend to kiss the S. Heart, I read the Funeral inscription—"Well it's too bad but goodby"—I feel happy, it is like a sign thru death here for me—the cosmic joke's come true in happy way—the wonderworld where Man knows he's in a dream—I pass on to a square where with big candles the bodies are on display on wooden scaffolds, covered with white sheet & guarded by Army soldiers in White—I'm amazed by this street display—Next I realize this front Street is only the thin layer of money people, but there are great probably cheap apartments for rent here—I'll settle down like Gregory in one, with my

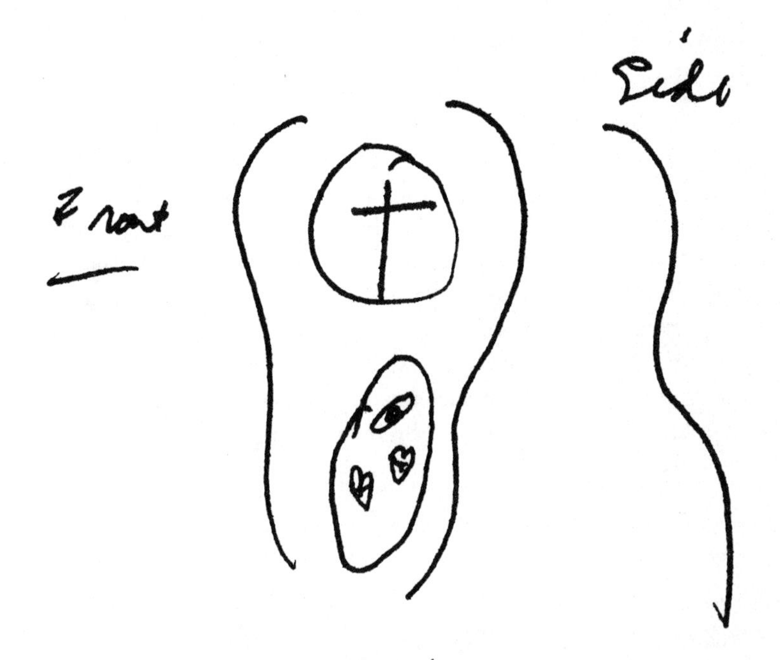

Premonition dream

own kitchen, and a white suit, and live free—Then behind these streets must be the filthy hovels I'll explore, I'll walk there tomorrow, I shiver with fear and say, The Bombay seems endless, I never realized how it would feel, first those nites of old city waterfront, then the Great All India Gate to the New City I'm in now which goes on miles too—here's a big hotel, I enter later & get lost in green lobby-garage—I'm wandering in India, it's like a new earth—I'm happy—I wake—Morning in Haifa, my ass aches from a colitis or clap or Amoeba—morn light—time to get up soon it's 6:45—light to write this prophecy by.

Nov. 8—

Moved down from Haifa to Tel Aviv—met poet Maty Meged at Café, all night wandering. At apartment of Ethel Broido a dream fades out this morn in room with Gurdjieff who's disappearing talking about farewell to Peter—we both sentimentalize and agree Peter sure was the perfect

Russian servant of love—Gurdjieff behind a desk of the Commie Embassy, I in door saying goodbye and high—I had that nite given Meged mushrooms #7.

Nov. 9—

Dropped watch last nite, just before sleep—I had been writing poems in little backside pocket spiral note-book with soft white cover that turns page up from top spiral—I woke with dream—in house rented with Gregory sharing a room we both are writing, I fill the notebook with long poems, he comes upstairs and starts reading me his while I'm writing, I say No, don't interrupt me, so I go downstairs to kitchen and continue alone. Louis is there with his own writing I guess, and some pots on the stove.

— — —

Waking pondering first of all, that watch was Gregory's and after it hit the stone floor it don't work no more, still says quarter to two which is when I went to bed. Jack continues his confessions in Florida. Bill working on his cut-ups somewhere in U.S. now, an extended labor. Greg in London polishing his apples. Me, I'm getting vainer, more talkative & sloppier & don't do anything. Jerked off & fell asleep feeling good that for some reason I conjured up a blonde girl to fuck & that's what happened after dreaming Peter's farewell.

9 Nov. Dream—

To bed & immediate sleep—in a room with corpse of Naomi in bed—I in bed with that—or live—she rises up—maybe stiff—Louis is in room—I get up, turn down Spirit lamp—you know kerosine—it sprays all over me, I crouch & cry to Louis the figure at side—then I wake.

The tomb of Reb Meir Ba'al Haness on Galilee shore, Tiberias in the scenery.

* * *

According to Israel Vekselman in Tel Aviv, who is my father's father's sister's son, I am descended from a Russian writer Achad Aham Ahad 'Haam né Ginsberg from Russia.

Dream—

in bed in large dark room with younger man, a cousin or friend, I roll over on him and roll him up at my hips, and he is passive but friendly, I feel hot, I start to push him down to blow me—someone else in room disturbs this presumption of mine—but it feels good and the bed mate may comply, I lift him physically in bed to put his mouth at my hips—and the effort of lifting wakes me up with a start Sunday morn in Tel Aviv.

20 Nov. Dream—

Asked for Bill Burroughs' passport by young fellow, I gave it over, but then worried after they picked up mail, that Ian Summerville wouldn't return it to me. But he did in the dream.

Woke depressed, that is hemmed in by inconsequence of my life, that is metabolically brought down, faced by Burroughs.

To Peter Orlovsky

When we parted in Tanger
We said ten years or perhaps a few months.
Whatever fate and railroads bring, whatever cities or deserts—
Now I'm in the holy land, alone
Reading Cavafy— it's half past twelve.
My letters haven't reached you, yet you're somewhere here, Petra or Syria
Perhaps have entered the Gate to this land and are looking for me in Jerusalem—
I wrote to all your addresses and to your mother—
Tonite I am reading books & remembering our old nights together naked—
I hope fate brings us together, a letter answered, held in the red hand—
or crossing some modern streetcorner, look joyfully in each other's eyes.

Nov. 24 Dream—

Grand Reunion Ansen, Claude, Jack etc. all meeting in some N.J. Paradise town, in beds, lovemaking, & old eros nostalgia.

— — —

Neutron bomb is triumph of accumulated Capital: possessors of Capital annihilated, Capital eliminates all but itself in the universe.

* * *

Cracks, leaks, crunches, Creeps, Craps, Crops, Chips, spray. Chop chop. Fuck you.

Time to destroy this notebook with some scribbling. All leading up to this moment. Opium. In Ethel Broido's apartment, Tel Aviv Hayarkon St. overlooking the orange-purple sunset over Egyptian horizon. With Bernard Kops folksinging all afternoon. Read about Zoroaster. Talked philosophy with 18-year-old kid visitor & read him Marvell's "Garden" & Smart's Cat Jeoffry [1] lines.

Peter leant on couch reading a contemporary play (by Englishman Kops), the transistor playing Arab music, me with book on lap, heater on floor with red electric bar radiating warmth in the stone-floor Israeli room. I am too comfortable in this body, I hardly want to move out. Thought of getting psychedelic high is a disturbance—the discomfort to the spirit, to be detached from habit, wakened and made to gaze around in a room on the world's edge at the mediterranean near-East shore.

Yet I been talking Transcendency to everyone from Morocco to Palestine. Endless jabber about drugs, like the Ancient Mariner with his albatross.

Pink-thank-thunk of Arab ouads over Transistor coming in from the couch. Alvar-ar, alvar-shmuhadi. Aaaah, the schlopsy voice of Arabic announcers.

Aoch machem desu macaw horrim. Likiat a shaham shivu mein hakoleli rosh shana. A pif gan me assal a parisiana. A quom no megin schmoumin, hashifel zo discor bictora, levadel levagel ahanim. Schehim Bram et heitum cameo mishana arbaka hagal schnatui, beshesh. Valuso de algirar al sabath. Tunis. Se fruit ha shabei pash too ta, gueyom adam a mutzalla ort, noch alumar, frudit de Tunis. A danzi fruit a folklore hagiographic.

That's the radio.

And a pipe of Egyptian hash. And Beethoven violin entering vibrations in the air centered on the little black Sony I bought in

---

[1] From Christopher Smart's *Jubilate Agno.*

Gibraltar, a memento & totem for $21 dollars. Chorus of orchestra one section flowing after another, mounted, & sewed by the needle silver solo violin, scaled.

"Man is the Messiah" saith the worm.

"They put them into the hospital today" saith Peter.

Tell that to the Hassidim, bow down Naturai Karta, sing Poet. In this realm beauty & composure and death enter, cycles of colitis, headache, oversleep, anxiety, am I escaping oblivion?

Here too is oblivion, here too

where the page ends and a new begins, quick as the flash from one word to another. One world to another joined.

Only myself in this solitude. Be it the Skull Cathedral of Indies of Dream, towering grey in night-memory.

A sign, writhing fucking the bed calling the Lord. In my sleep.

Come thou X and be an X. The detective crossed the room & stared with a magnifying glass at the chalk which marked the spot where the Angel appeared. By the old brown closet, next to Beethoven's mahogany window.

Beethoven and Blake, seraphic incarnations . . .

"I am in! I am out!"

Echoing from Jerusalem, Belsen, Hiroshima, towns made holy by annihilation, burning, crucifixion in their turn, now memory.

Bruno Schwanz played the music over the radio. Eilat next, to wait for ships bound for East.

Buber advising against Vision, mouth hidden by his dear beard. Gershom Scholem wrapping his hand under his knee.

The gossip that is not written down, the arguments over Arabia & Egypt.

"Where's Ethel?" Honk Honk out the window, waltz on the radio, the return of the universe to itself. Kosmos the Magician is Born!

Behold, many babies are born in many Bethlehems, over the hills beyond the wall. By the barbed wire. The silence between Yiddish & Araby frontiers. Sad backdrops of the Old painted Comedy theaters. Faded applause.

I think I will write an article for a Newspaper. Mr. & Mrs. America, Hello. Hitler too was a poet, they said. I am Adolph Hitler in disguise, visiting campus.

Dr. Mabuse organized riots. The hawk nose & white hair and eyes staring into hypnotic walls, papers and madhouse bars.

Breughel's hypnotic needles, Beethoven's needles in his ears. He heard that music in his skull? Hypnotic Eternity, snakes and deserts, New York Herald Tribune Pravda, C.B.C., CBS, Times, Daily News, Fair Play for Cuba Committee, 100 against the Atoms.

The anti-Atom Bomb Party—an international movement. Licensed reproduction? Got to stop sex & reproduction to solve the population explosion. China & India & America, Russia Britain Israel, South Africa,

South USA,—white man must know black. The Hatikva. What'm I going to do, take them to court? Nathan Zak [Israeli poet] on mind.

Can Jehova fuck Buddha? Can Mohammed suck Christ? Zoroaster, Bh'ai, Gurdjieff, Subud, Sabbati Sevi, Isaac the Blind, what kind of mental daisychain weaving have they accomplished?

The atombomb will solve one aspect of the population explosion caused by Science. Are the Scientists in charge here? L.S.D.-25 another Atom Bomb. Inside & outside—an expanding universe. There are 10,000,000 possible inhabited planets? Plenty of room to spread. Sooner or later life will consume life. The secret of the universe is that it has no reason. No human comparison? Long ago and far away. Closing the eyes in question. Facing India.

Dream of Nov. 9 must be symbolic of early memory in bed with Louis & Naomi & she must have come over my face. Swathed in warm fleshy silk. Being born. Frightened, entering the world. I will leave life the same.

Straining to hear the Ahad Haam in the Music. What happens to everybody after they die? All the religions get the same treatment, Arab & Jew in Immortal dark—

"Take me by the hand
O baby
and lead me to
the promised land . . ."—Leadbelly to Blind Lemon Jefferson

The minstrels into the Deaf Ears. The Stroboscope fills the sky. How do we know we're not already under the Hypnotic spell of invisible Nerve Gas? No wonder my poor mother complained about wires in her head. After the lobotomy. And Elise said, "you haven't done with her, yet?" after typing the mss. of *Kaddish.* I'm attracted to intellectual madwomen.

Nov 29:

Emerson "Winter, night, sleep are all invasions of the Eternal Budh . . ." 1842–43. "This horrid infinite which circles us"—

1866—arriving at the contemplation of the Budh "and a perpetual approach and assimilation to Him, thus escaping new births . . ."

—[Emerson's] Journals

A Little Bit of Joy

Ho! Ho! This tree is an animal moving in Gan Eden, Folks.
That tree has a soldier at its trunk staring into the lighted café,
blindly startled, moving off in the green light—
This tree has five great arms sticking up into the darkness
and down out of the darkness, clusters of leaves, bunches of green berries
    are
hanging, and move their fingers in the automobile breeze—
This tree on main street in the Holy land has three streamers of moss
    under its arms—
This tree stands up like a ghost, solid and grey, after hours,
when the avenue's crowded with photographers, young men with black
    sweaters,
This tree leans against the striped tables of the café, and gossips with
    friends of the family,
this tree beckons, and flowers to all
waving with little movements in each long branch fellow leaves—
this tree is blind, this tree is dumb, this green madness at birth,
umbrella'd over the busses, branches sticking out by the delicatessen,
    innocent-tendril'd, knockneed & rough barked
Standing on the edge of the curb, flagpole of Eden and all the eyes of the
    dead—
This tree which I see for a minute is invisible to all who sit in the café.

Cassit [Café] Dec. 3, 1961
10–15 minute sketch

This tree will be visible when the future has passed by.

* * *

Salt slagheaps move down on Sodom
brackish water shifts, the slimy plain's cracked,
arid mud pods & sunken clay beds slick the feet—
iron machinery twists all rusted near piles of grey salt-ash,
sun sets violet and pink against the horizon's foreign
    cliffs & mountain tops.

Dream:

Looking up the places on the map written of by the old
Hebrew poet & weeping because I WAS THERE

"Between Island & Pallia
Poland and Kos
Kos & Chios
I go
between Poland & Ionia
Poros and Pharos
Io and Jove
I am born"

"Step by step
nobody follows
Place after place
No one will go
Karas to Petén
None to remember
Denver to Frisco is
one forever."

Dream—19 Dec. 1961—Acca (Acre)—Palestine—

Part of a newsreel taken Candid Camera of Peter during the regular filming of other movie by a Dutch or Polish cameraman—during filming of "Pull My Daisy"—as Peter who had small part in official film was horsing around trying to work himself up into spontaneous pantomime, he walks around the large studio set—Acca with Ruins or the Colosseum in Miniature—à la chorusgirl strut, sticking out chest and rubbing breasts (like Naomi), then passes into Pierrotesque melancholy droop realizing he's a man, then plays basketball with the air, circling the stage—a crowd is gathering, I'm watching from the infield—the cameraman is recording it all not just fragments, I'm amazed, that he had that much sense and it's worked out so now it's being shown to the public neighbors—Peter weaves about the stage, half transformed, not yet in the role, showing it, so that his role is to demonstrate his search for a role—he bicycles around

Dream, Acco:

Earlier, broke my sunglasses in dream.

the stage with his hair long and aspect transformed to that of a plump breasty breathless Jewish virgin who teaches arts and crafts to children in a nervous breakdown Academy—I dislike this aspect and wish he'd drop that role, he's swung into it unconsciously and I don't want to be associated with that—he glances up at me—I'm standing arms folded on chest with a frightened cold eye on him, unmoved—he supplicated toward me with his arm, I stare back cynically—now he's making fun of me, the camera is recording it all—he makes champagne gestures to infinity, he pantomimes a weep, he wriggles his ass, he comes up to embrace me in flashy queen red sweater like greek whore Janos, he turns tender, I turn tender, we kiss, his leg between my thighs, in a Faust-Marguerite seduction scene from opera—that is the close up and end of the pantomime, I'm playing along not to disappoint his art and so as to impress camera audience with our rapport in heaven, despite cynical eyebrow raised by my conscience and whatever the spectators may think.—

* * *

Floating bodiless above the world
(my head on a pillow in Acre
    inside the Crusaders walls
        ruined in the rain,
        electricity cut from Haifa
    Josephus' Jewish wars on the quilt—
waiting for Sabbath to pass me by)

What was the War in Korea?

How many millions died? What for? Only ten years ago!
All newspapers portrayed this new war as a Just War. Portugal took part!
The last three American Wars were Just! War I, War II, Korea.
I say none of them were just wars.
I say whoever preaches War preparedness is a self-interested murderer.
Truman's a murderer, Eisenhower murderer, Kennedy's preparing murder.
What motive? What they gain?
They're out to make war rather than surrender opinions, sensory impressions, selfskins to oblivion.
Millions of citizens be dragged thru mud-fires so Truman believe he's really Truman,
Ike be Ike of his dreams, Kennedy satisfy his father's ambition.
I am Nobody has no left or right, anyone who's a power is a murder power.
What's any war ever accomplished but contagion gangrene & vomit?
Whose trickery illusions' Heroes? Why's that taught to Children?
What do 1926 History books say about the Opium Wars?
What will the History books 1990 say about Korea, Algeria, Formosa, Cuba, Laos, Congo?
Reader of Jewish Wars knows it was all a lot of A.D. shit,
Bar-Kochba no hero, big-headed suicidal nut sold on his own importance—
Herod an egotistical fanatic—Rabbi Akiba full of shit—

"The grass will grow out of his jaws before the Messiah comes"—
All think they are Messiahs, Truman & Kennedy & Khrushchev all think Messiahs,
all Messiahs including me equally smart in our own stupid brains.
2 thousand year succession of mad bureaucrats,
Pillaging, raping, brainwashing, spying, stealing, bleeding,
Lying— whole populations think the way they do—
popular propaganda gossips influencing electricity, talking radios,
TV leering in bedrooms, splashing blood all over the newspapers—
Big speeches justify themselves— "You dont realize all my problems" they all complain
to the masses hypnotized smiling on chicken feather sofas or boney starving in Chile coal mines—
Khrushchev orating Kennedy orating— big mouths open, both same—
Chiang Kai-shek de Gaulle— showing their tongues to the microphone— 48 sets of teeth flash an identical idea—
Nasser and Ben-Gurion, one big mouth hates Arabs, one big mouth hates Jews— Which is which, anyway—
Adenauer the Catholic, fawned on by reformed Storm troopers & businessmen who ate jewish genitals during the wartime shortage—
Ulbricht the atheist summoning the glory of communist Gefilte Fish for which he is willing everybody should die with him—
Allessandri of Chile, trickery and oily manners, Castro of Cuba, a big cigar and he wants to be hero too,
He thinks of his name in the future & shuts down the Moons of the revolution [1]—
The moon of the Cuban rebellion's gone under the laughing Carib!—
Mao Tse-tung just shat on Tibet, everybody thinks National Sovereignty violated—
he proposes Communist self-determination— everybody's reincarnation's extended another Kalpa to Aleph.
Clinging to his ideological bones! Couldn't leave those prayer wheels alone?
No! Had to ban the Ghost Traps! He was against Mandalic boneyards!
What's happening in Siam? Who's paying whose spy blood?

---

[1] *Lunes de Revolución:* a literary newspaper in Havana circa 1960 closed by Castro.

Who's screaming murder in Pentagon again? Does anybody know what
FBI knows?
Anybody ware of CIA plots? Who knows what evil lurks in the hearts of
the C.I.A. Men—
I say all these bastards have taken over the world, & not one of them is
right!
We're all wrong! Take the armaments manufacture out of the
Government Councils—

* * *

The Moon of the Cuban
Revolution's gone under
the Laughing Carib—
I told you so!

Pierrot Lunaire's been
banned from the stands
for seraphim tendencies—
Wouldnt you know!

What'll we do for new
hope for the masses now
politics shows its tricks—
How Should I know?

Communists, Capitalists
play up to the Masses
and both are sincere but
Business is slow!

LeRoi Jones president
I'll be the treasury,
we'll reform the world, with
our stupid noses in a row!

Cut up the world, and
You'll see the right answer,
Words are the Weapons,
The Weapons must go!

* * *

Rhythmic Paradigm: *National Anger*

Blasted be Congress and doom on the White House and cursed are the
works of our Mayors and Priests—
Shit on the face of the Governors Senators Moviestar Banks and the
N.B.C.!
Hypocrite Gold freaks' newspaper death-traps advertize Crap-suck
asshole cops!
Teachers in business suits, Lawyers in money pants, Dynamite stinks in
your nostril war—
Shit on all your dollars! Megaton yr. boneyards! Billions for Starvation!
Man wants to die!
Arabs want power! Jews want their Jaweh! Pope wants Apocalypse! God
wants to be God!
Hitler never dies! Stalin's on the rise! Franco eats our eyes! Nixon's on the
Air!
Now I drop the mental bomb that blows our heads apart from God!
Lie! steal! fly! Hide! shout! cry! Creep! dream! curse! Drop dead! Mad
Earth!

* * *

Lying here on the couch
my head propped by white pillow
my feet on a worn armchair,
cigarettes, ashtray, poems of Cavafy to
read a year later—
looking up at the glass doors to the
balcony, sea rush below,
Mediterranean night darked from here
to the pillars of Hercules—
It is a rest in my travels, busses,
my arm leaning on boat rails—
a long ocean way to India— from
there back to my Paterson,
or a New York—
I would like to live here now, alone,
rested, my head against this pillow
facing the bookshelves by the glass door,

relaxed, nowhere to go, long nights
    hearing this water roar
Except my head on this pillow's filled
    with war, revolution,
metallic snakes with thousand-folded
    skin-plates
circling aether darkness— Hermes the
    youth speeding a new message—
bearded oraters in the tropics, palm trees,
    riots, newspaper presses turning like
    windmills of skin—
I would like to stay here and do nothing,
make no move to future, let be
    Whatever come— long nights
with my feet against the worn easychair,
my head against the white pillow
    —eyes closed to rest.

* * *

Anthology of English Folk Songs

Tune: *After the Ball*

After the ball was over
Didn't we have some fun?
Taking the girls in the corner
Fucking them one by one?
Brought out my hairy monster,
Shoved it between her thighs—
Oh, tickle me Charlie,
See her belly rise!

Tune: *Unknown*

When I was only just 13
I found I had a quim,
I stood before the looking glass
And stuck my finger in—
And now I just turned 23
And youth has lost its charm,
For I can get 5 fingers in
And half my bleeding arm.

Tune: *Unknown*

Bums, bellies & tits
Bums, bellies & tits
There's nothing so pleasing
as constantly squeezing
Bums, bellies & tits

Bums, bellies & tits
Bums, bellies & tits
and a hole in the middle
for someone to piddle
Bums, bellies & tits

Bums, bellies & tits
Bums, bellies & tits
There's nothing so pleasing
as constantly squeezing
Bums, bellies & tits

Tune: *Dixie*

I'm a fellow what makes his living
Tossing off men what don't like women
  with me hand, with me hand,
  with me little bunch of five–
I'm a fellow what don't like Nick
I'd rather have a big fat prick
  with me hand, with me hand
  with me little bunch of five.

Tune: *Unknown*

Four and twenty virgins
Came down to Inverness
And when the ball was over
There were four and twenty less
Singing "Balls to your partner,
Ass against the wall,
If you never get fucked on Saturday night
You'll never get fucked at all!"

Here's the Village Idiot
doing his favorite trick,
pulling his foreskin over his head
and yodeling down his prick.
[Chorus: *Balls to your partner, etc.*]

The Village Parson he was there,
he was mighty proud
swinging on the Chandelier
and peeing on the crowd. [Chorus]

There was fucking in the parlour
Fucking on the stairs,
You couldna see the staircase
for the mass of curly hairs— [Chorus]

Tune: *Schubert's "The Trout"*

There was a fair young maiden
who had a double cunt
One was set behind her
& one stuck out in front

She went out for to seek a fellow
to sate her twofold lust
Who could make love behind her,
And kiss her panting bust

She traipsed the world ah! vainly,
and even tried a pair of twins
But each of them resigned her
two unsatisfied quims.

At last she came upon a family
of fairies with aethereal cocks,
Who cast a spell to bind her
inside a single box
(words by A.G.)

Tune: *On the Good Ship Lollipop*

On the good ship Lollipop
Won't you come and suck my cock
Wontcha gobble it please
I'll be glad to give you alla my cheese.

On the good ship Lollipop
You can fuck me with a mop,
You can lick my ass
on the poopdeck or the top of the mast.

On the good ship Lollipop
We can make love round the clock,
When we get to Japan
You can jerk me off with your other hand.

On the Chinese, Indian seas
We'll get naked in the breeze—
Drop the anchor there!
We could stop & shit in each other's hair.
(words by A.G.)

Dream—20/Dec/61

"It's Gripmunk, Munch! Munch!"

The outgoing Ike administration: chaos in the huge battleship building as the administration moves out of its multi-story offices on the shores of huge lake in the bottom of the Southern Hemisphere—

I had had my bunk & files way upstairs in the Scholars Newspaper Department—I have enormous files I've been accumulating sloppily on everybody's private gossip & state secrets, as an unattached bohemian sleeping free in the reporters' dormitory.

At dawn everyone had woken for reveille and on top of this tower of Babel in a Dorm room lined up in underwear with their files. Forrestal had jumped out of a window around here. I decided to play it smart & get my papers in order and infiltrate the new administration. In fact I knew so much I could make believe I was the President's Secretary—permanently attached to all presidents. An Inside job. While the others were putting on their clothes I was already in sport clothes doing my homework, preparing a report summarizing the National Situation from my files.

We all went downstairs on the elevator thru the glass doors of receptionist-telephone waiting rooms to join the motorcade of the retreating president. I spotted Ike as he was leaving down the stairway in his black felt hat and business suit. "Hey Ike" I shouted behind him. He turned around perplexed & gratified. Why & who would anybody be friendly to him now he was retiring. "I'll see you around! I'll come visit you!" I shouted. He was gratified! Not many people were so nice to him anymore. He was a little confused but vaguely recognized me—I'd been hanging around the corridors so long. He smiled & waved & said "See you soon—be sure to come, just phone me up anytime." The guards saw it all & saluted me as I left the building myself to get a ride on one of the limousines of the new administration that was entering the building. There'll be no FBI check now, I smiled to myself.

I came inside thru police cordon, thru the downstairs traffic lanes and gates on foot, and went into the secondary waiting room where all the confetti from the elections & torn paper & orange peels were all over the floor. I brought this girl in with me. I don't know what she was doing there—maybe looking for a place to spend the day—up all nite. I sneaked her in thru the guards & glass doors, feeling good—I had a new job as President's Secretary which meant I'd be permanently attached to the inside office upstairs, be able to worm in on everybody's private life and watch the president & know all the state secrets.

"Are you prepared to live way out here & travel around the world like that? The job requires that sacrifice" someone had advised me, and I'd nodded yes to myself happily.

Meanwhile the girl is looking for a place to hide in the room—I try to lead her over to an easychair & settle her there while I go upstairs, but she's afraid & goes thru dark door into a bathroom closet—I say no, not necessary—just then the Broom Closet Janitor comes in & sees her—His eyes gleam with Mexican rape: "Just leave her with me, I'll take care of her."

I look him over, he's snickering at me & looking for his fellow janitors to arrive for a gang bang.

"Right!" I greet him. "Just give me the money in advance." He looks perplexed. I continue my strategy, besides, he's not bad looking . . . "or better still I'll take it out in trade"—and I go over and start feeling him up. He retreats. Just then a gang of lost FBI men come in the disused messy cloakroom-waiting room to change into their Fuzzy Clothes. One has his fly open & taking down his pants reveals a bump in his jockey shorts.

The girl dashes forward & points to his thighs—"It's Gripmunck, Munch! Munch!" she cries—She's a nurse or licensed practitioner of some kind, now she swings into action to cover her presence—"It's crabs" she means, some kind of rash or V.D. or crabs—He looks down hurriedly alarmed. I wake.

* * *

There was a "Superintendent of the Curtains" in the 3rd temple at Jerusalem.

* * *

1958, Adam the first young "hip" Londoner that Gregory & I met, worked in the complaint department of a pyjama factory. I learned this month he was in looney bin nowadays.

Dream, Thursday—21 Dec 61—

In a tourist hotel office, with Marianne Moore—conversation about how I was going to, and she was not going to, glimpse the white peaks of the Himalayas. I thought of mentioning how bad her review of the Don Allen Anthology was, but didn't.

Dream—Dec. 24, 1961

In Haifa—left on my own, wandering—I leave my rich apartment as guest—it's a holiday—wander on up narrow hill streets—Pass by garden homes I've "visited before socially." Passing Mrs. Arnon's society home, on the left, on the right Mrs. Kirshner where all the ladies are gathered typing with Negro secretary lady—come to top side of hill—ashamed to go in to the ladies who'd been hospitable before—the road branches off an area I'd never seen before—I ask in the hospital house before the 2 alleys that divide—They laugh at me—"on the right is the road thru the Defective Children's Hospital. Mongol land to you"—one of them warns me angrily—"See that sign?—Well follow it"—I look at the sign with a picture of invading horns & rocks of Mongolian Precipices—with the legend "Accept all incoherent Speech as an attempt at Communication."—All language means something to the speaker in other words. I'm amazed. I walk on and notice a peg where old shopping bags and ancient veils are hung—This is explained as my family portrait—My mother's Mongol black veil—originally she was of Mongolian inferior class "but as you can see her black hairnet fitted in with your father's lines' shopping bag without bride price because of her exceptional beauty." I glimpse children playing in high amphitheater on the right into which one road leads—I go with it—Wake up. Time to leave Acca where I'd been reading about Crusaders Mongols & Fatimids & go to Tel Aviv arrange money & ship to Orient.

Ship thru Red Sea to Mombasa

29 Dec. 1961

Woke in stupor more absorbed in books I'm reading than the trip: water on deck & passing thru gulf of Aqaba saw on both sides the cragged low brown mountains. Later a vast beach in Egypt, backed by the mountains with a little blue UN hut at the narrows of the gulf leading into the Red Sea.

Irritated all day by book on comparative religion—Zaehner's Mescaline book—periodically put it down to look at the landscape. At dusk reading an official guide to Abyssinia, the afternoon vast blue, colored at the western horizon by red sun left violet & orange glow at length along Egypt flatland. Now in Red Sea which at dusk reflects reddish.

At the mouth of Aqaba had been a circle of green shallows in the azure water and the stream out of that (caused by a wrecked iron ship) a feather current of iridescent malachite, shining & unreal as a hummingbird's wing. Behind that a long way over the flat calm water, Arabian beaches & a promontory mount, desolate &—

Quiet in the afternoon. Last night read Arthur C. Clarke's *Childhood's End.* Before that the last weeks, *Hitler's Table Talk* (Bormann)—

That nite, after finishing book, I stood on the prow, eyeing the huge space between Big Dipper down behind me and Orion high up before me, the twinkle of a meteor, white band of stars, swash of black water, ship gliding evenly thru the narrow sea,—A gleam of light on the horizon I thought might be a star rising—Closer, was a ship, the semaphore blinks of white light pinpointed far away—then in silence a glare near behind me blinked on and off our bridge with silent reply again from far way—

in stillness a conversation of lights blinked from one end of the sea of night to another.

The Rules of the Happy Law

Majingo area outskirts of Mombasa Sat & Sun Nite 6–9 Drumming & Dancing.

From a book of Swahili Proverbs:

The torment of the grave is known by the corpse.
Brains are like hair (every one different kind).
A person who dislikes company is a wizard.
He who wanders around a lot by day, he knows (i.e. learns a lot).
Stangaye sana na jua, huja.
The skin of yesterday's sugar cane is a whole harvest to an ant.
If you do not know death, look at a grave.
Every boat has its own waves.
To every child his own neck ornament. *Kila mtoto na koja lake.*
A new thing is a source of joy even if it be a sore.
When the lips die, the saliva is scattered.
You don't take vengeance on silliness. *Maafoo hapatiliziwi.*
Why drive chickens away from shit you don't eat yourself?
Old shit doesn't stink?
You aint the only fisherman who knows where to look for an octopus.
A dying ear does not feel the medicine.
Don't argue with the coconut-palm climber, the coconut has been eaten by the moon.

* * *

"Fearing Death I sought God, and found God in Death."
—Sankara, 9th Cent. India

4 a.m. Jan 1, 1962—Dream off coast of Abyssinia

Living in old broken down house in Fredericksburg, Va., as a suburb of Washington—in the top floor of the condemned building (huge concrete rock structure five stories high with huge loft flats up & down the halls, vast rooms inside like N.Y. 23rd Street Cannastra [peace to his soul!] lofts). This is perhaps the site of many earlier dreams of apartments and elevated trains to high flats in Brooklyn, for the first time seen from the empty lot outside, in isolation where I got a good look at it—the dreamworld runs thru the future as well as the past in that case—Always before uneasy feeling I couldn't locate but had not yet the memory *where* the place was—at close of this dream I was passing by the building in a car with the fat doctor, or a trolley—and looked up and saw the structure—could see thru the windows—part of the right hand side of the building had collapsed, it's an old cheap place to live—but my sublet digs are safer because it is a sort of recessed penthouse loft—

Well I'd been upstairs & there was a big New Years party there, lots of couples I half-knew, mostly beat & bohemian acquaintances of the former owner who'd given me the key—in fact none of them knew who was really living there—

At one hour toward the end I was forced to sit in the lap of a big elderly woman who wanted to make love. I was tired & unwilling, she was resentful—I had a big handful of dripping cherry sandwich—Some I gave her, some I tried to eat, a lot of it dripped all over the couch & on her dress, off the sandwich & out of my mouth I was stuffing it into—We wrassled over the dripping sandwich, it distracted her from her unwanted lovemaking—

Late in the evening people started to go home & I got separated out as the owner of the apartment, or the man in residence—with some embarrassment at being discovered so possessive of the abandoned flat—it used to belong to Terry Fredericks [1]—that's why he has this strange Fredericksburg slum address—young Fredericks the stutterer—

Car riding trying to escape with the phony threat of murder on my trail—à la John O'Hara, along California-style seaside highways—

5 a.m.— Long mountainous sea coast, white snow patches low on the mts. Horse carts, without reins, the driver standing in animal furs, swaying back and forth on one leg on the cart platform, calling for customers—when none came she swayed forward as before & shouted to the horse to move.

---

[1] "Went Princeton or Yale circa 1960; helped Tambimuttu edit *Poetry New York* London issue"—A.G. 1976.

Jan 1, 1962—11 PM

Massawa all day, blasting sun shielded by clouds, strange thin green fish skimming the surface of the bay water by the long road from dock Island to mainland where the road embankment divided two villages of wooden shacks, one green mosque of wood with a two-story balcony—Minaret—a huge teahouse with large narghile [water pipe] & flowery paintings of leaves & vases & branches delicate on the whitewashed slat wall—and a main street with shoemakers, cripples, blacks bent over canes, runts in white rags & cloth turbans sloppy, splaylegged & thin black skin & bones—boys with hair cut bald or along center a tuft or ladies with curled rows of hair against dark skull. The shoemaker sewing the red sneakers, a cigarette hung out his mouth—Passerby wrapped in red silk shirts, light emerald gauzy veils on little girls—the raucous Hey Joe come here Friend titsy insistence—to a cocoacola beer bottle—with green tables & soda—

Late nite, high on the deck, Orion over head South before the prow—and moved over to the right as we turned a corner in the Red Sea, toward the pocket of Djibouti where Rimbaud landed & blacked his skin in nearby quarries—Harrar inland—across from dreary Aden—

Exciting days sailing down coast here—the lighthouse at night seen far behind in Massawa—flies on the table and a cool breeze back in the hold-dormitory—light on the ship-stairs shines in the room all nite—

Bomba the sailor who scored & was strange hearted—thought himself slave to the company & shit union; tender.

Djibouti—Jan. 3—

Ship docked 7 a.m.—went off by taxi at 8 to center of Ville, past Messageries Maritimes building—then wandered afoot into huge empty paved square several blocks wide—on one corner a stubby squat thick white-coned Afric Mosque Minaret and large elevated courtyard, across the street a vegetable & fish market—rays, swordfish, crabs—the other end of the Place Arthur Rimbaud congregations in tea shops—black woolly haired, curled-haired & some red haired shades—We wandered up the blocks of tin & wood shacks, here and there an older 2 story green & orange painted rack-house with delicate slat-windows—almost like a

Chinese Junk in style—The area of mud streets extending 5 blocks in each direction—another huge square filled with goats & an overturned car—Several mosques—Went back to Tourist Info office to look up traces of Rimbaud—None, he'd lived across the gulf in Tadjoura.

Dream—Morn 9-10 Jan 5 after rounding Cape Guardafui—

An international European city 1962—Berlin—Jerusalem—Warsaw—walking around in streets, I go upstairs top floor studio big apartment building with a gang of young kids—playwrites & poets & their girlfriends with flowers—looking down on the desolate arcaded streets below—walls pockmarked with bullet holes—

A young man salutes me artistically and says "I want you to hear the words of my play"

And begins the first song of his International Review (Intnl. Death Review):

"I want you to hear the words of my play—
Ack-ack-ack-ack-ack-ack-ack-ack-ack-ack
I want you to know what I'm feeling today—
Ack-ack-ack ack-ack-ack ack-ack-ack ack"

(The bursts of machinegun fire that punctuate the lines fall rhythmically with accent on the last "ack" in a sentimental love song tune.) Machine gun fire from street below—

I wake up in bed with Elise Cowen, she's humming "you do something to me"—my head's on her breast. I feel good with her—I try to explain to her and her Polish friends what I just dreamed and in the dream effort to say ack ack I wake up. And tell the dream to Peter.

Reprise of play—huge stalking Buchenwald figures like ghosts float thru stage at opportune times, Roosevelt, Stalin, Hitler conspiring in background as part of phantom sub-plot.

Final chorus, Russian Communists—

"We will have our victory"

A huge deathshead projected in center of stage blinking at 13 cycles per sec stroboscope.

Capitalist chorus, Negro chorus, Yellow race chorus, Arab and Jewish chorus all pointing up to skull

"We will have our victory"

Jan. 5—Morn, waking dream

Peter in inner room at typewriter, Lafcadio pulls a strange gun with short wide barrel & gleam of light in center of bore like diamond plate—

Peter throws the change in the cash register, the whole handful at once (might be a signal to Burroughs?) and adds the last pence in the right cash-pocket in the register drawer, & closes it—he does this last to show Lafcadio he's not trying to betray him, so the cash register is in normal condition. He's trapped.

I get up to leave the room suddenly, Lafcadio stunned because he can't shoot me, I go out the door into adjoining room & summon the other docile Lafcadio & order him outside with a message (which he doesn't understand)—as he leaves, the first Lafcadio follows me with the gun—which he has changed & adjusted so it has long wiry protrusion from muzzle, 3 feet long—I grab the iron wire & swing the gun out of his hands, he's disarmed—he's now bewildered, his scheme failed. "You're not going to shoot anybody" I tell him.

7 Jan— Finished *Hitler's Table Talk* as recorded by Martin Bormann—600 pages of ideas. Annoyance at the end with bad art & waltzes and autobahns materialisms and all that egotism. Yet like a dream he could have existed as if Ubu Roi became real & were in charge of History.

God: celestial telepathy—To get in contact with "God"—as if we were individual units of the grand assemblage of Telepaths—total contact or immersion on all the lines at once—annihilate that individuated consciousness—some method of practical research to be devised for purpose of telepathic communication with God, once & for all—Prayer is the form, or Yogic meditation.

Under the stars ½° below the equator, on the bridge, looking at astronomical charts, & stepping out to the rail with binoculars to look into the star populations around Canis Major—thinking of celestial telepathy on the side, in the abstract, in answer to the Mate's sudden question—"What religion are you"—posed tenderly, curious—and "Do you believe in God?" 2:30 a.m.

Two more days to Dar es Salaam. Lying most of the day in the empty dormitory reading books on Buddha and Hitler, all this week thru Red Sea and around Cape Guardafui & down the East Afric coast, each night staring up from the deck, or climbing to the prow, to find out where Orion's belt is set, or where tips the big dipper in the blackness.—

Where the big dipper tips the blackness into the Void.

Jan. 8, '62—Reading concentration camp and Nazi memoirs—feeling nervous, went up to brush teeth & take Aralen pill, which stuck in back of my throat, I vomited, could not get the bitterness out of the windpipe and regurgitated several times—then slowly recovering, in the night, in jockey shorts & sneakers, on the deck, looking up saw the arch of the Milky Way directly overhead suddenly loom vast upward like a rainbow, soft & colossal, the pattern of this nebula revealed for an instant, like a huge veil around reality, a luminous Halo of Astronomy seen from the girdle of the earth 2 degrees below the equator. Went up on prow and leaned my face flat upward to rest my eyes on it more, looking south into the cloudiest part of the galactic spiral where the center must be. An impersonal presence curves itself too huge to be seen over Earth's concentration camp.

Spread over us like Asia on the maps, or aurora, rainbows, shimmering light at giant distance.

Dream Jan 9, 1962—Dawn, approaching Dar es Salaam:

I

In a huge apartment full of people, in a building (from earlier dreams) used as an anonymous flop, hide out, with furnished rooms, corridors, apartments, closets, porches, attics—the underground social building—where alternately in other dreams Eugene had apartment (near Bway 115 St.) to study law, I had bed there then, or another time dream I had key to dark small room where I kept old cans of sardines & dirty pillow & never went there; or had high attic apartment; or traveled there by Elevated thru Bklyn—recurrent archetype—to live there anonymous—

Well in this dream, it's a place where I have my own room & go visit some wino-type friends—whom I find have a huge three-bed furnished room—I notice it's an extremely large, high ceilinged place with French window—but closed in with curtains. A small door into the hotel corridor—you wouldn't expect them to live in such huge space—they share it together, I realize they pay about 60 a week—several hundred a month—but shared three ways it's possibly cheap individually—how they get their money I wonder they seem like tired flops—I realize while I'm visiting them they're in the Junk business. They're turning on. I'm interested and a little scared, back on that scene, but they've worked out a real hide out den for themselves.

II

I'm back in my own apartment in a building—also Elise & maybe Janine, also Francesca & Lucien and several others are there—it's also an office at 8 a.m.—my apartment is leased out during the day. Office hours are beginning, there is some confusion—I have a daily school job somewhere else, so I don't stay there all day—in fact I am sort of janitor there & work morn & afternoons late—but leave around 9 a.m. for my other job.

Before office hours begin I'm sitting around thinking, worried—Francesca seems also to be a Junkie, or a lesbian,—it disturbs me as I wonder how she can stand this change of outlook—except I say to myself, this is just the kind of anarchic freedom I've been prophesying and preaching to people, & she's got some individual strength over the years from contact with me & my kind. Still I feel sad to see her apart from society & life, on her own, as it were, in the underground. Elise also, is preparing an injection—a sort of Methadone syringe of plastic, not exactly needle but plastic grooved spike you stick in upper arm—new German synthetic stuff & new style disposable works—I'm surprised she's on this kind of kick, but it seems everyone including Cessa is—it's a game, not without danger, but not very habit forming they tell me, I'm too anxious—they even prepare a shot for me—I'm aloofly going about my business cleaning up the place preparing for office occupancy in a few hours, they're getting ready to get out & meanwhile Elise kindly goes about, nurse-like, giving me an extra shot like everyone else got, because I'm me & she respects me & feels duty to keep me going OK.

The officials of the new German-style bureau come in for office hours & the day begins. I'm cleaning up, I'm the janitor, emptying wastebaskets. After awhile I finish, in all the confusion of friends leaving & officials entering & getting down to their desks & compartments in the room shuffling papers. I have a school job, as I said, elsewhere—mainly because I want to have two different scenes ready for the new political dictatorship that's slowly evolving in society. I have got permission to work a double job, so that covers me with the bureaucrats in my home office—The other school assignment is actually an excuse for me to get away & do underground work & study.

A friend, a hepcat beatnik from Idaho who has just crossed the Atlantic, recognizes me and asks me, on the side, as he offers me a war-style rough tobac Idaho roll-yr-own (commercial brand) "Well how's the trip from abroad?" I nod & try to escape attention further. I want not to be recognized, I want to be totally anonymous—janitor with double job—because I realize the new Fascist state will eliminate me as a loudmouth immediately if I keep up previous public poesy activities.

In fact I realize with regret all previous "beat" scene I'd been making was just a stupid way of betraying myself & other good people to public notice so that now when the heat—which I never suspected would become real—is on & the whole world has become a police state I'm in a dangerous position unable to fight it or hide from it, I'd betrayed myself long ago not realizing the seriousness of the "coming struggle for power" with the Control forces. However I'd got myself straight in time—this apartment & cover job as a janitor & the side job to escape to & make other underground connections there—

I go to the desk to sign out—it's actually my first day in this new system—the lady there is not sure—but arrangements had been made so my leaving the office is in order—I'm hoping everything runs smoothly this first day—Her desk is piled with papers, it's a travel bureau actually—I put away my mop & bucket to prepare to go crosstown to the school where I have another apartment hideout. I maintain a double work & home life. They probably have office hours at nite, as they have day hours here—I live both places & plot my underground activities when I have the 2 places to myself, and maintain the fiction that I work at each during the time they're open.

That is, the place I'm leaving is where I have my own pad at nite—it's an office in the day where I work an hour or so then leave for real work office crosstown—But when I get crosstown that office is closing down and afterwards I have the place to myself for the rest of the day.

I realize what a mistake I'd made in giving away all my thoughts & feelings since now that makes me a naked man. I hadn't realized that all I'd been intemperately prophesying—police state, thought wash, control—would soon become true & everybody connected with my type of activity be in danger.

I saw the wisdom of Bill's silent organization.

8:30—Same morning, after going back to sleep after last pages writing.

On a bus, later. I've been on a picnic trip to another city. There in another room where the travellers hang out I have my old clothes on the floor—including protective fur collar mountain-coat I'd had for years & gave away in Tanger—I'd moved into this city, and brought a huge wobbly desk arrangement with chair & bookshelves & plastic mirrors & pigeonholes attached, along with me. I figured it be useful in any apartment I occupy.

Now on bus going back talking with a friend who's warning me how evil Himmler was—the Bus stops to pick up a new passenger—friend of Nicholas Calas and Meyer Schapiro—My friend recognizes it's Himmler entering the bus, Himmler himself, just back from liquidating a whole echelon of concentration camp revolutionaries—But this Himmler is someone I've very familiar with—I'd been joking intimate relations with for a long time—I'm confused but at the same time feel the advantage. He sits in seat opposite me on bus, across the aisle, I turn to him greeting & smiling. "Still up to your old dirty tricks, eh?" Everyone else on the bus is horrified & frightened of the bad taste of this presumptuous joke—Himmler turns, wearily, & salutes me—I offer to introduce him to the friend who'd been describing him so heatedly before—They tentatively exchange hands, in embarrassed flattery to be introduced to each other, Himmler somewhat wearily, my friend a little confused. I don't know what this situation is all about, if it is dangerous for me or not, but I feel a certain confidence in Himmler that I have him under *my* power in the long run, thru my "innocence."

* * *

The Theory and Practice of Hell—Eugen Kogon [1]

"Shiftless elements"
S.S. Death-Head Units
"Röhm's Avengers"
The "Singing Horses" of the Sachsenhausen camp
& Buchenwald

[1] Originally published by Farrar, Straus and Giroux in 1950; later in the 1958 Berkeley Medallion edition.

"An especially popular procedure for entertaining visitors to the camps was to have the Jews line up in the roll call to the left of the tower and sing the vile tune"—

Jew Song

"And now, with mournful crooked Jewish noses,
We find that hate and discord were in vain"

Prisoner "implored & reproached by
members of his own family, especially
his mother"

"... making him strip to the skin, climb
a tree and call down: 'I am a filthy
Jewish swine!' "

Dachau: "Labor means liberty"
Buchenwald: "Right or Wrong—my Country!" was centered
around the "Goëthe Oak" on Ettersberg
The "Rose Garden" (of barbed wire) at Buchenwald

"parachute troops"—the suicides who jumped into the
quarry at Mauthausen.
Dachau's Sky Ride Wagon. "... the blood does not yet
boil at an altitude of 70,000 feet—under simulated
conditions of experiment."
"Division for Typhus and Virus Research" at Buchenwald of
the Institute of Hygiene of the Waffen S.S.

The whipping rack in the roll call area at Buchenwald: "The rack was carried in by four prisoners lifted up high like a throne ... on a big stone mound ... [the band was then ordered] to strike up a march. On one occasion at Buchenwald S.S. Major Rödl actually stationed an opera singer by the rack and had him accompany the performance with operatic arias."

"... recaptured prisoners had a sign placed round their
neck reading 'I am back.' "

* * *

Himmler's signs posted:
"There is a road to freedom.
Its milestones are: obedience,
hard work, honesty, sobriety,
cleanliness, devotion, order,
discipline and patriotism."—Himmler

The Gypsy in chicken wire cage with nails: "His dreadful screams
had long since lost any semblance of humanity."

Total inmates 1933–45 7,820,000
Survivors 700,000

" 'you'll be hitting the grate' "—or—
" 'you'll be going up the stack.' "
A written report on methods of shrinking human heads
to the size of an orange, requested by Chief Medical
Officer Lolling.
" 'Corpse carriers to the gatehouse!' "
Prisoners bent, heads in toilet full of shit, for 25
lashes on buttocks.
"Night & Fog Shipments"

* * *

Peter Orlovsky, ice cream, snot, heroin, movies
Asthma & Chapattis, pushing me around by the shoulders in Mombasa,
What a queen! What an angel! with his bar bells and cant play the guitar
and his voice like a calf that's lost his mother
bawling in the barnyard, "You're sweeter than a flower,"
Taking a shower with his belly stuck out like a big baby,
with a hundred dollars a month from the U.S. Govt. for being crazy
which he spends in Egypt, on which he walks in red sneakers
which get dirty in Africa which he visits without seeing an elephant
which he didn't care because he already kist the sphinx
which he saw en route to Palestine to meet me which am his friend.

Tom M' Boya's Wedding Party Sat Jan 20, '62

Dance— Chattas Room City Hall
10 AM
Raimtula

Trustee Hall Jawanjee St
next to Info. office
7PM–11PM
we got kicked out for not having coats & ties.

* * *

Kanu Rally— Jomo Kenyatta speaker
Nairobi Stadium— 1PM
Durham Rd.
Sunday Jan 21
My Amex wallet was stolen, Peter & I the only whites there.

Jan 24, 1962—Nairobi Dream, Hotel Hamhadrut

Going to sleep, I lay in bed by window looking up at dull dark sky, wondering where I was, lost, feeling dull in Africa, lost my way not got to India, hung on sex with Peter playing with his boogers, made the wrong turn somewhere, accept patiently, Burroughs killed my love, what is there to love in people, they're not really there to begin with, Mahatma Gandhi & Hitler—Gandhi preaching faith—I have no faith—so how operate on that—first time, I confess to myself I'm an atheist—universe machine—not even that—just "special conditions" for accident of life that break down—the purpose of life?—a snout emerging—as Buddha says—so fell to sleep.

Later in night, series of dreams. First, with great excitement—I'm setting off on a new historic trip for myself—going to settle awhile in London & see Nordic countries—on to big boat as of yore that'll bring me to parapets of Buckingham Street'd London—The shoppes & British Museum & English Speech & societies & buses & crumpets & friends & freedom then—a happy vision—great difficulties getting thru the boat, having to float & swing to the boat, huge Queen ship—arriving there, to make arrangements, call up the past, Call Seymour Wyse, make old contacts again, get a flat, settle in and prepare further travel & settling down in London—a long intimate season there—I feel happy, starting a new life. This on way to India.

I am to meet Gregory—it's a later part of the dream—to go there. Where shall we go? I guess I had woken realized I'd *already* been to England & in real life there's no thrill there—or *is* there?—anyway, why not meet him on the road to India further East—in the Balkans say—I don't know anything about the Balkans, I have to look them up—I've never been there, good place to start out afresh & strange—go there & encounter Gregory anew—I go to old school-teacher (who was Greek who taught me odyssey in Central H.S.?) (The man with lower eyelid skin mottled under his eyeglasses, Mr.——?) has books, I see him somewhere in library or school or roof reading room—I can't find the right books—Maybe I should meet further East of Israel, in Persia? or Arabia? I look on the map, Roumania, Bulgaria, Albania—grey places—why should I go there—I can't even get in with my passport there! Why those lands? Something wrong? I wake? And realize in any case why go *back* there, why not go further to Arabia on the way instead of back to England or the Balkans? I forget completely I'm as far as E. Africa already. What kind of reversed dream is this? A prophecy! Like earlier exciting dreams which I'd believed. Parapets of Europe, weeping with joy. I realize these dreams are mechanical hope for prophetic voyage happiness thrill—Even after I've been to Europe & got bored there I have repeat dreams of going there for first time. In the dark, awake, something's wrong, my dreams are misleading me.

Then asleep again, more dreams—I'm visiting whom—Peggy Guggenheim or Dorothy Thompson [1] or Elise Cowen—some rich queen lady—We're talking—a murder has taken place, or a suicide or scandal—The police have been & gone—I go upstairs to the elevator & car on the roof to see what's happened—the lady hasn't even cleaned out her car since it's happened, she's been so upset. I go look in the car—preparations for a party abandoned—old tins of food & towels & newspapers to throw out or rescue & use now, not waste—a carton of little milk wax cardboard tubes—The milk's too old & probably spoiled, can't have that at all. Luxurious car with rugs, and all those things scattered and hid on seat & underfloor—I'm taking charge of situation to clean up & make myself indispensable strong man after the scandal which has confused the lady.

A conversation with Thompson-Guggenheim about Dorothy Norman—Yes, she's o.k., but "too constantly full of activity"—"Of course she's on the Way, and very deep—but there is this constant chatter & activity—There's no withdrawal, not much silence, no darkness, no individual strangeness about her—all sweetness & light & receiving good people as guests—" I wonder about the qualifications of the speaker—yes

[1] Newspaper columnist, ex-wife of Sinclair Lewis.

she's Thompson, who brooded & *was* full of sex anarchy individual darkness & drunk—à la Guggenheim. A judgement on Norman, that she was O.K. but not truly Indic silent dark enuf—that is she talked & was sociable always & too well arranged.

Finally in a big apartment as of a dream several days ago while I was sharing a huge room in a house with some Turkey girls. It's now my apartment. There are a few people there—perhaps Michael Portman & some other Burroughs disciples. Eugene comes in too, and on the wall there's a miniature Puppet stage, with little living figures enacting their roles. They are cartoonish caricatures of real people, odd ones & very personal, quite live—strange & funny. Like Tableaux Vivants but dwarfish & cloaked schoolteachers acting obsessed with themselves. What are they pantomiming? What's the action.

Eugene looking at them says they're meaningless & uninteresting & begins a speech about ignoring them & getting on with consciousness destruction. As I hear him, he sounds like Burroughs. I say "Shut up, Burroughs" to him sharply—he is speaking as B's Replica & even in B's tone of voice & even begins to look like B. He protests he's not a replica but is shocked & stoned by my abrupt pointing the finger "You've been invaded by Burroughs." He argues that the pantomime is not funny—I look to check if it is or not with my own senses—it seems funny to me—I get annoyed—he's merely talking to distract attention from the pantomime saying it's meaningless dull—I take charge & get aggressive—"It looks as if we have need of an 'Excision operation' here to exorcise Burroughs Ghost from your mind"—he is shocked—I'm delighted to have found the way of counter exorcism in the dream—Who is it? Slow paying attention to everything he says, examining it in detail/contradicting what's untrue or not reasonable, step by step, pointing out where the voice & ideas are merely replicas of B and not conformable to actual circumstances, like the puppet show which *is* funny and rather odd & not to be ignored. Strange that he should have got Eugene.

* * *

Mombasa—Jan. 27, 1962, Dream

Going to big party—someone's house some fairies in New York, Ned Rorem I think, into the front door, I think I'm on time tho not exactly invited—a vast apartment it is too—you go thru loft or run-down tenement upper flat entrance door and enter huge living room with velvet sofas à la Virgil Thomson's place—then extending outward under a glass roof you get to a parquet or tile floor—just a special nearly jeweled Indian tile—a rectangular section of it half buried in the grass, then a block-long field that extends out thru the backyard maybe to the river—and this is the interior of the apartment—

Thru a door to the kitchen, they're looking at big pots full of spare ribs, don't offer me any, so I climb up on top of the icebox & stick my hand into a vat & grab a boiled rib—if anybody notices me I'll brazen it out after all I'm a friend of Paul's—Finally I find Bowles in one of the rooms and sit down with him friendly—

We're walking down a big street in foreign city together, sightseeing—suddenly a party in rich evening dress comes up the street to the Ritzy apt. Hotel our party was at—glittering Evening dresses and the fellow in tie & tales—talking animatedly—Suddenly in the street light day, he starts a funny walk flapping his feet back in forth in & dowt rapidly like a fan, like a super Chaplin walk, it's a brilliant conversation & style he has. Bowles leans toward me loverly & says in Peter's voice—"I'd like to play with him"—I am embarrassed by Bowles' intimate childlike weakness confidence—it reminds me of Peter's snot eating intimacy—I reply "Well, it wouldn't be hard to meet him." and wake, 3 AM in mosquito net. Up to write, & mosquitoes bite my ankle.

Reading Gandhi's ideas on chastity in autobiography.

* * *

Hydro hotel, granite floor,
white sneakers, round table with
hat knife grey typewriter paper
plate ink book on India— noise
from the kitchen radio & rapping pans—
and knives on aluminum, chopping blocks,
voices in Swahili— Hong Kong on the
radio somewhere?— chirp of insects
buzzing thru the air with cheeps &
electric sizzlings of sweet sound,
—Peter sitting up in bed "You oughta
be ashamed of yourself"— reading whomdoyucallit
Saints politico details— ambiguous in

Peter Orlovsky, Hydro Hotel, Mombasa

books as ever— black rose Streets weaving
somewhere in the kingdom of Kāshī.
("Instant mixed cutups with sonnets.")
Wrote Bill Burroughs the other day,
whoever that be. In a palmeraie
near Marrakesh, in Hotel Albert, Hydro,
Saint-Tropez & Mycenae Ngoma
across the river where the tall
palms rose against the silver sky,
blackmuscled sweating statues on the
docks rolled ivory & bales of sisal
& German machinery—The ships up to
dock seven, English & Indian lines—
is it proper thus to kill the Mosquito?
Slam my hand against the wall, an itch
on my right foot— disappointment realized

it's not a bloodyd blot— looks a little
mechanical, a living toylet sleeping
sickness tsetse fly, bugs' death—
the lizard & spider-roach that hang
around in the Hindustani toilet bowl fixed
down in the floor— the squat ache in the
stiff knees to empty my insides on the
ground, the wretching spasm of the
mouthed intestine as it vomits shit back
to earth
. . .—Creatures whirling in
a mandala in the mosquito net—
Under what shade sleeps the mosquito at
midday?— folded in a leaf on a pond?—
Any memory of the day before? Sally
forth a few days & meet death in my
palm— Mankind like a cloud of mosquitoes
thinking up a God—Communication
in Chandragupta's times—Mosquito bites
on the left shoulder— "You must be
a mosquito, Allen!" Is that a prophesy
of my actual karma. Mosquito Sonnets.
Because I hate them so, I fear
their buzz before my eyes & hovering over
my brow. Brush him gently off my neck.
Protect myself in a mosquito net. Introduce
new animals. Bacteriological warfare next.
Invent a saint bacteria. Or Heroin?

The Gold Bomb.

Dream—Feb 1—

In Motel at Mombasa, all imaginary, or out in modern houses in Nyeri beach, a party of us—I get caught up waiting for the Devil in one of the houses—it's a woman, I'm not frightened—big hard city woman with her fatherless kids—gets in bed with me (rather like Helen Parker [1] in general appearance, red head)—later I miss her, go to another house where we

[1] The "H.P." of "Transcription of Organ Music" (see p. 26, *Howl and Other Poems.)*

have date, she's in bed in downstairs apartment of huge building, with new Negro friend. I go in to interrupt them—Jealous!—I say "To err is human which I've done—but you are *all* jealousy & you're divine so you have no excuse not to forgive my intrusion."

Dream, S.S. Amra, Feb. 9, 1962

A small amphitheater in Paterson—I've been back in that house-apartment of previous dreams—in the auditorium perhaps of the Y—Dr. Mahler's family is seated upstairs, I watch them (upstairs along the rows of circular seats)—

Later in the house, Louis & the Newark family not yet returned—Peter & I finally go to bed in the small bed, tho there are several other beds & people around & we could have used a big fold out double bed. I bring the vaseline & hide it in the bed under mattress where I can get it—

Suddenly the family enters finally, so we all get up again—tho I'd been feigning sleepiness—to greet them, Louis & Clara & Claire & husbands—

I'm about to get into a fight with Clara about Israel—I hold back because I realize she's probably better equipped with facts than I am—

Then I recount—for my prospective employer—my previous interviews with employers & teachers, & come up with this Buchmanite advertisement—

"I used to see God in the faraway sense and this memory has always been my deepest inspiration."

* * *

Yesterday dreamt something about Tibet which I neglected to write & as a result about 3 dreams went down the drain. Something about Caterpillars?

Feb 11—

No it was a lamb, a baby brown-grey lamb I was carrying—and I began feeling up its ass, it got feeling sexy in my arms, the lamb in the dream.

Then last night, a huge tureen of urine that I had to remove—I even tasted it, bitter, and so high to the edge of the thick heavy tureen that moving it would have spilt the surface—finally Bill Keck who studied

Gurdjieff dancing I think he showed me a sort of dustpan-shaped ladle that was full of urine, gold urine sloshing about, also—but that was useful to empty the pots—and a recollection of the bitter tearful taste of urine somewhere from the past—Fair Street childhood eras.

Woke depressed, as if again bankrupt on the India bound ship—no motif, no goal again, no god—the puzzling breaks of continuity with Burroughs—tho strangeness of Keck's different road—I'm surrounded by Muslims & Sikhs and hindu vegetarians and dozens of indic babies—and the boy with the brown tennis legs—fucking Peter's white back bent over in the shower room—the stars out of the window vent in the ship's dormitory—eating with the fat pink Englishman who'd walked 7 months thru the geologies of Southern Africa—the piles of shit in the hindustani squat toilets, water always on the floor—the Gujarati movies under the canvas on the fantail—my lower bunk and air mattress where I lay all day & read up on India Kipling's Kim, Hemingway & James as a last look backward to the West—and despair but so cold not to know my way anymore, and nothing to say.

Dream—Mon Feb 11, 1962—

Up north, in the junk pad—a huge Siberian studio—with Sheri, Heine, various ex or present dead or alive junkies—selling it in the form of blotting paper or licorice—I'm there often about to buy, but prevented by some kind of suspicion—a big geography is going on—explanations of the trade route in ancient times from Scandinavia to Africa and around the Horn again up to Siberia & China & back to Scandinavia—selling junk? I'm on a trip of my own.

INDEX